ON TO C++

Patrick Henry Winston

Professor of Computer Science

Massachusetts Institute of Technology

▲▼ Addison-Wesley Publishing Company

Reading, Massachusetts ■ Menlo Park, California ■ New York
Don Mills, Ontario ■ Wokingham, England ■ Amsterdam ■ Bonn
Sydney ■ Singapore ■ Tokyo ■ Madrid ■ San Juan ■ Milan ■ Paris

Library of Congress Cataloging-in-Publication Data
Winston, Patrick Henry.
    On to C++ / Patrick Henry Winston.
        p.   cm. -- (Programming languages library)
    Includes index.
    ISBN 0-201-58043-8
    1. C++ (Computer programming language).   I. Title.   II. Series.
QA76.73.C153W59   1994
005.13'3--dc20

                                                        93-49605
                                                        CIP

Reprinted with corrections August, 1994

Reproduced by Addison-Wesley from camera-ready copy supplied by the author.

2 3 4 5 6 7 8 9 10-CRW-969594

CONTENTS

ACKNOWLEDGEMENTS

The cover photograph, the cover design, and the interior design are by Chiai Takahashi, with counsel from Karen A. Prendergast. The engine in the photograph was kindly positioned for Ms. Takahashi by three gracious employees of a local railroad.

Lyn Dupre was the developmental editor, and Boris Katz was the chief technical editor. Both have a special gift for rooting out problems and suggesting improvements.

In addition, Sundar Narasimhan provided invaluable advice on C's subtleties, Thomas Stahovich helped to test the programs, and Lisa Freedman found grammatical and typographical errors that were introduced in final editing.

1 HOW THIS BOOK TEACHES YOU THE LANGUAGE

1 The purpose of this book is to help you learn the essentials of C++ programming. In this section, you learn why you should know C++ and how this book is organized.

2 The C++ programming language is related to C. Because ++ is C's increment operator, and because the developers of C++ viewed C++ as an incremental augmentation of C, rather than as a completely different language, they decided to use C and ++ in C++'s name.

3 In the vernacular of programming, an **object** is a packet of information stored in a chunk of computer memory. Every object is associated with a data type, and the data type determines what can be done to an object. All programming languages have built-in data types, such as the integer data type and the character data type.

4 An **object-oriented programming language** encourages you to design programs around data types and data-type hierarchies that you define yourself. Typically, you define data types and data-type hierarchies so that you can describe individual nails, horseshoes, horses, kingdoms, or whatever else happens to come up naturally in your application.

In contrast, **procedure-oriented programming languages** encourage you to think in terms of procedures, instead of in terms of data types and data-type hierarchies.

In this book, you learn more about what *object-oriented* means and why many programmers prefer object-oriented languages. For now, it suffices to know that C++ is an object-oriented programming language, whereas most other programming languages are *procedure-oriented* programming languages.

5 C++ became a popular object-oriented programming language because its parent language, C, was already popular. C, in turn, became popular by virtue of attractive characteristics, such as the following:

- C is easy to learn.

- C programs are fast.

- C programs are concise.

- C compilers—programs that translate C programs into machine instructions—are usually fast and concise.

- C compilers and C programs run on all sorts of computers, from small personal computers to huge supercomputers.

- UNIX, a popular operating system, happens to be written in C.

6 There are two principal reasons to learn C++:

- The productivity of C++ programmers generally exceeds the productivity of C programmers. Hence, C++ programmers are in demand.

- The supply of powerful off-the-shelf C++ software modules, both free and for sale, is increasing rapidly. The supply of off-the-shelf C modules, most of which you can incorporate into C++ programs, is already huge.

Also, because C++ is the most widely used object-oriented programming language, you often hear programmers debate the merits of other object-oriented languages in terms of advantages and disadvantages relative to C++.

7　Four principles determined this introductory book's organization and style:

- The book should get you up and running in the language quickly.

- The book should answer your basic questions explicitly.

- The book should encourage you to develop a personal library of solutions to standard programming problems.

- The book should deepen your understanding of the art of good programming practice.

8　To get you up and running in C++ quickly, the sections in this book generally supply you with the most useful approach to each programming need, be it to display characters on your screen, to define a new function, or to read information from a file.

9　To answer your basic questions explicitly, this book is divided into parts that generally focus on one issue, which is plainly announced in the title of the section. Accordingly, you see titles such as the following:

- How To Write Arithmetic Expressions

- How To Define Simple Functions

- How To Create Classes and Objects

- How To Benefit from Data Abstraction

- How To Design Class Hierarchies

- How To Organize a Multiple-File Program

10　To encourage you to develop a personal library of solutions to standard programming problems, this book introduces many useful, productivity-increasing, general-purpose, templatelike patterns—sometimes called **cliches** by experienced programmers—that you can fill in to achieve particular-purpose goals.

Cliches are introduced because learning to program involves more than learning to use programming-language primitives, just as learning to speak a human language involves more than learning to use vocabulary words.

11　To deepen your understanding of the art of good programming practice, this book emphasizes the value of such ideas as *data abstraction* and *procedure abstraction*, along with principles such as the explicit-representation principle, the no-duplication principle, the local-view principle, the look-up principle, the need-to-know principle, and the keep-it-simple principle.

12 In this book, single-idea segments, analogous to slides, are arranged in sections that are analogous to slide shows. The segments come in several varieties: **basic segments** explain essential ideas; **sidetrip segments** introduce interesting, but skippable, ideas; **practice segments** provide opportunities to experiment with new ideas; and **highlights segments** summarize important points.

13 Finally, the book develops a simple, yet realistic C++ program, which you see in many versions as your understanding of the language increases. In its ultimate version, the program reads information from a file describing a railroad train, computes the load-bearing volume of each box car and tank car using formulas drawn from descriptions of boxes and cylinders, and displays a car-by-car report. Programs similar to the one developed can help you to manage a railroad, either model or real.

14

- C++ is an object-oriented programming language. Object-oriented programming languages emphasize user-defined data types and data-type hierarchies, rather than computations to perform.

- C++ descends from C, an already-popular programming language; thus, heredity is the most conspicuous reason why C++ itself enjoys considerable popularity.

- This book gets you up and running in C++ quickly; it answers your basic questions explicitly; it equips you with program patterns that you can adapt to your own purposes; and it deepens your understanding of the art of good programming practice.

2 HOW TO COMPILE AND RUN A SIMPLE PROGRAM

15   In this section, you learn how to compile and run a simple program that computes the volume of a railroad box car. You also review a lot of standard terminology used throughout the rest of this book.

16   Working with C++ is like working with most programming languages. First, you **write** a program using an editor. Next, you **compile** your program, translating it into machine instructions.

In its original form, your program is **text** or **source code**. Once translated, the source code becomes **object code**.

Your program's source code may be distributed among several files, which you can compile into separate object-code files. Subsequently, you **link** the separately compiled object-code files to produce **executable code**.

Finally, you **run** your executable code, or, said another way, you **execute** your program.

17   As usual, you generally go around two key loops many times as you search for bugs:

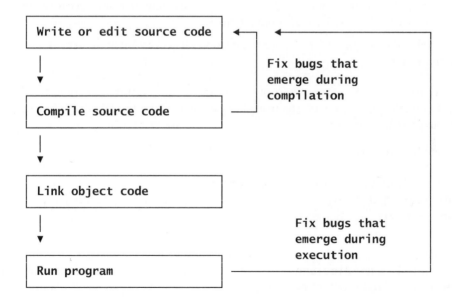

18   Typical C++ programs contain many **function definitions**, each of which contains a sequence of **variable declarations**, which tell the C++ compiler about the variables you intend to use, and **statements**, which tell the C++ compiler about the computations to be performed.

Every C++ program must contain a definition for a function named `main`. When you start a C++ program, that program starts to perform the computations specified in the `main` function.

In mathematics, a *function* is a set relating input variables uniquely to output variables. In C++ programming, the word *function* is used differently, inasmuch as the functions in C++ programs may have side effects, or may not produce consistent outputs for all inputs, or may not even produce outputs at all. Accordingly, many authors of books on programming prefer to use the word *procedure* instead of the word *function*. Recognizing, however, that the word *function* is solidly entrenched in the vernacular of C++ programming, this book uses *function* throughout.

20 The following program, which computes the volume of a typical railroad box car, consists of just one function, the `main` function:

```
main ( ) {
  11 * 9 * 40;
}
```

This `main` function consists of the **function name**, `main`, followed by matched parentheses—which you should ignore for now—followed by a single statement sandwiched between matched braces that delimit the function's **body**.

The one and only statement in the body of the `main` function contains two instances of the **multiplication operator**, `*`. Note that this statement, like most C++ statements, is terminated by a semicolon.

The semicolon, the parentheses, and the braces act as punctuation. Occasionally, such symbols, in such contexts, are called **punctuators**.

Note also that the sample program is quite catatonic: It accepts no input data and produces no output result.

21 To relieve the sample program of part of its catatonia, you can provide statements that tell the C++ compiler that you want the results of the multiplication to be displayed, as in the following revised program:

```
#include <iostream.h>
main ( ) {
  cout << "The volume of the box car is ";
  cout << 11 * 9 * 40;
  cout << endl;
}
```

The revised program introduces several concepts and syntactical markers, and forces the introduction of the line `#include <iostream.h>`. Accordingly, you need to zoom in, and to look at the revised program piece by piece.

22 The **output operator**, `<<`, also known as the **insertion operator**, always stands between a data-producing expression, located on the right, and a name that specifies a place to put those data on the left. When you want characters displayed on your screen, for example, you use `cout` as the name that specifies the place to put the data.

In the sample program, there are three output statements, each identified as such by the output operator. In the first instance, the output operator displays a **character string**; in C++, character strings are delimited on both ends by double-quotation marks:

```
cout << "The volume of the box car is ";
```

23   In the second instance, the output operator displays the result of an arithmetic computation:

```
cout << 11 * 9 * 40;
```

24   In the third instance, the output operator appears with endl, an acronym for *end line*, which causes the output operator to terminate the current line and to start a new one.

25   To use the output operator, you must inform the C++ compiler that you plan to use C++'s standard input–output library by including the following line in your program:

```
#include <iostream.h>
```

There is more to be said about such lines; for now, however, just include the prescribed line before the first instance of the output operator appears.

26   Note that C++ is **blank insensitive**; C++ treats all sequences of spaces, tabs, and carriage returns—other than those in character strings—as though there were just a single space. Thus, the following are equivalent:

```
#include <iostream.h>

main ( ) {
  cout << "The volume of the box car is ";
  cout << 11 * 9 * 40;
  cout << endl;
}


#include <iostream.h>

main ( )
{
  cout << "The volume of the box car is ";
  cout << 11 * 9 * 40;
  cout << endl;
}


#include <iostream.h>
main ( ) {
    cout << "The volume of the box car is ";
    cout << 11 * 9 * 40;
    cout << endl;
    }


#include <iostream.h>
main ( ){cout << "The volume of the box car is ";
        cout << 11 * 9 * 40;
        cout << endl;}
```

7

None of these layout options can be said to be "best" or "official." In fact, some experienced C++ programmers argue heatedly about how to arrange functions so as to maximize transparency and to please the eye. In this book, the functions are written in a style that both uses paper efficiently and lies within the envelope of common practice.

27 Note, however, that C++ is **case sensitive**; for example, if you write `Main` or `MAIN` when you mean `main`, C++ cannot understand your intent.

28 At this point, you have seen sample uses of two C++ operators: the multiplication operator and the output operator. These particular operators are built-in functions that work on inputs supplied to them according to the conventions of arithmetic: such functions are interspersed among their inputs, and those inputs are called **operands**.

29 Generally, you choose a source-code file name, such as `box_car`, to describe the file's contents, and you choose a source-code extension, such as `cxx`, to indicate that the file contains source code, producing a complete file name, such as `box_car.cxx`. Conventions on file extensions for C++ source code vary: some programmers prefer—and some compilers require—`C`, `cc`, or `cpp`.

The `cxx` variant is supposed to suggest two plus signs rotated 45°: many operating systems do not permit real plus signs to appear in names.

30 Unfortunately, the correct way to compile and link your source code files depends on your C++ supplier and on your operating system. For example, the name of the program that compiles and links may be `CC`, `g++`, or `cxx`, just to mention a three popular examples. Accordingly, you many need to refer to your compiler manual, or to ask a local wizard, if the instructions given in the following segments do not work for you.

31 On UNIX systems, one representative way to initiate compilation and linking is as follows, assuming that your program is in a file named `box_car.cxx`:

```
CC -o box_car box_car.cxx
```

Such an instruction to the operating system has several parts:

- `CC` means use a program that includes the C++ compiler and linker.
- `box_car.cxx` means work on the source-code file named `box_car.cxx`.
- `-o box_car` means put the executable code in a file named `box_car`.

32 On DOS systems, you compile and link programs a little differently. Assuming that your program is in a file named `box_car.cxx`, you produce executable code as follows:

```
CC -o box_car.exe box_car.cxx
```

The file name `box_car.exe` appears, instead of `box_car`, because DOS, by convention, requires files containing executable code to have an `exe` extension.

33 Once the C++ compiler and linker have placed executable code in the file named `box_car` (UNIX) or `box_car.exe` (DOS), you can run that executable code by just typing that file's name, followed by a carriage return:

34   Although the sample program communicates with you by way of output data displayed on your screen, it does not receive any input data after it is compiled. Instead, it works with data that were supplied as the program was written. Such data are said to be **wired in** or **hard coded**.

35   In this book, you see many templatelike, general-purpose program patterns that you can fill in to suit your own specific purpose. In these patterns, each place to be filled in is identified by a box that contains a description of the item to be inserted, `such as this`.

When you fill in a pattern, replacing descriptions with specific instances of the general categories described, you are said to **instantiate** the pattern.

36   Write a program that computes the volume of the Earth in cubic feet.
PRACTICE

37
HIGHLIGHTS

- When you work with C++, as with most programming languages, you write source code, the C++ compiler translates source code into object code, the C++ linker then links object code into executable code, and your computer runs that executable code.

- C++ functions contain sequences of computation-specifying statements.

- All C++ programs contain a function named `main`. When you run a C++ program, you initiate the computations specified in that `main` function.

- Many statements involve built-in operators, such as the multiplication operator, `*`, and the output operator, `<<`. Operators do their work on operands.

- To test simple programs, you often use data that you supply when you write the program. Such data are said to be wired in.

- If you plan to use the output operator, **then** you must inform the C++ compiler of your intention by including the following line near the beginning of your program:

  `#include <iostream.h>`

- If you wish to display characters, **then** use an output statement:

  `cout <<` `expression whose value is to be displayed` `;`

- If you want to terminate a line, **then** include an output statement with `endl`:

  `cout << endl;`

3 HOW TO DECLARE VARIABLES

38   In this section, you learn how to declare variables in C++. You also continue to review a lot of standard terminology used throughout the rest of this book.

39   A C++ **identifier** is a name consisting of letters and digits, the first of which must be a letter, with underscore, _, counting as a letter.

A **variable** is an identifier that serves as the name of a chunk of computer memory. Thus, each variable **refers to** a chunk of memory.

The variable's **data type** determines the size of the chunk and the way the bits in the chunk are interpreted. If the variable belongs to the `int` data type, a kind of *int*eger, the chunk of memory involved is likely to contain 32 bits, one of which determines the integer's sign and 31 of which determine the integer's absolute value.

The chunk of memory named by a variable is said to hold that variable's **value**. As a program runs, a variable's value may change, but a variable's data type never changes. Thus, the value of an integer variable named `length` could be the integer 40 at one time and the integer 41 at another, but `length`'s value could never be a floating-point number, such as `40.5`.

40   Because every variable is typed, the C++ compiler can allocate a memory chunk of the right size for each variable, once and for all, taking advantage of the fact that the value of the variable always will fit within the allocated memory chunk.

41   When you tell the C++ compiler the type of a variable inside `main`, you are said to **declare** the variable. Thus, the following program exhibits three variable declarations—all three variables are declared to be integer variables, because each is preceded by the data-type–declaring `int`.

```
main ( ) {
  int height;
  int width;
  int length;
  ...
}
```

42   You can combine several separate variable declarations into one, more concise variable declaration as long as each variable belongs to the same data type. In the following program fragment, for example, all three variables are declared to be integer variables in a single declaration:

```
main ( ) {
  int height, width, length;
  ...
}
```

Note the obligatory, variable-separating commas.

43 Storing a value in the memory chunk allocated for a variable is called **variable assignment**. Accordingly, whenever C++ places a value in such a memory chunk, the variable is said to be **assigned a value** and the value is said to be **assigned to the variable**.

44 You can **initialize** variables, as in the following program:

```
main ( ) {
  int height = 11;
  int width = 9;
  int length = 40;
  ...
}
```

You can combine several initializations into one, more concise variable declaration, as in the following example:

```
main ( ) {
  int height = 11, width = 9, length = 40;
  ...
}
```

Again, note the obligatory commas.

45 For the moment, the sample programs use test data that are wired in by way of initialized variables. Later on, in Section 5, you learn how to use test data that you provide via your keyboard or a file.

46 To change the value of a variable, you use the **assignment operator**, =. Three assignment statements appear in the following program:

```
#include <iostream.h>
main ( ) {
  int result, height = 11, width = 9, length = 40;
  result = height;
  result = result * width;
  result = result * length;
  cout << "The volume of the box car is ";
  cout << result;
  cout << endl;
}
```
————————————————— Result —————————————————
```
The volume of the box car is 3960
```

Of course, this program is a bit awkward—the only reason to split the computation of volume into three separate statements is to demonstrate that a variable can be assigned and then reassigned.

47 For storing integers, C++ provides a range of data-type possibilities, including char, short, int, and long. C++ compiler writers are free to choose the number of bytes associated with each type, provided that the following constraint is obeyed:

The number of bytes for the char type

$\leq$ The number of bytes for the short type

$\leq$ The number of bytes for the int type

$\leq$ The number of bytes for the long type

The char data type ordinarily is used for storing characters, but because character codes can be viewed as integers, char is viewed as one of the **integral data types**, along with short, int, and long.

48   For storing floating-point numbers, C++ also provides a range of type possibilities, including float, double, and long double, which obey the following constraint:

The number of bytes for the float type

$\leq$ The number of bytes for the double type

$\leq$ The number of bytes for the long double type

49   The implementation used to test the programs in this book allocates bytes as follows for the various data types:

Type	Bytes (typical)	Stores
char	1	character
short	2	integer
int	4	integer
long	4	integer
float	4	floating-point number
double	8	floating-point number
long double	8	floating-point number

50   For most integers, the short integer type is a bit small, and any data type larger than int is unnecessarily large. Analogously, for most floating-point numbers, the float floating-point type is a bit small, and any data type larger than double is unnecessarily large. Consequently, most programmers use int and double more than they do any other integer and floating-point types, and all the programs in the rest of this book use int and double for all integers and floating-point numbers.

51   Because the long and long double data types usually are unnecessarily large, and not
SIDE TRIP   supported directly by instructions in computer hardware, many C++ compiler writers arrange for long to be synonymous to int, and for long double to be synonymous to double.

52   Experienced programmers occasionally use short or float when maximum execution speed is of prime importance.

53   You can include **comments** in C++ programs in two ways. First, whenever the C++ compiler encounters two adjacent forward slashes, //, C++ ignores both the slashes and the rest of the line on which the slashes appear:

```
// Short comment.
```

Second, whenever C++ encounters a slash followed immediately by an asterisk, /*, C++ ignores both the /* characters and all other characters up to and including the next asterisk followed immediately by a slash, */.

```
/*
Long comment ···
that just goes on ···
and on ···
*/
```

If you wish to test how a program works without certain lines of source code, you can hide those lines in a comment, instead of deleting them.

54 Note that you cannot place a /* ··· */ comment inside another /* ··· */ comment. If you try, you find that the inner comment's */ terminates the outer comment, and your C++ compiler cannot compile your program:

```
/*  ←─────────────────────────────────┐
                                       │
First part of outer comment ···        │
                                       │    */ of inner comment
/*  ←── Commented out                  │    terminates /* of
                                       │    outer comment
Inner comment ···                      │
                                       │
*/ ────────────────────────────────────┘
Second part of outer comment ···
*/  ←── Dangles
```

55
SIDE TRIP 55 If you are curious about how much memory your C++ implementation allocates for the various data types, you can compile and execute the following program, which uses the sizeof operator to determine data-type size:

```
#include <iostream.h>
main ( ) {
   cout << "Data Type     Bytes" << endl
        << "char          " << sizeof(char) << endl
        << "short         " << sizeof(short) << endl
        << "int           " << sizeof(int) << endl
        << "long          " << sizeof(long) << endl
        << "float         " << sizeof(float) << endl
        << "double        " << sizeof(double) << endl
        << "long double   " << sizeof(long double) << endl;
}
```

56 Write a program that computes the volume of the Earth in cubic feet. Wire in the radius
PRACTICE of the Earth using a variable, r.

- A variable is an identifier that names a chunk of memory.

- If you wish to introduce a variable, **then** you must declare the data type of that variable in a variable declaration:

  `data type` `variable name` ;

- If you wish to provide an initial value for a variable, **then** include that initial value in the declaration statement:

  `data type` `variable name` = `initial-value expression` ;

- If you wish to reassign a variable, **then** use an assignment statement:

  `variable name` = `new-value expression` ;

- The integral data types are `char`, `short`, `int`, and `long`.

4 HOW TO WRITE ARITHMETIC EXPRESSIONS

58 In Section 2, you saw sample expressions involving the multiplication operator, *, and the output operator <<. In this section, you learn about additional operators and about the way C++ handles operator precedence and associativity.

59 You arrange for basic arithmetic calculations using the +, -, *, and / operators for addition, subtraction, multiplication, and division:

```
6 + 3          // Add, evaluating to 9
6 - 3          // Subtract, evaluating to 3
6 * 3          // Multiply, evaluating to 18
6 / 3          // Divide, evaluating to 2
6 + y          // Add, evaluating to 6 plus y's value
x - 3          // Subtract, evaluating to x's value minus 3
x * y          // Multiply, evaluating to x's value times y's value
x / y          // Divide, evaluating to x's value divided by y's value
```

60 When an integer denominator does not divide evenly into an integer numerator, the division operator truncates, rather than rounds, the result, producing another integer. The **modulus operator**, %, produces the remainder:

```
5 / 3          // Divide, evaluating to 1, rather than 2 or 1.66667
5 % 3          // Divide, evaluating to the remainder, 2
```

Of course, when dividing floating-point numbers, C++ produces a floating-point result:

```
5.0 / 3.0      // Divide, evaluating to 1.66667
```

61 Arithmetic expressions can contain one operator, but they also can contain no operators or more than one operator:

```
6              // Constant expression
x              // Variable expression
6 + 3 + 2      // Produces 11
6 - 3 - 2      // Produces 1
6 * 3 * 2      // Produces 36
6 / 3 / 2      // Produces 1
```

62 C++ follows standard practice with respect to the syntax rules that dictate how the C++ compiler crystallizes operands around operators. In the following, for example, the C++ compiler takes 6 + 3 * 2 to be equivalent to 6 + (3 * 2), rather than to (6 + 3) * 2, because multiplication has **precedence** higher than addition:

```
6 + 3 * 2          // Equivalent to 6 + (3 * 2), rather than (6 + 3) * 2
                   // Equivalent to 12, rather than 18
```

63   When an expression contains two operators of equal precedence, such as multiplication and division, the C++ compiler handles the expression as in the following examples:

```
6 / 3 * 2       // Equivalent to (6 / 3) * 2 = 4,
                // rather than 6 / (3 * 2) = 1
6 * 3 / 2       // Equivalent to (6 * 3) / 2 = 9,
                // rather than 6 * (3 / 2) = 6
```

Thus, in C++, the multiplication and division operators are said to **associate** from left to right. Most operators associate from left to right, but some operators do not, as you learn in Segment 72.

64   Of course, you can always deploy parentheses around subexpressions whenever the C++ compiler's interpretation of the entire expression is not the interpretation you want:

```
6 + 3 * 2       // Value is 12, rather than 18
(6 + 3) * 2     // Value is 18, rather than 12
```

You can also use parentheses to make your intentions clearer. In the following, for example, the parentheses are not required, but many programmers insert them anyway, just to make the meaning of the expression absolutely clear:

```
6 + 3 * 2       // Value is clearly 12
6 + (3 * 2)     // Value is even more clearly 12
```

Inserting such parentheses is a good idea, especially when you are working with less familiar operators, such as the output operator, or when you are working with large expressions.

65   Most operators are **binary operators**; that is, they have two operands. In C++, those two operands are found on the immediate left and immediate right of the operator. Some operators, such as the negation operator, -, and unary plus, +, have just one operand, found on the immediate right of the operator. Such operators are **unary operators**.

You can always determine whether the - and + denote unary or binary operators by looking to see whether there is any constant, variable, or subexpression to the immediate left. If there is, then - denotes subtraction and + denotes addition; otherwise, - denotes negation and + is handled as if it were not there at all.

66   The precedence of the negation operator is higher than that of +, -, *, or /:

```
- 6 * 3 / 2     // Equivalent to ((- 6) * 3) / 2 = -9
```

67   When arithmetic expressions contain a mixture of data types, they are called **mixed expressions**. The general rule about mixed expressions is that C++ attempts to convert one number into another in a way that does not lose information. Thus, when given a mixed expression that multiplies a floating-point number by an integer, C++ converts the integer into a floating-point number first, before multiplying.

68   Sometimes, however, C++ must do a conversion that loses information, as when an integer variable is assigned a value derived from an expression that produces a floating-point number. Many C++ compilers issue warnings when they are asked to perform such information-losing, **narrowing conversions**.

18

69 If you want to tell C++ to convert an expression from one type to another explicitly, rather than relying on automatic conversion, possibly avoiding a quarrelsome compiler warning, you can **cast** the expression. To do casting, you prefix the expression with the name of the desired type in parentheses.

If, for example, i is an integer and d is a double, you can cast i to a double and d to an integer as follows:

```
(double) i        // A double expression
(int) d           // An int expression
```

Note that the original types of the i and d variables remain undisturbed: i remains an int variable, and d remains a double variable.

70 Generally, you should avoid casting, because your C++ compiler probably will make conversion choices that are as good or better than those you force by casting.

71 The assignment operator, =, like all operators in C++, produces a value. By convention, the value produced is the same as the value assigned. Thus, the value of the expression y = 5 is 5.

Accordingly, assignment expressions can appear as subexpressions nested inside larger expressions.

In the following assignment expression, for example, the assignment expression, y = 5, which assigns a value to y, appears inside a larger assignment expression, which assigns a value to x as well:

```
x = (y = 5)
```

When the assignment expression is evaluated, 5 is assigned to y first; then, the value of the subexpression, which is also 5, is assigned to x.

72 The assignment operator, =, in contrast to all the other operators that you have seen so
SIDE TRIP far, associates from right to left. Accordingly, the expression x = y = 5 is equivalent to the expression x = (y = 5).

Fortunately, x = y = 5 *does not* mean (x = y) = 5, because the value of an assignment statement, such as x = y, is *not* a variable name. Thus, (x = y) = 5 makes no sense, and if the assignment operator were to associate left to right, x = y = 5 would make no sense either.

73 You can have several output operators in the same output statement, as in the following program:

```
#include <iostream.h>
main ( ) {
  cout << "The volume of the box car is " << 11 * 9 * 40 << endl;
}
```
——————————— Result ———————————
```
The volume of the box car is 3960
```

19

Because the output operator associates left to right, the preceding program is equivalent to the following program:

```
#include <iostream.h>
main ( ) {
   ((cout << "The volume of the box car is ") << 11 * 9 * 40) << endl;
}
```

———————————— Result ————————————
The volume of the box car is 3960

To see how C++ handles such output statements, you need to take a fresh look at cout and at the output operator. So far, you have viewed cout merely as a symbol that specifies that you want the data handed to the output operator to be displayed on your screen. More precisely, however, cout is a variable, and like all variables, it is the name of a chunk of memory, and that chunk of memory tells C++ the place where you want to put data.

Next, you need to know that each output expression refers to the same chunk of memory that is referred to by the output expression's left-side operand. Accordingly, the output expression cout << "The volume of the box car is " refers to a chunk of memory that specifies a place to put data, and that chunk of memory is the same chunk of memory that is named by cout.

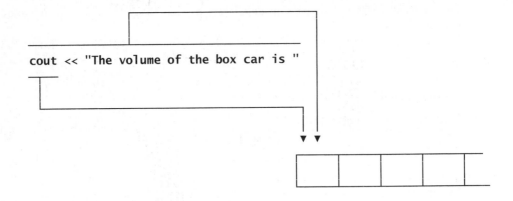

74 The chunk of memory named by cout contains not only an output-place specification, but also state-describing information of various sorts. Inside that memory chunk, the state-describing information changes as computing progresses, but the output-place specification does not change.

75 Unlike the values of most variables, the value of the cout variable is not displayable on your screen. The value of cout is contained in a chunk of memory that is meaningful to only the output operator.

76 Aligning the output operators in long output statements makes those output statements easier to read:

```
#include <iostream.h>
main ( ) {
  cout << "The volume of the box car is "
       << 11 * 9 * 40
       << endl;
}
```
———————————————— Result ————————————————
The volume of the box car is 3960

77   From the perspective of operator precedence, you should remember that the output operator has precedence lower than that of all the arithmetic operators. Accordingly, no parentheses are needed to keep all the arithmetic operations together.

78   On the other hand, the assignment operator has precedence lower than that of the output operator. Accordingly, the parentheses are essential in the following program.

```
#include <iostream.h>
main ( ) {
  int volume;
  cout << "The volume of the box car is ";
  cout << (volume = 11 * 9 * 40);
  cout << endl;
  // ... Statements using the volume variable go here ...
}
```

If you wrote cout << volume = 11 * 9 * 40;, C++ would try to make sense of the statement as though you had written (cout << volume) = 11 * 9 * 40;, which makes no sense.

79   The reason that the assignment operator has precedence lower than that of the output operator is that << has another meaning for which high precedence makes sense. In particular, when the operand on the left is an integral data type, << denotes the **left-shift operator**, a meaning C++ inherits from C. In Section 9, you learn that C++ allows functions and operators to have more than one meaning, which C++ keeps sorted out through what is called function and operator overloading.

SIDE TRIP

80   So far, you have learned about arithmetic operators, +, -, *, /, and %, the output operator, <<, and the assignment operator, =. In general, an **operator** is a symbol, or combination of symbols, that is treated by the compiler in a special way.

Most operators are special in that they receive arguments via flanking operands, rather than via the parenthesized argument lists used by ordinary functions. Some operators, such as the new operator, which you learn about in Section 27, and the delete operator, which you learn about in Section 43 are special in that they do not evaluate their arguments. Still others, such as the conditional operator, which you learn about in Section 18, are special in that they evaluate some arguments, but not others.

81   The precedences and associativity of the operators that you have learned about so far are given in the following table, arranged from highest precedence to lowest. Appendix A provides a complete table.

Operators	Associativity
- (unary) + (unary)	right to left
* / %	left to right
+ -	left to right
<<	left to right
=	right to left

- C++ offers negation, addition, subtraction, multiplication, division, output, and assignment operators, and C++ follows standard precedence and associativity rules.

- If you want to make your arithmetic expressions clearer, **then** use parentheses to create subexpressions.

- The output operator has precedence lower than that of the arithmetic operators. The assignment operator has still lower precedence.

- If you wish to combine several output statements into one, **then** instantiate the following pattern:

```
cout << first expression
     << second expression
     << ...
     << final expression ;
```

5 HOW TO WRITE STATEMENTS THAT READ INFORMATION FROM YOUR KEYBOARD

83   In this section, you learn how to use the input operator, >>, which enables your programs to obtain information from your keyboard, thus eliminating the need to use wired-in data when you experiment with programs.

84   The **input operator, >>**, also known as the **extraction operator**, is the complement of the output operator.

When used with the cout output-place specification, the output operator displays the value of an expression on your screen. When used with the cin input-place specification, the input operator picks up a value for a variable by watching what you type on your keyboard. In the following program, for example, each input expression picks up an integer and assigns that integer to a variable:

```
#include <iostream.h>
main ( ) {
  int height, width, length;
  cout << "Please type three integers." << endl;
  cin >> height;
  cin >> width;
  cin >> length;
  cout << "The volume of a "
       << height << " by " << width << " by " << length
       << " box car is " << height * width * length << endl;
}
```

85   When you execute the volume-computing program, presuming that you have named it box_car, you could witness the following:

```
box_car                                        ←— You type
Please type three integers.                    ←— Your program types
11 9 40                                        ←— You type
The volume of a 11 by 9 by 40 box car is 3960. ←— Your program types
```

When you use the box_car program, you can use spaces, tabs, or carriage returns to separate the integers and to mark the end of the final integer.

Note that, if you are using the UNIX operating system, the characters that you type accumulate temporarily in an **input buffer** before delivery to your program. Delivery occurs only when you type a carriage return. Accordingly, the box_car program lies inert until you not only type three integers, but also supply a carriage return following the third one.

```
Spaces separate integers
    │ │
    ▼ ▼
11 9 40 ←— Carriage return marks the end of a line of input and
         delivers the accumulated characters to your program
```

86 Just as an output statement can contain many output operators, an input statement can contain many input operators. The following program picks up three values and assigns those three values to three variables.

```cpp
#include <iostream.h>
main ( ) {
  int height, width, length;
  cout << "Please type three integers." << endl;
  cin >> height >> width >> length;
  cout << "The volume of a "
        << height << " by " << width << " by " << length
        << " box car is " << height * width * length << endl;
}
```

space or <cr> are token boundaries for inputs

87 You can incorporate multiple input operators into one input statement for the same reason that you can include multiple output operators into one output statement: In C++, each input expression refers to the same chunk of memory that is referred to by that input expression's left-side operand. Accordingly, the input expression `cin >> height` refers to a chunk of memory that specifies an input place, and that chunk of memory is the same chunk of memory that is named by `cin`:

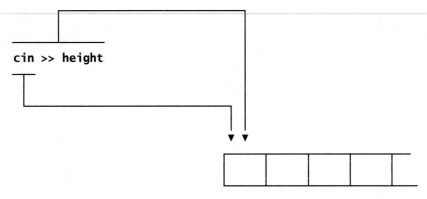

```
cin >> height
```

88 Later on, in Section 21, you learn about mechanisms that enable you to read data from
SIDE TRIP files. Meanwhile, if you happen to be using UNIX or DOS, you may wish to take advantage of the **input-redirection mechanism** that enables you to tell your program to accept input from a file as though that input were coming from your keyboard.

To supply information from a file, you first prepare a file containing the characters that you would have supplied from your keyboard:

11 9 40

The command line that redirects input from your keyboard to the file is as follows, assuming that your program's name is `box_car`, and that your data file's name is `test_data`,

box_car < test_data

89 Write a program that computes the volume of any planet in cubic meters. Arrange to
PRACTICE provide the radius of the planet at run time.

24

- If you plan to use the input operator, **then** you must inform C++ of your intention by including the following line near the beginning of your program:

  ```
  #include <iostream.h>
  ```

- If you wish to read data from your keyboard, **then** use an input statement:

  ```
  cin >> variable whose value is to be assigned ;
  ```

- If you wish to combine several input statements into one, **then** instantiate the following pattern:

  ```
  cin >> first variable
      >> second variable
      >> ...
      >> final variable ;
  ```

- If you wish to redirect input from your keyboard to a file, **then** instantiate the following pattern:

  ```
  program name < file name
  ```

6 HOW TO DEFINE SIMPLE FUNCTIONS

91 In this section, you learn how to define C++ functions in addition to the required `main`
function. In the process, you learn how to work with arguments, parameters, and returned
values.

92 The following program computes the volume of a box car:

```
#include <iostream.h>
main ( ) {
  cout << "The volume of the box car is " << 11 * 9 * 40 << endl;
}
```

Of course, if you propose to compute the volumes of many box cars, of varying length, you
certainly should define a volume-computing function, perhaps named `box_car_volume`,
to do the work:

```
#include <iostream.h>
// ... Definition of box_car_volume function will go here ...
main ( ) {
  cout << "The volume of the box car is "
       << box_car_volume (11, 9, 40)
       << endl;
}
```

In this example, the `box_car_volume` function has three arguments—11, 9, and 40. As
illustrated, C++ requires function arguments to be separated by commas.

93 In the example shown in the previous segment, the arguments are all constant expressions,
but, of course, arguments can be variable expressions, such as `height`, `width`, and `length`,
or expressions containing operators, such as `length + stretch`:

```
#include <iostream.h>
// ... Definition of box_car_volume function will go here ...
main ( ) {
  int height = 11, width = 9, length = 40, stretch = 10;
  cout << "The volume of the standard box car is "
       << box_car_volume (height, width, length)
       << endl
       << "The volume of a stretched box car is "
       << box_car_volume (height, width, length + stretch)
       << endl;
}
```

94 Whenever a call to the `box_car_volume` function appears, the C++ compiler must arrange
for the following to be done:

- Reserve chunks of memory for the values of the argument expressions.

- Write the values of those argument expressions into those memory chunks.

- Identify the memory chunks with parameters—say, h, w, and 1.

- Evaluate the expression h * w * 1.

- Return the value of h * w * 1 for use in other computations.

95 You define the box_car_volume function as follows:

```
int box_car_volume (int h, int w, int 1) {
   return h * w * 1;
}
```

Here is what each part of a function definition does:

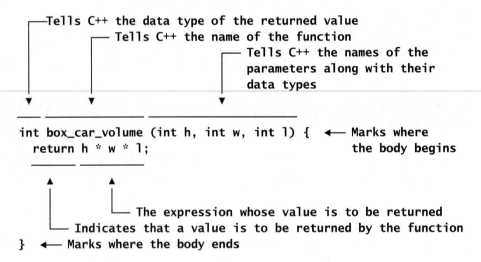

96 Note that a function's **parameters** are just variables that are initialized with argument values each time that the function is called.

97 Note also that you must declare data types for parameters and returned values when you define a C++ function:

- You declare the data type of each parameter in each function at the place where you introduce the parameter.

- You declare the data type of the value returned by each function in every C++ program at the place where you name the function to be defined.

98 In the following example, the definition of the box_car_volume function appears in a complete program:

```
#include <iostream.h>
// Define box_car_volume first:
int box_car_volume (int h, int w, int l) {
   return h * w * l;
}
// Then, define main:
main ( ) {
   int height = 11, width = 9, length = 40, stretch = 10;
   cout << "The volume of the standard box car is "
        << box_car_volume (height, width, length)
        << endl
        << "The volume of a stretched box car is "
        << box_car_volume (height, width, length + stretch)
        << endl;
}
```

———————————————————— Result ————————————————————

```
The volume of the standard box car is 3960
The volume of a stretched box car is 4950
```

99   Note that you must declare the data type of each parameter individually, because data types in parameter declarations, unlike data types in variable declarations, do not propagate across commas. Thus, the following is wrong:

┌─── **Wrong, data type does not propagate**

```
int box_car_volume (int h, w, l) {
   ...
}
```

100   The C++ compiler ordinarily requires C++ programs to be ordered such that each function's definition appears before calls to that function appear. Thus, box_car_volume must be defined before main is defined, because main contains a call to box_car_volume.

The reason for requiring programs to be so ordered is that such ordering simplifies the development of efficient compilers.

Later, in Section 23, you learn that function prototypes make it possible to write programs in which function calls do appear before definitions. Until then, be sure each function's definition appears before calls to that function appear.

101   You can leave out the declaration of a function's return value data type if that value is to be
SIDE TRIP an integer, because if there is no data-type specifier, the C++ compiler assumes, by default, that the returned value is to be an integer. Generally, however, most good programmers declare the return data type for every function, except for the main function, as explained in Segment 105.

102 When `box_car_volume` is called with three integer variables as arguments, a copy of the value of the first argument becomes the value of the first parameter, h; a copy of the value of the second argument becomes the value of the second parameter, w; and a copy of the value of the third argument becomes the value of the third parameter, l. Assuming, for example, that the value of the variable `height` is 11, that the value of `width` is 9, and that the value of `length` is 40, then the copying works like this:

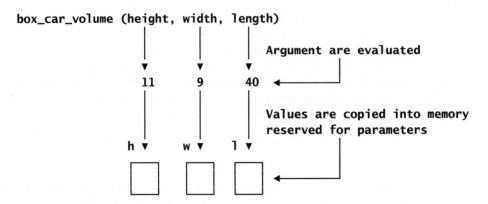

103 Some functions *do not* return values used in other computations. Instead, they are executed for some other purpose, such as displaying a value.

Accordingly, C++ allows you to use the `void` symbol as though it were a data type for return values. When C++ sees `void` used as though it were a return value data type, C++ knows that nothing is to be returned.

For example, in the following variation on the program in Segment 98, display is handled in the `display_box_car_volume` function, so there is no value to be returned. Accordingly, `void` appears instead of a data-type name in the definition of `display_box_car_volume`, and `display_box_car_volume` contains no `return` statement:

```
#include <iostream.h>
// Define display_box_car_volume first:
void display_box_car_volume (int h, int w, int l) {
  cout << "The volume of the box car is " << h * w * l << endl;
}
// Then, define main:
main ( ) {
  int height = 11, width = 9, length = 40;
  display_box_car_volume (height, width, length);
}
———————————————— Result ————————————————
The volume of the box car is 3960
```

104 Because `display_box_car_volume` has no return statement, it is said to **fall off its end**, returning nothing, which is allowed for only those functions that have a `void` return type.

Some programmers think it inelegant to have functions that fall off the end. Accordingly, those programmers write empty `return` statements, as in the following amended version of `display_box_car_volume`:

```
void display_box_car_volume (int h, int w, int l) {
  cout << "The volume of the box car is " << h * w * l << endl;
  return;
}
```

105 Many programmers treat the `main` function specially in that they omit the return type declaration and include no return statement. Such `main` functions are treated by the C++ compiler as though there were an `int` type declaration in front of `main` and a `return 0;` statement at the end of `main`. The 0 tells the operating system that the program terminated in the expected way, rather than with some sort of error.

Some C++ compilers issue warnings whenever either the type declaration or the return statement are missing.

106 Note that, because C++ is case sensitive, the function name `display_box_car_volume` is different from the function name `Display_box_car_volume` and different from the function name `DISPLAY_BOX_CAR_VOLUME`. Most C++ programmers use all-lower-case function names.

107 Unlike most languages, C++ allows you to define multiple functions with the same name, as long as each version has a different arrangement of parameter data types.

Whenever there is more than one definition for a function, the function name is said to be **overloaded**. The use of the word *overloaded* is unfortunate, because the word *overloaded* usually suggests abuse, as in *the overloaded circuit blew a fuse*. In C++, no suggestion of abuse is intended, however. Instead, the ability to handle function overloading is a distinctive feature of the language.

108 You can, for example, define one `display_box_car_volume` function that handles integers, and another `display_box_car_volume` function that handles floating-point numbers:

```
// Define integer display_box_car_volume function:
void display_box_car_volume (int h, int w, int l) {
  cout << "The integer volume of the box car is "
       << h * w * l
       << endl;
}

// Then, define floating-point display_box_car_volume function:
void display_box_car_volume (double h, double w, double l) {
  cout << "The floating-point volume of the box car is "
       << h * w * l
       << endl;
}
```

Then, you can put both functions to work in the same program:

```
#include <iostream.h>
// ... Define integer display_box_car_volume function here ...
// ... Define floating-point display_box_car_volume function here ...
// Then, define main:
main ( ) {
  int int_height = 11,
      int_width = 9,
      int_length = 40;
  double double_height = 10.5,
         double_width = 9.5,
         double_length = 40.0;
  display_box_car_volume (int_height, int_width, int_length);
  display_box_car_volume (double_height, double_width, double_length);
}
```
——————————————— Result ———————————————
```
The integer volume of the box car is 3960
The floating-point volume of the box car is 3990
```

109 From this point on, most of the examples in this book deal with floating-point numbers, largely because many examples will involve the computation of cylinder volumes, which requires the use of a floating-point value for π.

110 Write a program that computes the volume of any planet in cubic meters. Have the volume
PRACTICE computation performed by a function named sphere. Arrange to provide the radius of the planet at run time.

111 The energy of a moving mass is given by the formula $\frac{1}{2}mv^2$. Write a program that deter-
PRACTICE mines the energy ratio of a car moving at two speeds provided at run time. Write and use a function name square in your solution. Use your program to determine how much more energy a car has when moving at 80 miles per hour than when it is moving at 55 miles per hour.

112
HIGHLIGHTS
- Whenever a function is called, the function's arguments are evaluated and copies of the resulting values are assigned to the function's parameters. Then, the statements in the function's body are evaluated. When a return statement is evaluated, the argument of the return expression is evaluated, and that value becomes the value of the function call.

- When you define a function, C++ requires you to declare a data type for each parameter and for the value that the function returns.

- If you want to define a function that does not return a value, **then** supply void in place of an ordinary data-type declaration.

- You can define many identically named functions, as long as each of those identically named functions has a unique pattern of parameter data types.

- **If** you want to define your own function, **then** instantiate the following pattern:

```
data type  function name  (data type 1  parameter 1,
                           ...,
                           data type 1  parameter 1) {
   declaration 1
   ...
   declaration m
   statement 1
   ...
   statement n
}
```

7 HOW TO BENEFIT FROM PROCEDURE ABSTRACTION

113   In this section, you review what procedure abstraction is and how procedure abstraction increases your efficiency and makes your programs easier to maintain.

114   When you move computational detail into a function, you are said to be doing **procedure abstraction,** and you are said to be hiding the details of how a computation is done behind a **procedure-abstraction barrier.**

     The key virtue of procedure abstraction is that *you make it easy to reuse your programs.* Instead of trying to copy particular lines of program, you—or another programmer— arrange to call a previously defined function.

115   Another virtue of procedure abstraction is that *you push details out of sight and out of mind*, making your programs easier to read and enabling you to concentrate on high-level steps.

116   Another virtue of procedure abstraction is that *you can debug your programs more easily*. By dividing a program into small, independently debuggable pieces, you exploit the powerful divide-and-conquer problem-solving heuristic.

117   Still another virtue of procedure abstraction is that *you easily can augment repetitive computations*. For example, you have seen the floating-point version of box_car_volume defined this way:

```
double box_car_volume (double h, double w, double l) {
  return h * w * l;
}
```

You easily can add a line that displays the volume every time that the volume is computed:

```
double box_car_volume (double h, double w, double l) {
  cout << "The volume is " h * w * l << endl;
  return h * w * l;
}
```

Thus, you do not need even to bother to find all the places where a volume is computed, because you need only to change the box_car_volume function's definition.

118   Another virtue of procedure abstraction is that *you easily can improve how a computation is done*. You might decide, for example, that it is wasteful for your box_car_volume function to multiply out height, width, and length twice. Accordingly, you might decide to do the computation just once, using a variable, named result, to hold on to the value:

```
double box_car_volume (double h, double w, double l) {
  double result = h * w * l;
  cout << "The volume is " result << endl;
  return result;
}
```

Again, you do not need to bother to find all the places where the volume is computed using the `box_car_volume` function; you need only to change the `box_car_volume` function's definition.

119   Still another virtue of procedure abstraction is that *you easily can change the way a computation is done.* If you decide to measure size the way the U.S. Postal Service measures size, instead of by computing volume, you easily can redefine `box_car_volume`.

```
double box_car_volume (double h, double w, double l) {
  double result = h + w + l;
  cout << "The post-office size is " << result << endl;
  return result;
}
```

At this point, of course, you should also rename your function to bring the name into line with what the function does.

120   Write a function named `c_to_f` that transforms an integer argument into twice that integer
PRACTICE plus 30.

Next, amend your `c_to_f` function such that it displays "Performing an approximate temperature conversion" every time it is called.

Next, improve your `c_to_f` function by having it add 40 to the argument, multiply by 9/5, and subtract 40.

Finally, adapt your `c_to_f` function such that the argument is in Celsius degrees relative to absolute zero and the result returned is in Fahrenheit degrees relative to absolute zero. Absolute zero is -273 degrees Celsius.

For each change, comment on the corresponding benefit provided by function abstraction.

121
HIGHLIGHTS

- *Procedure abstraction* hides the details of computations inside functions, thus moving those details behind an abstraction barrier.

- You should practice procedure abstraction so as to take advantage of the following benefits:

  - Your programs become easier to reuse.

  - Your programs become easier to read.

  - Your programs become easier to debug.

  - Your programs become easier to augment.

  - Your programs become easier to improve.

  - Your programs become easier to adapt.

8 HOW TO WORK WITH LOCAL AND GLOBAL VARIABLES

122   The **extent** of a variable is the time during which a chunk of memory is allocated for that variable. The **scope** of a variable is that portion of a program where that variable can be evaluated or assigned.

In this section, you learn how C++ handles extent and scope. In particular, you learn that you can reuse names for parameters and local variables, as long as you do not try to use any name more than once per function.

123   It is important to know that the parameter values established when a function is entered are available only inside the function. It is as though C++ builds a isolating fence to protect any other uses of the same parameter name outside of the function. Consider `box_car_volume`, for example:

```
double box_car_volume (double h, double w, double l) {
  return h * w * l;
}
```

When `box_car_volume` is used, any existing values for other variables that happen to be named h, w, and l are protected:

```
box_car_volume fence
   The value of h, w, and l inside
   this fence are isolated from
   values outside

   Function computes the value of
   h * w * l using the values of
   h, w, and l inside this fence
```

```
The values of h, w, and l
outside the fence, if any,
are not affected by the
values inside
```

124   The reason C++ acts as though it builds an isolating fence around each function's parameters is that C++ reserves a chunk of memory for each parameter every time the corresponding function is called. In the `box_car_volume` example, a new chunk of memory is reserved for the parameters, h, w, and l, and the arguments' values are placed in those chunks, as shown here for l:

```
Memory reserved for l,
a variable in main
```
```
Memory reserved for l,
a parameter in box_car_volume
```

Thus, the reassignment of the parameter, l, inside the function has no effect on the value of the variable, l, outside, even though the names, l and l, happen to be the same.

Because C++ generally reserves new chunks of memory for parameters and variables, into which values are copied, C++ is said to be a **call-by-value** language.

125 In the following program, for example, 1's value is 40 before box_car_volume has been entered, 1's value is 50 as box_car_volume is executed, and 1's value is 40 after the execution of box_car_volume.

```
#include <iostream.h>
// Define box_car_volume first:
double box_car_volume (double h, double w, double l) {
  cout << "The value of l inside box_car_volume is "
      << l << endl;
  return h * w * l;
}
// Then, define main:
main ( ) {
  double l = 40.0, volume;
  cout << "The value of l outside box_car_volume is "
      << l << endl;
  volume = box_car_volume (10.5, 9.5, l + 10.0);
  cout << "The volume of a stretched box car is "
      << volume << endl;
  cout << "The value of l outside box_car_volume is still "
      << l << endl;
}
```

────────────── Result ──────────────
```
The value of l outside box_car_volume is 40
The value of l inside box_car_volume is 50
The volume of a stretched box car is 4987.5
The value of l outside box_car_volume is still 40
```

126 Because parameters are just variables that happen to be initialized by argument values, you can change the value of any parameter using an assignment statement. For example, you could amend the box_car_volume function as follows:

```
double box_car_volume (double h, double w, double l) {
  l = h * w * l;
  return l;
}
```

Using 1 as a name for the volume is bad programming practice, however, because such use leaves 1 with more than one meaning.

127 Here are two other important consequences of parameter isolation:

- The values of a function's parameters are not available after that function has returned.

- When one function calls another, the values of the parameters in the calling function are not available during the execution of the called function.

128 In the following program, box_car_volume is redefined, yet again, albeit awkwardly, to illustrate the limited availability of parameter values:

```
#include <iostream.h>
// Define multiplier and box_car_volume first:
double multiplier ( ) {
  return h * w * l;                                          // BUG!
}
double box_car_volume (double h, double w, double l) {
  return multiplier ( );
}
// Then, define main:
main ( ) {
  cout << "The volume of the box car is "
       << box_car_volume (10.5, 9.5, 40.0) << endl;
  cout << "The value of the parameters are "
       << h << ", " << w << ", and " << l                   // BUG!
       << endl;
}
```

In this program, box_car_volume asks multiplier—a function with no parameters—to perform the actual computation of h * w * l. However, the C++ compiler cannot compile multiplier, because no values for the h, w, or l parameters of box_car_volume are available to multiplier.

Moreover, C++ cannot compile the second output statement in the main function. The reason is that h, w, and l exist only during the execution of the function in which they appear as parameters; h, w, and l no longer exist once that function has returned.

129   In general, a **declaration** is a program element that provides a compiler with essential information or useful advise. In C++ programming, the word *declaration* is most often used for program elements that inform the compiler about the data type associated with an identifier. For example, when you specify the type of a variable or parameter, you are said to *declare* the variable or parameter.

A **definition** causes a compiler to set aside memory at compile time. For example, when you introduce a variable *outside* of any function body, you both *declare* and *define* the variable, because you inform the compiler about the variable's type and you cause the compiler to set aside memory for the variable at compile time.

On the other hand, when you introduce a variable *inside* a function, you only *declare* that variable, because the compiler does not set aside memory for that variable at compile time.

Generally, when a variable is both declared and defined, you say, as a sort of shorthand, that it is defined; otherwise, it is declared.

Functions are both *declared* and *defined*, because you must specify their return type and because the compiler sets aside memory for functions at compile time.

130   A variable *declared* inside a function definition is said to be a **local variable**; some programmers prefer to call such a variable an **automatic variable**. A variable *defined* outside of any function definition is said to be a **global variable**.

131   What you have learned about parameters also applies to local variables:

- Local variables are available only inside the function in which they are declared. Thus, the assignment of a local variable has no effect on other, identically named variables or parameters that appear in the definitions of other functions.

- The values of a function's local variables are not available after that function has returned.

- When one function calls another, the values of the local variables in the calling function are not available during the execution of the called function.

132 The rules for global variables—those defined outside of any function—are quite different:

- Global variable values are available to all functions that are defined after the global variable is defined, except in functions in which there is a parameter or local variable that happens to have the same name. Such parameters or local variables are said to **shadow** the corresponding global variables.

- In places where a global variable value is not shadowed, its value can be changed by an assignment statement. The change affects all subsequent evaluation of the global variable.

133 The memory set aside for a global variable is never reallocated, so global variables are said to have **static extent**. The memory allocated for parameters and local variables is reallocated as soon as the corresponding function has finished executing, so parameters and local variables are said to have **dynamic extent**.

Global variables can be evaluated and assigned at any point in a program after they are defined, so global variables are said to have **universal scope**. Parameters and local variables can be evaluated and assigned only in the function in which they are declared. Accordingly, parameters and local variables are said to have **local scope**.

134 Suppose that you want to perform certain computations involving the mathematical constant π. You could use 3.14159 explicitly in such places, but a more elegant alternative is to define a global variable, pi, with the appropriate value:

```
#include <iostream.h>
// First define pi to be a global variable:
double pi = 3.14159;
// Then, define tank_car_volume, a function that uses pi:
double tank_car_volume (double r, double l) {
  return pi * r * r * l;
}
// Then, define main:
main ( ) {
  cout << "The volume of a standard tank car is "
       << tank_car_volume (3.5, 40.0) << endl;
}
——————————————— Result ———————————————
The volume of a standard tank car is 1539.38
```

135   Because pi is not only a global variable, but also a mathematical constant, it is best to add `const` to the definition:

```
const double pi = 3.14159;
```

With the definition marked by `const`, your C++ compiler should complain if pi ever appears on the left side of an assignment statement.

```
pi = 3.0  ← Will not compile; pi is supposed to be a constant
```

136   Rather than define pi yourself, you can rely, if you wish, on C++'s library of mathematics

SIDE TRIP   constants and functions, which contains various **macros**.

Before the main work of translation to machine code begins, the C++ compiler replaces each instance of each macro identifier by a character sequence prescribed in the macro's declaration. Thus, the C++ compiler replaces the four characters in M_PI—a macro available in most modern versions of the C++ mathematics library—by the seven characters in 3.14159 (or probably by a longer, machine-dependent sequence of characters).

Note that M_PI is an upper-case-only identifier, because C++ programmers generally adhere to an upper-case-only convention when declaring macros.

To use the M_PI macro, you replace the definition, `const double pi = 3.14159`, with a line that loads information from the mathematics library:

```
#include <iostream.h>
// Use the mathematics library, which contains a declaration for M_PI:
#include <math.h>
// Then, define tank_car_volume, a function that uses M_PI:
double tank_car_volume (double r, double l) {
  return M_PI * r * r * l;
}
// Then, define main:
main ( ) {
  cout << "The volume of a standard tank car is "
       << tank_car_volume (3.5, 40.0) << endl;
}
———————————————— Result ————————————————
The volume of a standard tank car is 1539.38
```

137   A **compound statement**, also known as a **block,** is a group of statements surrounded by braces. A compound statement can have its own variable declarations.

The scope of the variables declared in a compound statement is the compound statement itself. The extent of such variables is the time during which the compound statement is executed.

Note that function bodies are compound statements. You see other examples in Section 18, because compound statements are used liberally inside C++'s `if` and `while` statements.

Static global variables are variables whose scope includes one file of a multiple-file program. Hence, a static global variable can be evaluated and assigned at any point in one file, after it is defined, but that same static global variable cannot be evaluated or assigned at any point in any other file. Static global variables are discussed in Segment 705.

Scope issues also arise in connection with class member variables and class member functions. You learn about member variables and member functions—and their corresponding scope properties—throughout the remainder of this book.

Amend the temperature conversion function that you were asked to write in Segment 120 such that, each time it is called, it reports the number of times it has been called.

- A local variable is a variable that is declared inside a function definition. A global variable is a variable that is defined outside of any function definition.

- C++ isolates parameters and local variables, enabling you to reuse their names. Accordingly, the values of a function's parameters and local variables are not available after that function has returned. Also, when one function calls another, the values of the parameters and local variables in the calling function are not available during the execution of the called function.

- You can obtain a value for a global variable everywhere, except in functions in which there is a parameter or local variable that happens to have the same name. You can assign a value to a global variable anywhere that you can obtain a value for that variable.

- You can obtain a value for a global constant everywhere, except in functions in which there is a parameter or local variable that happens to have the same name, but you cannot reassign global constants anywhere.

9 HOW TO CREATE CLASSES AND OBJECTS

141   To describe a box car, viewed as a container, you think naturally in terms of its height, width, and length. To describe a tank car, viewed as a container, you think naturally in terms of its radius and length.

Thus, the numbers that describe a particular box car or tank car constitute a natural bundle—a bundle of three numbers for each individual that belongs to the box-car category, and a bundle of two numbers for each individual that belongs to the tank-car category.

In this section, you learn that C++'s great virtue is that C++ offers programming-language mechanisms that enable you to describe, construct, and manipulate bundles of descriptive data items that mirror real-world **individuals** and **categories**. These special mechanisms set C++ apart from most other programming languages, including C, C++'s parent language.

142   C++ encourages you to define C++ **classes**, such as the box-car class and the tank-car class, that correspond to naturally occurring categories. Once you have defined a class, you can construct any number of **class objects** that belong to that class, each of which corresponds to an individual that belongs to the corresponding category.

When you define the `box_car` class, for example, you indicate that all boxes have a height, width, and length. Then, you can construct box objects with particular heights, widths, and lengths.

Thus, the employment of classes enables you to create information bundles in your programs that describe naturally occurring individuals. Consequently, classes help you to produce clearer, easier-to-understand programs.

143   The basic data types—such as character, integer, and floating-point number—are categories too. Thus, the basic data types could be called **built-in classes**, and classes sometimes are called **user-defined data types**.

Analogously, individuals belonging to C++'s basic data types—such as characters, integers, and floating-point numbers—are objects. Thus, those individuals sometimes are called *data-type objects*.

144   In contrast to data-type objects, class objects generally have multiple parts, and you can work with each part separately. Accordingly, characters, integers, and floating-point numbers sometimes are called **atomic objects**, and class objects sometimes are called **compound objects**.

Generally, you can refer to objects of all types by the word **object**, leaving it to the context to establish the precise kind of object you mean. Sometimes, you may want to be more precise by adding a specializing word, producing combinations such as class object, data-type object, atomic object, and compound object.

145   When you define a class, you tell C++ about the variables that describe the objects that belong to that class. Note that you also can define functions that work with those objects. You might, for example, define a `volume` function that knows how to find values for any

box-car object's `height`, `width`, and `length` variables, and that knows how to use those values to compute the box-car object's volume.

Thus, in the following diagram, the `box_car` class description contains descriptions of variables and class-specific functions, whereas the descriptions of particular `box_car` objects contain variables values.

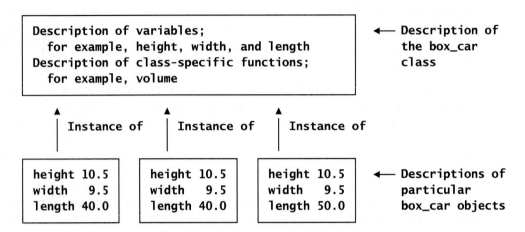

146 The following is a C++ definition of the `box_car` class; evidently, the chunks of memory that describe box cars hold values for three floating-point numbers—namely, height, width, and length:

```
class box_car {
  public:
    double height, width, length;
};
```

Here is what each part of the definition does:

```
class           ←— Tells C++ that a class is to be defined
      box_car   ←— Tells C++ the name of the class
            {   ←— Marks the beginning of the body
  public:       ←— Specifies where variables can be referenced
    double ···; ←— Introduces variables
}               ←— Marks the end of the body
  ;             ←— Marks the end of the class definition
```

This definition of the `box_car` class describes `height`, `width`, and `length` variables only; no function definitions appear. Furthermore, this definition of the `box_car` class indicates, via the `public:` symbol, that all the variable values describing a `box_car` object will be available, and changeable, anywhere after the class named `box_car` has been defined.

147 In Segment 129, you learned that a **declaration** is a program element that provides a compiler with information or advice, whereas a definition causes the compiler to allocate storage. Class definitions may or may not cause storage to be allocated. Accordingly, some purists prefer to use the phrase **class declaration** unless storage actually is allocated.

Nevertheless, the declaration–definition distinction tends to be blurred when programmers talk about classes, and the phrase **class definition** tends to be used whether or not storage is allocated.

148 The variables that appear inside class definitions—such as `height`, `width`, and `length`— are called **member variables**.

In other programming languages, member variables are called **fields** or **slots**. The virtue of such alternative terms is that they encourage you to think of class definitions as patterns and of class objects as filled-in patterns. Bowing to convention, however, this book uses the term *member variable* throughout.

149 Once the `box_car` class is defined, you can introduce a variable with `box_car` as the variable's data type:

```
box_car x;
```

The syntax is the same as that you use when you introduce a variable with `int` or `double` as its data type.

150 Once you have created a `box_car` object by defining a variable of the `box_car` class, you can refer to that `box_car`'s own `height`, `width`, and `length` member variables. To refer to a member variable, you join the name of the `box_car` variable, via the **class-member operator**, a period, to the name of the member variable in which you are interested. Thus, `x.height` produces the value of the `height` member variable of the `box_car` object named by x.

Once you know how to refer to a `box_car` object's member variables, you are free to assign values to those member variables and, subsequently, to retrieve those values.

151 In the following program, a `box_car` object is created, values are assigned to the member variables, and the `box_car` object's volume is computed by an ordinary function named `box_car_volume`.

```
#include <iostream.h>
class box_car {
  public: double height, width, length;
};
double box_car_volume (double h, double w, double l) {
  return h * w * l;
}
main ( ) {
  box_car x;
  x.height = 10.5; x.width = 9.5; x.length = 40.0;
  cout << "The volume of the box_car is "
       << box_car_volume (x.height, x.width, x.length)
       << endl;
}
———————————————————— Result ————————————————————
The volume of the box_car is 3990
```

Why, you might ask, do class definitions end with a semicolon. After all, the final brace makes it clear where the class definition ends.

```
class box_car {
  public:
    double height, width, length;
};
```
▲
└── Semicolon

One reason is that the semicolon syntax allows you to describe a class and to define global variables using that class in a single statement. In the following, for example, in a single statement, the box_car class is defined and global variables b1 and b2 are defined that belong to the box_car class.

```
class box_car {
  public:
    double height, width, length;
} b1, b2;
```

Thus, the semicolon tells C++ where the list of defined variables ends.

153 Instead of handing three double-type arguments to box_car_volume, you can write a new function, volume, that takes just one argument, which you declare to be a box_car object. If you choose this approach, you need to change the body: instead of height, width, and length parameters, the body must refer to the box_car object's height, width, and length member variables:

```
double volume (box_car b) {return b.height * b.width * b.length;}
```

154 With volume redefined to operate on box_car objects—instead of on a height, width, and length combination—you can rewrite the program in Segment 151 as follows:

```
#include <iostream.h>
class box_car {
  public: double height, width, length;
};
double volume (box_car b) {
  return b.height * b.width * b.length;
}
main ( ) {
  box_car x;
  x.height = 10.5; x.width = 9.5; x.length = 40.0;
  cout << "The volume of the box_car is "
       << volume (x) << endl;
}
```
———————————————— Result ————————————————
The volume of the box_car is 3990

155   Now suppose that you want to deal with tank cars as well as box cars. You need to add only another class and another definition of volume.

```
#include <iostream.h>
const double pi = 3.14159;
class box_car {public: double height, width, length;};
class tank_car {public: double radius, length;};
double volume (box_car b) {
  return b.height * b.width * b.length;
}
double volume (tank_car t) {
  return pi * t.radius * t.radius * t.length;
}
main ( ) {
  box_car x; x.height = 10.5; x.width = 9.5; x.length = 40.0;
  tank_car y; y.radius = 3.5, y.length = 40.0;
  cout << "The volume of the box car is " << volume (x) << endl
       << "The volume of the tank car is " << volume (y) << endl;
}
```
———————————————— Result ————————————————
```
The volume of the box car is 3990
The volume of the tank car is 1539.38
```

Because there is more than one definition of the volume function, volume is said to be **overloaded**. Wherever an overloaded function appears, the C++ compiler determines which version is to be used by looking for the function definition in which the parameter data type matches the data type of the argument that appears in the function call.

156   In the program shown in Segment 155, C++ copies the box_car and tank_car objects as
SIDE TRIP   those objects are passed to their volume functions. In this respect, passing a class object is just like passing an ordinary integer or floating-point argument. Such copying is to be expected, because C++ is a call-by-value language, but such copying is not necessarily desirable, especially when class objects are large.

In Section 10, you learn about member functions and you learn that C++ passes one class object to each member function without copying. In Section 44, you learn that it is possible to arrange for C++ to prevent you from inadvertently writing a function that copies a class-object argument.

157   Devise a class, flat_car, for flat cars. Note that flat cars have no height.
PRACTICE

158   Devise a volume function for the flat_car class. Assume that flat cars are loaded to a
PRACTICE   maximum height of 8.25 feet.

159
HIGHLIGHTS

- C++ classes correspond to categories, and C++ class objects correspond to individuals.

- You can view data types as built-in classes, and you can view classes as user-defined data types.

- Class definitions generally include member variables, also known as slots or fields.

- If you want to define a simple class, with member variables only, **then** instantiate the following pattern, in which the member variable declarations consist of a data type, followed by one or more comma-separated member variable names, followed by a semicolon:

```
class class name {
  public:
    member variable declaration 1
    ...
    member variable declaration n
};
```

- If you wish to use a class object's member-variable value, **then** instantiate the following pattern:

```
class object's name . member-variable name
```

- If you wish to assign a class object's member-variable value, **then** instantiate the following pattern:

```
class object's name . member-variable name = expression ;
```

- C++ allows you to overload functions; C++ selects the right function, from among those with identical names, by matching argument classes and data types with parameter classes and data types.

10 HOW TO DEFINE MEMBER FUNCTIONS

160   In this section, you learn how you can define a class-specific function inside a class definition. Such functions become part of the class definition, and they are called in a special way that reflects their class membership.

161   In the program in Segment 155, you saw the `volume` function defined as follows for `box_car` objects:

```
double volume (box_car b) {
  return b.height * b.width * b.length;
}
```

You can define `volume` to be even more specific to `box_car` objects by moving its definition into the definition of the `box_car` class. Such functions, like member variables, are said to be **member functions** of the classes in which they are defined.

162   By convention, small but important changes in syntax distinguish member-function calls from calls to ordinary functions. In particular, each member function has one special argument:

- The special argument's value is a class object that belongs to the same class as does the member function.

- The special argument does not appear in parentheses with other, ordinary arguments. Instead, it is joined, via the class-member operator, a period, to the name of the member function, in a manner reminiscent of member variable references.

For example, to call the `volume` function—the one that is a member of the `box_car` class—to work a `box_car` object named by a variable, x, you write the following:

```
x.volume ( )
```

Note that the `volume` member function happens to have no ordinary arguments.

163   Member-function definitions differ from ordinary function definitions in the following respects:

- Member functions have no parameter corresponding to the special, class-object argument.

- In member functions, there are no parameters or variables connected to member variables via the class-member operator; instead, all member variables are taken to belong to the special, class-object argument.

Thus, you define `volume` as a member function as follows:

```
class box_car {
  public: double height, width, length;
          double volume ( ) {
             return height * width * length;
          }
};
```

When this volume member function is called on a particular box_car object, the height, width, and length variables appearing in the definition of volume automatically refer to the height, width and length member variables associated with that particular box_car object.

164 Now you can rewrite the program in Segment 155 with one version of volume defined as a member function of the box_car class and another version defined as a member function of the tank_car class. C++ picks the right function on the basis of the class-object argument.

```
#include <iostream.h>
const double pi = 3.14159;
class box_car {
  public: double height, width, length;
          double volume ( ) {
             return height * width * length;
          }
};
class tank_car {
  public: double radius, length;
          double volume ( ) {
             return pi * radius * radius * length;
          }
};
main ( ) {
  box_car x; x.height = 10.5; x.width = 9.5; x.length = 40.0;
  tank_car y; y.radius = 3.5, y.length = 40.0;
  cout << "The volume of the box_car is " << x.volume ( ) << endl
       << "The volume of the tank_car is " << y.volume ( ) << endl;
}
```
———————————————————— Result ————————————————————
```
The volume of the box_car is 3990
The volume of the tank_car is 1539.38
```

165 Note carefully that C++ does not copy the class-object argument of a member function when the member function is called. Consequently, when you reassign a member variable inside a member function, you change the value of the member variable in the class-object argument.

166 Member functions can have ordinary arguments in addition to the special class-object argument. You might, for example, have a member function named scaled_volume that

multiplies the volume of its class-object argument by a scale factor supplied as an ordinary argument:

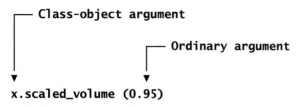

```
x.scaled_volume (0.95)
```

The definition of a `scaled_volume` member function is similar to that of a `volume` member function. The only difference is the addition of an ordinary parameter, `scale_factor`:

```
class box_car {
  public: double height, width, length;
          double scaled_volume (double scale_factor) {
            return scale_factor * height * width * length;
          }
};
```

167 Class definitions can grow large, making it difficult and error prone to define many large member functions within a class definition. Accordingly, C++ allows you to provide just a preview of a member definition within the class definition itself, in the form of a **function prototype**. Then, you can define the function itself outside of the class definition.

A *function prototype, definition of* is like a function definition without a body. By supplying a function prototype for a member function, you supply only what the C++ compiler needs to know about a function's argument types and return type in order to compile calls to the function. The following, for example, is the function prototype for a volume member function:

```
double volume ( );
```

168 Note that a function prototype is a declaration, rather than a definition—a function proto-
SIDE TRIP type only provides the C++ compiler with information about a function for which memory is allocated when a definition is processed elsewhere.

169 Once you have introduced a function's prototype, you can define the function outside of the class definition. Note, however, that C++ requires you to indicate to which class such an externally defined function belongs by prefixing the function name with the class name and two colons:

```
class box_car {
  public: double height, width, length;
          double volume ( );
};

double box_car::volume ( ) {
  return height * width * length;
}
```

The class names and colons preceding the member-function definitions have two purposes:

- They signal that the definitions are definitions of member functions.

- They establish to which classes the definitions belong.

The colons are called the **class-scope operator**.

170
SIDE TRIP Later, in Section 45, you learn about **inline functions**, and you learn that the C++ compiler tries to compile member functions defined inside class definitions as inline functions. No effort is made to compile externally defined member functions as inline functions.

171
SIDE TRIP The function prototype for the `volume` function is particularly simple, because there are no ordinary arguments. In general, function prototypes must include a data-type declaration for each ordinary argument.

> `return data type` `function name` (`data type of parameter 1` ,
>   . . . ,
>   `data type of parameter n`);

The following, for example, is a function prototype for a `scaled_volume` function:

```
double scaled_volume (double);
```

172 At this point, you have seen that you can define `volume` as an ordinary function with *one explicit parameter*, a particular `box_car` object. You refer to the `box_car` object's member variables using class-member operators:

```
double volume (box_car b) {
   return b.height * b.width * b.length;
}
```

Thus defined, `volume` is called with an argument that is a particular `box_car` object:

```
volume (x)
```

You can also define `volume` as a member-function with *no explicit parameter*:

```
double volume ( ) {
   return height * width * length;
}
```

Remember that, by convention, the member-variable values used in this definition of `volume` are the values associated with a particular `box_car` object—the one that is identified by the `box_car` variable that appears joined, via the class-member operator, to the function call:

```
x.volume ( )
```

173 Defining `volume` as a member function has several advantages relative to defining `volume` as an ordinary function. For example, the member-function definition is more streamlined because member variables are referred to by name only, without a prefixing name and class-member operator.

The most important advantage, however, is that member functions have special privileges with respect to member-variable reference and assignment. Later, in Section 14, you learn about the private portion of class definitions, and you see that the special privileges of member functions enable you to reference private member variables that are otherwise hidden from view.

174   Convert the `volume` function for flat cars, which you were asked to devise in Segment 158,
PRACTICE   into a member function.

175
HIGHLIGHTS

- If you want to make a function with a class-object parameter into a member function, **then** define the function inside a class definition as you would an ordinary function, **and** eliminate the class-object parameter from the parameter list **and** from the member variable references.

- If a member function is large, **then** move the definition outside the class definition, **and** leave behind a function prototype in the class definition,

  `return data type` `function name` ( );

  and indicate the class to which the moved member function belongs by joining the class name to the definition via two colons:

  `return data type` `class name` :: `function name` ( ) {···}

- If you want to call a member function, **then** use the class-member operator, a period, to identify the class object on which the function is to work, noting the following contrasts:

  `ordinary function` (`all arguments`)
  `class-object argument` . `member function` (`other arguments`)

11 HOW TO DEFINE CONSTRUCTOR MEMBER FUNCTIONS

176   In this section, you learn that **constructor member functions** are special member functions that are called when class objects are created.

177   In Section 9, you saw how to define a class-object variable in one statement and to initialize the corresponding class object's member variables in others. The following illustrates class-object declaration and initialization for a `tank_car` variable, `t`:

```
tank_car t;
t.radius = 3.5;
t.length = 40.0;
```

For many classes, member variables have predictable values, at least initially. Accordingly, C++ allows you to define a special member function, the **default constructor**, which is called automatically whenever a new class object is created. Such constructors enable you to initialize the member variables in new class objects.

178   In class definitions, default constructor functions stand apart from other member functions in three ways:

- The default constructor function's name is the same as the name of the class.

- The default constructor function has no return-value data type.

- The default constructor function cannot have a parameter.

179   In the following program, the `tank_car` class definition includes a default constructor function that initializes the member variables in particular `tank_car` objects:

```
#include <iostream.h>
const double pi = 3.14159;
class tank_car {
  public:
    double radius, length;
    // Default constructor:
    tank_car ( ) {radius = 3.5; length = 40.0;}
    // Volume function:
    double volume ( ) {return pi * radius * radius * length;}
};
main ( ) {
  tank_car t;
  cout << "The volume of the tank car is " << t.volume ( ) << endl;
}
```
————————————————— Result —————————————————
```
The volume of the tank car is 1539.38
```

180 Good programming practice dictates that you should include a definition for a default constructor in every class that you define. The rationale is that C++ defines a default constructor for you if you do not define one, and it is better to have a default constructor that is visible and explicit than to have one that is invisible and implicit.

Note, however, that you can define default constructors that do not initialize member variables or perform any other computation; you can define default constructors with empty bodies.

181 Now suppose that you want to initialize the radius and length member variables when you declare certain tank_car objects. The first thing you need to do is to define a constructor with two parameters:

```
class tank_car {
  public:
    double radius, length;
    // Default constructor:
    tank_car ( ) {radius = 3.5; length = 40.0;}
    // Constructor with two parameters:
    tank_car (double r, double l) {radius = r; length = l;}
    // Volume function:
    double volume ( ) {return pi * radius * radius * length;}
};
```

Note that the constructor with two parameters, like the default constructor, is named for the class in which it appears. Also, there is no return data type.

182 To tell the C++ compiler to use the two-parameter constructor, blocking the involvement of the default constructor, you modify your tank_car variable declaration as follows:

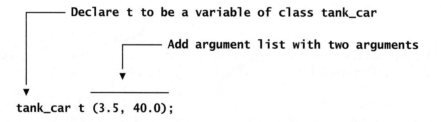

```
tank_car t (3.5, 40.0);
```

The parameters dictate that initialization is *not* to be done by the default constructor, because default constructors never have arguments. The default constructor is called whenever there is no argument list, as in the statement tank_car t;. The other, two-parameter constructor is called when there is an argument list, as in tank_car t (3.5, 50.0).

183 The following program deploys both the default constructor and a constructor with parameters:

```
#include <iostream.h>
const double pi = 3.14159;
class tank_car {
  public:
    double radius, length;
    tank_car ( ) {radius = 3.5; length = 40.0;}
    tank_car (double r, double l) {radius = r; length = l;}
    double volume ( ) {return pi * radius * radius * length;}
};
main ( ) {
  tank_car t1;
  tank_car t2 (3.5, 50.0);
  cout << "The volume of the default tank car is "
       << t1.volume ( )
       << endl
       << "The volume of the specified tank car is "
       << t2.volume ( )
       << endl;
}
```
————————————————— Result —————————————————
```
The volume of the default tank car is 1539.38
The volume of the specified tank car is 1924.22
```

184
SIDE TRIP
You must include a definition for a default constructor function in a class definition under the following condition: You define a constructor function with parameters, *and* you write declarations, such as tank_car t;, that do not include an argument list.

The rationale is that, if you have not defined a default constructor, then the lack of an argument list suggests that you have forgotten to include arguments for the parameter-bearing constructor that you have defined.

185
PRACTICE
Devise a default constructor and a two-parameter constructor for the flat_car class that you were asked to design in Segment 158.

186
HIGHLIGHTS

- Constructors perform computations, such as initial member variable assignment, that you want to occur when your program creates a class object.

- Each constructor is named for the class in which it is defined, and no constructor has a return-value data type.

- The default constructor has no parameters. You should include a definition of a default constructor in every class that you define.

- If you want to initialize a class object's member-variable values using the default constructor, **then** use the following pattern:

  `class name` `variable name` ;

57

- If you want to initialize a class object's member-variable values using another constructor, with parameters, **then** use the following pattern:

```
class name  variable name ( argument 1 , ···, argument n );
```

12 HOW TO DEFINE READER AND WRITER MEMBER FUNCTIONS

187 In Section 11, you learned that constructor member functions can help you to establish initial member-variable values. In this section, you learn that reader and writer functions can help you to refer to member-variable values and to assign values to member variables subsequent to initialization.

Note that reader and writer functions, as described in this section, have nothing to do with input–output programming, even though the words *reader* and *writer* are common in discussions of input–output programming.

Note also that the use of constructor functions is inescapable in C++ programming, whereas you do not have to write reader or writer functions. You should understand, however, that the use of reader and writer functions, as explained in this section, is recommended by many expert programmers, no matter what programming language you happen to use. You learn why in Section 13.

188 You know that you can refer to a member-variable value directly by using the class member operator. In particular, you know that you can refer to the value of the `radius` member variable of a particular `tank_car` object named `t`:

t.radius

Alternatively, you can refer to a member-variable value indirectly by defining a member function that returns the member-variable value. In the following `tank_car` class definition, for example, the addition of a definition for a member function named `read_radius` indicates that `read_radius` returns the value of the `radius` member variable:

```
class tank_car {
  public:
    double radius, length;
    tank_car ( ) {radius = 3.5; length = 40.0;}
    tank_car (double r, double l) {radius = r; length = l;}
    double read_radius ( ) {return radius;}
    double volume ( ) {return pi * radius * radius * length;}
};
```

Accordingly, with `read_radius` defined, you have another way to refer to the value of the `radius` member variable of a particular `tank_car` named `t`:

t.read_radius ( )

189 A **reader** is a function that extracts information from an object. One reason that you may wish to use a reader, rather than referencing a member variable directly, is that you can include additional computation in a reader. For example, if you are concerned about how often your program references the `radius` member variable, you can add a statement to the `read_radius` reader that announces each reference:

```
class tank_car {
  public:
    double radius, length;
    tank_car ( ) {radius = 3.5; length = 40.0;}
    tank_car (double r, double l) {radius = r; length = l;}
    double read_radius ( ) {
      cout << "Reading a tank_car's radius ..." << endl;
      return radius;}
    double volume ( ) {return pi * radius * radius * length;}
};
```

190 You may also wish to use readers to provide access to imaginary member variables that exist only in the sense that their values can be computed from member variables that do exist. For example, you can create read_diameter, which seems to refer to the contents of an imaginary diameter member variable, but which actually refers to the contents of the radius member variable:

```
class tank_car {
  public:
    double radius, length;
    tank_car ( ) {radius = 3.5; length = 40.0;}
    tank_car (double r, double l) {radius = r; length = l;}
    double read_radius ( ) {return radius;}
    double read_diameter ( ) {return radius * 2.0;}
    double volume ( ) {return pi * radius * radius * length;}
};
```

191 Analogously, you do not need to assign a member-variable value directly. Instead, you can assign a member-variable value indirectly by defining a member function that does the actual value assigning. In the following tank_car class definition, for example, the addition of a definition for a member function named write_radius indicates that write_radius assigns a value to the radius member variable:

```
class tank_car {
  public:
    double radius, length;
    tank_car ( ) {radius = 3.5; length = 40.0;}
    tank_car (double r, double l) {radius = r; length = l;}
    void write_radius (double r) {radius = r;}
    double volume ( ) {return pi * radius * radius * length;}
};
```

With write_radius defined, you have another way to assign a value to the radius member variable of a particular tank_car object named t:

```
t.write_radius (4.0)
```

Because the only purpose of write_radius is to assign a value to a member variable, write_radius is marked void, indicating that no value is to be returned.

192   A **writer** is a function that inserts information into an object. One reason that you may wish to use a writer, rather than writing into a member variable directly, is that you can include additional computation in a writer. In Segment 189, you saw how to add a statement to the `read_radius` reader that announces each reference. The following provides the same enhancement to the `write_radius` writer:

```
class tank_car {
  public:
    double radius, length;
    tank_car ( ) {radius = 3.5; length = 40.0;}
    tank_car (double r, double l) {radius = r; length = l;}
    void write_radius (double r) {
        cout << "Writing a tank car's radius ..." << endl;
        radius = r;}
    double volume ( ) {return pi * radius * radius * length;}
};
```

193   You may also wish to use writers that pretend to write into imaginary member variables, but that actually dictate values for member variables that do exist. For example, you can create a `write_diameter` member function, which seems to write into an imaginary `diameter` member variable, but which actually writes into the `radius` member variable:

```
class tank_car {
  public:
    double radius, length;
    tank_car ( ) {radius = 3.5; length = 40.0;}
    tank_car (double r, double l) {radius = r; length = l;}
    void write_radius (double r) {radius = r;}
    void write_diameter (double d) {radius = d / 2.0;}
    double volume ( ) {return pi * radius * radius * length;}
};
```

194   The naming of the `read_radius`, `write_radius`, `read_diameter`, and `write_diameter` functions, with the `read_` and `write_` prefixes, makes it clear that they are reader and writer functions, but using `read_` and `write_` is a personal convention, rather than a convention of C++.

195   Write readers and writers for the `flat_car` class that you were asked to design in Seg-
PRACTICE ment 158.

196
HIGHLIGHTS

- Reader and writer member functions provide an indirect route to member variable reference and assignment.

- You can define reader and writer member functions for imaginary member variables.

- If you want to refer to a member-variable value using a reader, **then** instantiate the following pattern:

  `class object` `. reader function` `( )`

- If you want to assign a member-variable value using a writer, **then** instantiate the following pattern:

  `class object` `. writer function` `( expression )`

13 HOW TO BENEFIT FROM DATA ABSTRACTION

197 You now know how to use constructor, reader, and writer member functions. Moreover, you have seen how readers and writers make it easy to add computation at the point where information is read from or written into objects, and how readers and writers can be defined for imaginary member variables. In this section, you learn how constructors, readers, and writers help you to practice data abstraction, thereby increasing your efficiency and making your programs easier to maintain.

198 Suppose that you develop a big program around a `tank_car` class definition that includes readers and writers for `radius` and `length` member variables, as well as for an imaginary `diameter` member variable:

```
class tank_car {
  public:
    double radius, length;
    tank_car ( ) {radius = 3.5; length = 40.0;}
    tank_car (double r, double l) {radius = r; length = l;}
    double read_radius ( ) {return radius;}
    void write_radius (double r) {radius = r;}
    double read_diameter ( ) {return 2.0 * radius;}
    void write_diameter (double d) {radius = d / 2.0;}
    double read_length ( ) {return length;}
    void write_length (double l) {length = l;}
    double volume ( ) {return pi * radius * radius * length;}
};
```

Next, suppose that you discover that your program refers to diameters more often than radii. If speed is a great concern, you should arrange to store diameters, rather than radii, so as to avoid multiplication on reading and division on writing.

199 If you work with the member variables in `tank_car` objects using constructors, readers, and writers only, you only need to change what happens in member functions:

```
class tank_car {
  public:
    double diameter, length;
    tank_car ( ) {diameter = 7.0; length = 40.0;}
    tank_car (double r, double l) {diameter = r * 2.0; length = l;}
    double read_radius ( ) {return diameter / 2.0;}
    void write_radius (double r) {diameter = r * 2.0;}
    double read_diameter ( ) {return diameter;}
    void write_diameter (double d) {diameter = d;}
    double read_length ( ) {return length;}
    void write_length (double l) {length = l;}
    double volume ( ) {return .25 * pi * diameter * diameter * length;}
};
```

200 Suppose, for example, that your program contains a statement that reads the diameter of a particular `tank_car`, `t`. If you work with readers, you need to make no change to that statement to accommodate the switch from a radius-based class definition to a diameter-based class definition:

··· `t.read_diameter ( )` ···

On the other hand, if you do not work with the member variables in `tank_car` objects using constructors, readers, and writers only, you have to go through your entire program, modifying myriad statements:

··· `t.radius` ··· ⟶ ··· `.5 * t.diameter` ···

Thus, constructors, readers, and writers isolate you from the effects of your efficiency-motivated switch from a radius-based class definition to a diameter-based class definition.

201 In general, constructors, readers, and writers isolate you from the details of how a class is implemented. Once you have written those member functions, you can forget about how they refer to and assign values; none of the details, such as whether you have a `radius` or a `diameter` member variable, clutter the programs that use `tank_car` objects.

202 Collectively, constructors, readers, and writers sometimes are called **access functions**. When you move representation detail into a set of access functions, you are said to be practicing **data abstraction**, and you are said to be hiding behind a **data-abstraction barrier** the details of how data are represented.

Good programmers carefully design into their programs appropriate access functions so as to create data-abstraction barriers.

203 Because the virtues of data abstraction parallel those of procedure abstraction, the following discussion of the virtues of data abstraction is much like the previous discussion, in Section 7, of the virtues of procedure abstraction.

The key virtue of data abstraction is that *you make it easy to reuse your work*. You can develop a library of class definitions and transfer the entire library to another programmer with little difficulty.

204 Another virtue of data abstraction is that you push details out of sight and out of mind, making your functions easier to read and enabling you to concentrate on high-level steps.

205 Still another virtue of data abstraction is that *you easily can augment what a class provides*. You can, for example, add information-displaying statements to your readers and writers, as you saw in Section 12.

206 Another virtue of data abstraction is that *you easily can improve the way data are stored*. In this section, you have seen an example in which there is an efficiency-motivated switch from a radius-based class definition to a diameter-based class definition.

207 Most good programmers provide readers and writers for some member variables, but not for others. The choice is a matter of taste and style. Until you have developed your own taste and style, you should rely on the following heuristic:

- Whenever the detailed implementation of a class may change, provide member-variable readers and writers to insulate your class-using functions from the potential change.

208
PRACTICE Revise the readers and writers for the `flat_car` class such that they display messages when used.

209
PRACTICE Revise the readers and writers for the `flat_car` class such that global variables are incremented when corresponding member functions are called.

210
HIGHLIGHTS

- Constructors, readers, and writers are called access functions. When you move references and assignments into access functions, you are practicing data abstraction.

- Data abstraction has many virtues, including the following:

  - Your programs become easier to reuse.

  - Your programs become easier to read.

  - You easily can augment what a class provides.

  - You easily can improve the way data are stored.

- If you anticipate that the detailed definition of a class may change, **then** you should provide access functions for the member variables to isolate the effects of the potential changes.

14 HOW TO PROTECT MEMBER VARIABLES FROM HARMFUL REFERENCE

211 In Section 13, you learned that constructor, reader, and writer member functions help you to benefit from data abstraction. In this section, you learn how to ensure that all member-variable references and assignments are channeled through such member functions.

212 The data-abstraction benefits of access functions—constructors, readers, and writers—disappear if you or an associate writes functions that include direct member-variable references or assignments.

If, for example, you decide to switch from radius-based descriptions to diameter-based descriptions, then C++ cannot compile any function containing an expression of the form `tank_car object` . `radius`. On the other hand, if you prevent direct access to the `radius` member variable, no one can accidentally come to rely on such expressions.

213 You prevent direct member-variable access by declaring the member variables in a separate, private part of the class definition—the one marked with the `private:` symbol.

You can, for example, redefine the `tank_car` class as follows, with the `radius` and `length` member variables moved from the public part of the class definition into a part marked by the `private:` symbol.

```
class tank_car {
  public:
    tank_car ( ) {radius = 3.5; length = 40.0;}
    tank_car (double r, double l) {radius = r; length = l;}
    double read_radius ( ) {return radius;}
    void write_radius (double r) {radius = r;}
    double read_diameter ( ) {return radius * 2.0;}
    void write_diameter (double d) {radius = d / 2.0;}
    double read_length ( ) {return length;}
    void write_length (double l) {length = l;}
    double volume ( ) {return pi * radius * radius * length;}
  private:
    double radius, length;
};
```

With the `tank_car` class so redefined, future attempts to refer to a `tank_car` object's `radius` and `length` member-variable values via the class-member operator fail to compile.

```
t.radius      ◄── Evaluation fails to compile;
                  the radius member variable is in the
                  private part of the class definition
t.radius = 6  ◄── Assignment fails to compile;
                  the radius member variable is in the
                  private part of the class definition
```

214   Note, however, that all member functions have access to member variables declared in the private portion of the class definition. Thus, you can reference and assign values via member functions located in the public part of the class definition:

```
t.read_radius ( )    ←── Evaluation compiles;
                         the read_radius function is in the
                         public part of the class definition
t.write_radius (6)   ←── Assignment compiles;
                         the read_radius function is in the
                         public part of the class definition
```

215   The member variables and member functions in the public part of the class definition are said to constitute the class's **public interface**. Once you have moved the `radius` and `length` member variables to the private part of the class definition, the only way to get at them is via member functions that remain part of the public interface.

Later, in Section 44, you see an example in which a member function appears in the private part of the class definition. Thus, member functions are not necessarily part of the public interface, just as member variables are not necessarily part of the public interface.

216   You can start a class definition with either the private part or the public part. Most programmers put the public part first, on the aesthetic ground that what is *public* should be up front and open to view, whereas what is *private* should be not so up front and not so open to view.

You can also define classes without specifying the part that member variables and member functions belong to. By default, the C++ compiler takes such member variables and member functions to belong to the private part of the class definition.

217   Data abstraction and the notion of a public interface fit together as follows:

- Channeling member-variable references and assignments through access functions isolates you from the details of class implementation, thus providing a means to ensure that you can practice data abstraction.

- When you move member variables to the private part of a class definition, you force all member-variable references and assignments to go through the constructors, readers, writers, and other member functions in the public interface, thus providing a means to ensure that you benefit from your effort to practice data abstraction.

218   Revise the readers and writers for the `flat_car` class such that the member variables are
PRACTICE   protected from access, except via readers and writers.

219

HIGHLIGHTS

- Inadvertent member-variable references and assignments via the class-member operator can destroy your effort to practice data abstraction.

- You can prevent inadvertent direct access to member variables by moving their declarations into the private part of the class definition.

- Member functions in general, and constructors, readers, and writers in particular, have complete access to all member variables, public and private.

- The member variables and member functions in the public part of a class definition constitute the class's public interface.

- The public–private dichotomy helps to ensure that you can benefit from data abstraction.

15 HOW TO DEFINE CLASSES THAT INHERIT VARIABLES AND FUNCTIONS

220   In this section, you learn that you can tie together classes in hierarchies such that the member variables declared in one class automatically appear in objects belonging to another. Thus, you learn about *inheritance*, one of the key concepts that distinguish object-oriented programming from traditional programming.

221   So far, you have learned how you can define classes for two railroad-car types: box cars and tank cars. Now suppose that you want to add information that is common to all railroad cars.

One way to proceed is to start with the classes that you have already defined for box cars and tank cars, adding whatever information you need. The following, for example, is one way to augment the box_car class:

```
int current_year = 2001;
class box_car {
  public:
    // From a previous definition of the box_car class:
    double height, width, length;
    box_car ( ) {height = 10.5; width = 9.2; length = 40.0;}
    double volume ( ) {return height * width * length;}
    // New member variables:
    int percentage_loaded;
    int year_built;
    // New member function; relies on current_year, a global variable:
    int age ( ) {return current_year - year_built;}
};
```

The problem with this way of defining railroad cars is that the percentage_loaded member variable would have to be repeated in both the box_car and tank_car class definitions, and the year_built member variable and the age member function would have to be repeated not only in those classes, but also in classes defined for, say, engine and caboose classes.

222   Maintaining multiple copies of member variables and member functions makes software development and maintenance difficult as you try to correct bugs, to add features, to improve performance, and to change behavior. Adding multiple programmers and multiple years to the mix turns mere difficulty into certain failure.

Of course, with just two new member variables and one new member function about which to worry, you could cope. In a more complex example, every kind of container, from railroad car to cereal box, would have a percentage_loaded member variable, along with a variety of other member variables, capturing information dealing with such characteristics as durability and visual appeal. Similarly, every kind of railroad car would have not only a year_built member variable and an age member function, but also a variety of other member variables and member functions dealing with such characteristics as their weight, number, owner, and destination.

223 Fortunately, C++ encourages you to cut down on duplication, thereby easing program writing, debugging, and maintenance, by allowing you to arrange class definitions in hierarchies that reflect natural category hierarchies.

Using C++, you can say, for example, that box cars, tank cars, engines, and cabooses are railroad cars. Then, you can declare a `year_built` member variable and an `age` member function in the `railroad_car` class alone, because the `year_built` member variable will appear in each individual box car, tank car, engine, and caboose object, and the `age` member function will be available to all those `railroad_car` objects as though `age` had been declared four times.

224 You also can say, with some risk, that box cars are boxes, tank cars are cylinders, and both boxes and cylinders are containers.

The reason it is risky to say, for example, that a box car is a box is that the meaning of *is* is different from the meaning of *is* when you say that a box car is a railroad car. When you say that a box car is a box, you are really thinking of the entire box car as though it were one of its parts, which happens to be a kind of container. When you say that a box car is a railroad car, you mean that a box car, as a whole, is a kind of railroad car.

The reason the distinction is important is that properties of parts do not necessarily transfer to wholes—a box-car's door may be *new*, whereas the corresponding box car may be **ancient**. Accordingly, you must be exceedingly careful when you say that an object belongs to a class to which, more precisely, one of the object's parts belongs.

225 Although you must be careful when you make assertions such as *a box car is a box*, such assertions are often expedient, especially if the word *is* can be taken to mean *usefully can be viewed as*.

For example, the following are plausible reasons why you might want to view a box car as a box and a tank car as a cylinder:

- You may have various sorts of trucks or storage tanks that make use of the same member variables and member functions as do box cars and tank cars. By collecting those member variables and member functions into `box` and `cylinder` classes, you avoid needless duplication and simplify maintenance.

- You may already have defined fully debugged `box` and `cylinder` classes. To prevent the gratuitous introduction of bugs, you would want to use those class definitions as they stand, rather than, say, copying bits of those `box` and `cylinder` class definitions into the `box_car` and `tank_car` class definitions.

- You may have decided to purchase code for `box` and `cylinder` classes from a vendor, because you anticipate using the elaborate box and cylinder capabilities advertised by that vendor. Because the vendor supplies you with compiled code only, you cannot access the source code, so you cannot copy bits of the vendor's `box` and `cylinder` class definitions into your `box_car` and `tank_car` class definitions. You can only define new classes that use those compiled classes as base classes.

226 In the example used throughout the rest of this book, you are to assume that a box car usefully can be viewed as a box and a tank car usefully can be viewed as a cylinder.

Consequently, you can move the `height`, `width`, and `length` from the `box_car` class into the `box` class, along with the `volume` member function that uses those member variables, making those variables and that member function more generally available. Similarly, you can move the `radius` and `length` member variables from the `tank_car` class into the `cylinder` class, along with the `volume` member function that uses those member variables.

You can also declare a `percentage_loaded` member variable in the `container` class alone, because subclass–superclass relations extending from the `box_car` and `tank_car` classes, through the `box` and `cylinder` classes, to the `container` class, ensure that all individual `box_car` and `tank_car` objects will have `percentage_loaded` member variables.

227   Usually, it is a good idea to draw a **class-hierarchy diagram**, such as the following, to see how your classes fit together. All arrows represent subclass-to-superclass relations:

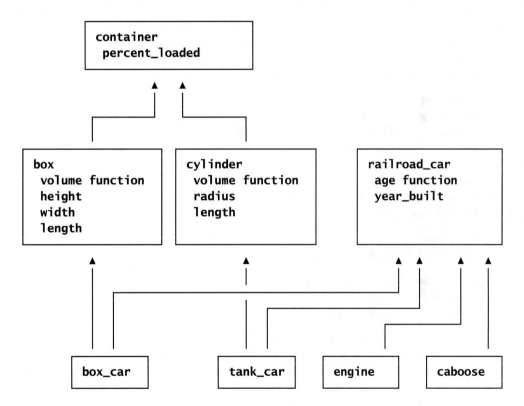

Such a class-hierarchy diagram helps you to see how to distribute member variables and member functions among the classes in the hierarchy. Such a class-hierarchy diagram can also expose semantic risks of the sort described in Segment 224.

228   Class objects **inherit member variables** from the class to which they belong, and from all that class's superclasses. Each `box_car` object, for example, has its own copy of every member variable declared in the `box_car`, `box`, `container`, and `railroad_car` classes.

Similarly, class objects **inherit member functions** from the class to which they belong, and from all that class's superclasses. You can, for example, work on a `box_car` object not only with member functions defined in the box_car class, but also with those defined in the box, container, and railroad_car classes, if any.

229 As a general rule, you should place member variables and member functions in classes such that two criteria are satisfied:

- There is no needless duplication of a member variable or member function.

- Each member variable and member function is useful in every subclass.

For example, the percentage_loaded member variable is in the container class, because it is useful for all container subclasses, although it is not useful for classes that are not container subclasses, such as the engine and caboose classes. Similarly, the year_built member variable and the age member function are in the railroad_car class, because they are useful for all railroad cars, rather than just for those railroad cars that happen to be containers.

On the other hand, there are two volume member functions, because the way that you compute the volume of a box is different from the way that you compute the volume of a cylinder. Thus, there is duplication, but there is no needless duplication.

230 Once you have decided where member variables and member functions should be declared and defined, you can proceed to define classes and to link them up in a hierarchy.

You can define the container and railroad_car classes readily, because neither is a subclass of any other class:

```
int current_year = 2001;
class container {
  public: int percent_loaded;
          // Default constructor:
          container ( ) { }
};
class railroad_car {
  public: int year_built;
          // Default constructor:
          railroad_car ( ) { }
          // Other member function:
          int age ( ) {return current_year - year_built;}
};
```

231 To specify a class's superclasses, you insert a colon, the symbol public, and name of the superclass just after the name of the class in the class's definition:

```
class  class name  : public  superclass name  {
  ...
};
```

For example, as you define the box class, you specify that container is a superclass as follows:

```
class box : public container {
   public: double height, width, length;
           // Default constructor:
           box ( ) { }
           // Other member function:
           double volume ( ) {return height * width * length;}
};
```

Note that the box class now contains the member variables and the member function formerly found in the box_car class.

232 Because the box class is directly under the container class in the class hierarchy, with no other class in between, the box class is said to be the **derived class**, relative to the container class, and the container class is said to be the **base class** relative to the box class.

233 The cylinder class, like the box class, is derived from the container class:

```
const double pi = 3.14159;
class cylinder : public container {
   public: double radius, length;
           // Default constructor:
           cylinder ( ) { }
           // Other member function:
           double volume ( ) {return pi * radius * radius * length;}
};
```

Note that the cylinder class now contains the member variables and the member function formerly found in the tank_car class.

234 So that the class definitions stay focused on the construction of a class hierarchy, none of the classes defined in this section include a private portion. Instead, all member variables and member functions are in the public interfaces. You could, of course, redefine the classes such that they have a private portion, adding appropriate readers and writers to the public interfaces.

235 Note that the container class must be defined before you define the box and cylinder classes. You cannot define a derived class until all its base classes have been defined.

236 Note also that none of the default constructors in the classes defined so far—container, box, cylinder, or railroad_car—initialize any member variables. These classes are too general to have sensible default member-variable values. After all, what could possibly be a default height for a box or a default radius for a cylinder.

237 Having defined the container, railroad_car, box, and cylinder classes, you can now define the classes at the bottom of the class hierarchy:

```
class box_car : public railroad_car, public box {
  public: box_car ( ) {height = 10.5; width = 9.2; length = 40.0;}
};
class tank_car : public railroad_car, public cylinder {
  public: tank_car ( ) {radius = 3.5; length = 40.0;}
};
class engine : public railroad_car {
  public: engine ( ) { }
};
class caboose : public railroad_car {
  public: caboose ( ) { }
};
```

Note that none of the class definitions just shown includes any member variables. All box_car, tank_car, engine, and caboose objects have member variables, however, because of the subclass–superclass relations that link the box_car, tank_car, engine, and caboose classes to various superclasses.

Note also that two of the four definitions specify two base classes; such definitions enable **multiple inheritance**.

Finally, note that the definitions of the box_car and tank_car classes include default constructors that initialize inherited member variables. These classes are sufficiently specific to have sensible default member-variable values. Later, in Section 32, you learn about another way to initialize inherited member variables using constructors that explicitly call other constructors.

238 In the class hierarchy as developed so far, each class exhibits only a default constructor. When you create an object in such a hierarchy, all the default constructors in the object's class and superclasses are called automatically, and each has the opportunity to contribute to the values of the member variables associated with the new object. In particular, the default constructors in all the box_car class and all superclasses of the box_car class are called whenever a box_car object is created:

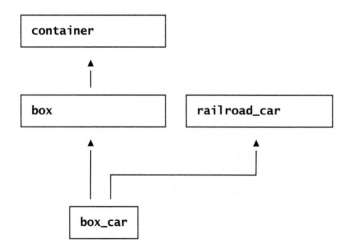

Thus, when your program creates a box_car object, the default box_car constructor is called, as well as the default constructors for the railroad_car, box, and container classes, as demonstrated by the output statements placed in the default constructors:

```cpp
#include <iostream.h>
int current_year = 2001;
const double pi = 3.14159;
class container {
  public: int percent_loaded;
          container ( ) {
            cout << "Calling container default constructor." << endl;
          }
};
class box : public container {
  public: double height, width, length;
          box ( ) {
            cout << "Calling box default constructor." << endl;
          }
          double volume ( ) {
            return height * width * length;
          }
};
// ... Cylinder definition goes here ...
class railroad_car {
  public: int year_built;
          railroad_car ( ) {
            cout << "Calling railroad_car default constructor."
                    << endl;
          }
          int age ( ) {return current_year - year_built;}
};
class box_car : public railroad_car, public box {
  public: box_car ( ) {
            cout << "Calling box_car default constructor." << endl;
            height = 10.5; width = 9.2; length = 40.0;}
};
// ... Other railroad car class definitions go here ...
main ( ) {
  box_car b;                 // Construct a box car
  b.year_built = 1943;       // Specify when it was built
  b.percent_loaded = 66;     // Specify how full it is
  // Display age using a railroad_car member function:
  cout << "The car is " << b.age ( ) << " years old." << endl;
  // Display how full using a container member variable:
  cout << "And " << b.percent_loaded << " percent loaded." << endl;
  // Display volume using a box member function:
  cout << "Its volume is " << b.volume ( ) << " units." << endl;
}
```

──────────────────── **Result** ────────────────────

```
Calling railroad_car default constructor.
Calling container default constructor.
Calling box default constructor.
Calling box_car default constructor.
The car is 58 years old.
And 66 percent loaded.
Its volume is 3864 units.
```

240 Sometimes, more than one member function with a particular name may show up in a subclass–superclass chain. Suppose, for example, that you must account for the tendency of railroads to pile material above the rims of gondola cars. Specifically, you must implement a volume member function for that kind of car, which is different from the volume member function defined in the box class:

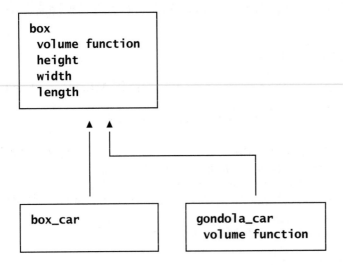

241 To decide which volume member function to use on, say, a box_car object, the C++ compiler searches up from the box_car object, through the subclass–superclass chain, to find the first member function named volume. For the box_car example, the only volume member function that the C++ compiler finds is the one found in the box class.

On the other hand, the volume member function selected by the C++ compiler to work on gondola_car objects is the one found in the gondola_car class, and the volume member function found in the box class is said to be **shadowed** by that lower-level member function.

Of course, if you happen to have a **box** object that is neither a box car nor a gondola car, and you want to compute the volume of that **box** object, then the volume member function found in the box class is the one that C++ selects for you.

242 If you really want to have your program call a shadowed member function, you can write statements that refer to that shadowed member function explicitly by prefixing the function name with the class name and two colons:

```
box::volume
```

Note that this notation is the same as that you use to identify the class associated with an externally defined member function.

243 Shadowing and explicit member function call are both illustrated in the following program:

```cpp
#include <iostream.h>
int current_year = 2001;
const double pi = 3.14159;
// ... Container and railroad car class definitions go here ...
class box : public container {
  public: double height, width, length;
          // Default constructor:
          box ( ) { }
          // The box volume member function;
          double volume ( ) {return height * width * length;}
};
// ... Cylinder definition goes here ...
class box_car : public railroad_car, public box {
  public: // Default constructor:
          box_car ( ) {height = 10.5; width = 9.2; length = 40.0;}
};
class gondola_car : public railroad_car, public box {
  public: // Default constructor:
          gondola_car ( ) {height = 6.0; width = 9.2; length = 40.0;}
          // The gondola volume member function;
          // gondola cars are loaded above their rims:
          double volume ( ) {return 1.2 * height * width * length;}
};
// ... Other railroad car class definitions go here ...
main ( ) {
  // Construct a gondola car:
  gondola_car g;
  // Display volume; use the gondola class volume function:
  cout << "Viewed as a gondola, the car's volume is "
       << g.volume ( ) << " units." << endl;
  // Display volume; use the box class volume function
  cout << "Viewed as a box, the car's volume is "
       << g.box::volume ( ) << " units." << endl;
}
```

─────────────────── Result ───────────────────
```
Viewed as a gondola, the car's volume is 2649.6 units.
Viewed as a box, the car's volume is 2208 units.
```

244 In the examples in this section, you have seen derived-class–base-class relations expressed using only the `public` symbol:

```
class <derived class name> : public <base class name> {
    ...
}
```

Such definitions are said to involve **public derivations**.

245
SIDE TRIP In addition to public derivations, there are **protected derivations** and **private derivations**, expressed by `protected` and `private`, which you learn about later, in Section 35. Protected and private derivations can combine with variable declarations and function definitions in public and private parts of class definitions as well as with another part, introduced in Section 34, called the **protected part**. Exploiting all these potential derivation-type–class-part combinations adds a dimension of complexity to C++ programming.

246
SIDE TRIP Also, you have seen, in this section, class hierarchies in which each class has a default constructor and no other. Adding other constructors introduces another dimension of complexity that you learn about later, in Section 32.

247
PRACTICE Tie the `flat_car` class into the hierarchy now populated by the `box_car` and `tank_car` classes.

248
PRACTICE Add a `sphere` class into the container hierarchy. Be sure to include an appropriate member variable, constructor member functions, and volume member function.

249
PRACTICE Create a class, `liquid_gas_car`, for cars that carry liquid gas. Assume that the cars carry the gas in two or three identical spheres. Include a member variable for the number and radius of the spheres, along with appropriate constructor member functions. Also include a `volume` member function that makes use of the member variables and the `volume` function in the `sphere` class.

250
HIGHLIGHTS
- Class hierarchies reflect subclass–superclass relations among classes.

- You have several reasons to arrange classes in hierarchies:

    - To parallel natural categories

    - To prevent avoidable duplication and to simplify maintenance

    - To avoid introducing bugs into previously debugged code

    - To use purchased code

- An object inherits member variables and member functions not only from the class to which it belongs, but also from all that class's superclasses.

- When a subclass–superclass chain contains multiple functions with the same name, the one closest to the object argument in the subclass–superclass chain is the one executed. All others are shadowed.

- When a subclass–superclass relation is direct, with no intervening classes, the subclass is called the derived class and the superclass is called the base class. The derived class is said to be derived from the base class.

- There are several types of derivations; so far, you know about only public derivations.

- **If** you want to create a class hierarchy, **then** draw a diagram that reflects natural categories, **and** populate the classes in that class hierarchy with member variables and member functions such that there is no needless duplication of a member variable or member function, and such that each member variable and member function is useful in every subclass.

- **If** you want to create a public derived-class–base-class relation, **then** augment the derived-class definition by instantiating the following pattern:

```
class  derived-class name  : public  base-class name  { ··· }
```

16 HOW TO DESIGN CLASSES AND CLASS HIERARCHIES

251   At this point, you have learned how to *define* classes and class hierarchies. In this section, you learn how to *design* classes and class hierarchies by observing several principles of representation design.

252   The principles described in this section are guidelines; they are not imperatives. Nevertheless, when you violate one, you should have a reason.

253   **The explicit-representation principle:** Whenever there is a natural category that your program needs to work with, there should be a class in your program that corresponds to that category.

In the railroad-car domain, for example, there are natural categories corresponding to the various sorts of railroad cars and containers. Accordingly, the program in Segment 239 has classes corresponding to those cars and containers.

254   **The no-duplication principle:** Member variables and function definitions should be distributed among class definitions to ensure that there is no duplication of identical code. Otherwise, duplicate copies are bound to become gratuitously different.

In the version of the program in Segment 239, for example, the `height`, `width`, and `length` member variables and `volume` member function reside in the `box` class, rather than in the `box_car`, making those member variables and member functions more generally available.

255   **The local-view principle:** Whenever related program elements are located close to one another on your screen, you can see at a glance how those program elements work together. Whenever related program elements cannot be made to appear on the same screen, you have extra difficulty understanding what is going on.

In the program shown in Segment 239, for example, the `box` volume function definition appears within a few lines of the declarations of the `height`, `width`, and `length` member variables.

256   **The look-it-up principle:** A program should look up a frequently needed answer, rather than computing that answer, whenever practicable.

Recall, for example, that a `radius` member variable was declared in one version of the cylinder class definition; a `diameter` member variable was declared in another. The right choice depends on whether cylinder-conscious functions are more likely to be interested in radii or diameters.

257   **The need-to-know principle:** Generally, when you design classes to be used by other programmers, your classes will contain many more member variables and functions than you expect to be accessed by the functions written by those other programmers. By restricting access to your classes to the member variables and functions in public interface, you can revise and improve the other member variables and functions without worrying about

whether other programmers have come to depend on member variables that disappear or functions whose behavior changes.

When you define a `cylinder` class, for example, you might choose to place a `radius` member variable in the private part, along with `read_radius` and `write_radius` functions in the public part. Your rationale would be that you could change later to a diameter-based definition without fear that anyone would have come to depend on direct access to the radius member variable. Instead, all cylinder users would have to use the `read_radius` and `write_radius` functions in the public interface, which you easily could redefine to work with a `diameter` member variable.

258   **The keep-it-simple principle:** In general, programs with complex program elements are difficult to write, to debug, to improve, and to maintain. Accordingly, when a class definition starts to be too complex to understand easily—certainly when it covers more than 20 lines or so—you should think about moving out the member-function definitions using the double-colon device for linking them into the class. Similarly, when a function definition of any kind becomes too complex to understand easily, you should think about breaking it up into smaller functions that you can debug and maintain independently.

259   When it comes to class implementation, you should adhere to a principle that applies not only to class implementation, but also to programming in general:

The modularity principle: Generally, you should divide your large programs into logically coherent modules, each of which occupies its own file. A first step to take in this direction is to separate your class definitions from your ordinary functions. A second step is to separate your class definitions along family lines.

As it stands, the program in Segment 239 is so short, many programmers would keep all of it in one file. On the other hand, were it to grow much larger, most programmers would divide the functions and class definitions of the program into files devoted to, say, the following program elements:

- The global variables and the `main` function

- The `box` and `cylinder` class definitions

- The `railroad_car`, `engine`, `box_car`, `tank_car`, and `caboose` class definitions

You learn about how to do such a division, using header files, in Section 45.

260   Design a class hierarchy for a dozen houses and buildings. At the highest level, place
PRACTICE   a member variable named `square_feet` and `age` and `location_multiplier`. Write a member function, `appraise`, for various classes in your hierarchy. Include classes such as `luxury_house`, `bungalow`, `skyscraper`, and `warehouse`.

261   Design a class hierarchy for a dozen occupations. At the highest level, place a member
PRACTICE   variable named `years_of_experience` and `location_multiplier`. Write a member function, `estimated_salary`, for various classes in your hierarchy. Include classes such as `physician`, `lawyer`, `engineer`, and `sports_hero`.

262

HIGHLIGHTS
- Programs should obey the explicit-representation principle, with classes included to reflect natural categories.

- Programs should obey the no-duplication principle, with member functions situated among class definitions to facilitate sharing.

- Programs should obey the local-view principle, with program elements placed to make it easy to see how the elements interact.

- Programs should obey the look-it-up principle, with class definitions including member variables for stable, frequently requested information.

- Programs should obey the need-to-know principle, with public interfaces designed to restrict member-variable and member-function access, thus facilitating the improvement and maintenance of nonpublic program elements.

- Programs should obey the keep-it-simple principle, with class and function definitions broken up when these definitions become too complex to understand.

- Programs should obey the modularity principle, with program elements divided into logically coherent modules.

17 HOW TO PERFORM TESTS USING NUMERICAL PREDICATES

263 In this section and the next several sections, you set classes and class objects aside, temporarily, to learn how to do routine testing and branching, iterating and recursing, and array access. You see that C++'s mechanisms for accomplishing such tasks are not much different from those that you would find in just about any programming language. In particular, in this section, you learn how to test numbers.

264 Functions that return values representing true or false are called **predicates**. C++ offers several predicates that test the relationship between pairs of numbers:

Predicate	Purpose
==	Are two numbers equal?
!=	Are two numbers not equal?
>	Is the first number greater than the second?
<	Is the first number less than the second?
>=	Is the first number greater than or equal to the second?
<=	Is the first number less than or equal to the second?

265 The value of the expression 6 == 3, in which the equality operator appears, is 0, which means **false** as far as C++ is concerned.

The value of the expression 6 != 3, in which the inequality operator appears, is 1, which means **true** as far as C++ is concerned.

Thus, the value returned by the == and != predicates may be either 0 or 1:

Integer Value	Meaning
0	False
1	True

266 A common error is to write =, the assignment operator, when you intend to check for equality. Be sure to remember that the equality predicate is written as a double equal sign, ==.

267 You now know that, whenever the character ! is followed immediately by the character =, the two characters together denote the inequality operator.

Note, however, that the ! character can appear alone, in which case the ! character denotes the *not* operator. The *not* operator is a unary operator that inverts true and false. Thus, the value of !0 is 1 and !1 is 0. Similarly, the value of !(6 == 3) is 1, meaning that it is true that 6 is equal to 3 is false. Also, the value of !(6 != 3) is 0, meaning that it is false that 6 is not equal to 3 is false.

268 Actually, C++ interprets any integer other than 0 as true. Accordingly, the not operator, !, turns any integer other than 0 into 0.

269   Note that you must have a program perform a cast, of the sort you learned about in Segment 69, if you want the program to compare an integer with a floating-point number. The following program illustrates how such comparisons must be performed:

```
#include <iostream.h>
main ( ) {
   int i = 50;
   double d = 50.0;
   cout << "i == (int) d    yields " << (i == (int) d)     << endl;
   cout << "(double) i != d yields " << ((double) i != d) << endl;
   cout << "i > (int) d      yields " << (i > (int) d)      << endl;
   cout << "(double) i < d  yields " << ((double) i < d)   << endl;
   cout << "i >= (int) d     yields " << (i >= (int) d)     << endl;
   cout << "(double) i <= d yields " << ((double) i <= d) << endl;
}
```

──────────────────── Result ────────────────────

```
i == (int) d      yields 1
(double) i != d yields 0
i > (int) d       yields 0
(double) i < d  yields 0
i >= (int) d      yields 1
(double) i <= d yields 1
```

270   Note that the parentheses surrounding the comparisons are required in the example, because the comparison operators, ==, !=, >, <, >=, and <=, have precedence lower than that of the output operator, <<.

```
                              Required       Required
                                 |              |
                                 ▼              ▼
...
cout << "i == (int) d yields " << (i == (int) d)    << endl;
...
```

You do not need the parentheses with ordinary arithmetic operators, because those operators have higher precedence:

```
                              Not            Not
                           required       required
                              |              |
                              ▼              ▼
...
cout << "i + (int) d yields " << (i + (int) d)    << endl;
...
```

To avoid stubbing your toe on such subtle distinctions, use parentheses liberally, whether or not you need them.

271   The energy of a moving mass is given by the formula $\frac{1}{2}mv^2$. Write a program that accepts
PRACTICE   the mass and velocity of two automobiles and displays 1 if the energy of the first is greater than that of the second; otherwise, your program is to display 0.

- A *predicate* is a function that returns 0 or 1.

- In C++, 0 means false, and 1 means true.

- The ! operator means not; the ! operator transforms 0 into 1 and any integer other than 0 into 0.

- **If** you want to force the conversion of a value of one type into the corresponding value of another type, **then** you must cast the value by instantiating the following pattern:

  `( type ) expression`

- **If** you want to compare two numbers of different types, **then** you must cast one to match the type of the other.

18 HOW TO WRITE ONE-WAY AND TWO-WAY CONDITIONAL STATEMENTS

273   In this section, you learn how to use conditional statements when the computation that you want to perform depends on the value of an expression, possibly an expression involving one or more predicates.

274   Conceptually, a **Boolean expression** is an expression that produces a true or false result. Reduced to practice in C++, a Boolean expression is an expression that produces either 0, meaning false, or any other integer, meaning true.

275   An `if` statement contains a Boolean expression, in parentheses, followed by an embedded statement:

```
if ( Boolean expression )
   embedded statement
```

When the Boolean expression of an `if` statement evaluates to *any integer* other than 0, C++ considers the expression to be true and executes the embedded statement; otherwise, if the Boolean expression evaluates to 0, C++ considers the expression to be false and skips the embedded statement.

276   Suppose, for example, that you want to write a program that displays a message that depends on the temperature of a refrigerator car. Specifically, if the temperature is greater than 50°F, you want your program to display `It is too warm!`, and if the temperature is less than 25°F, you want your program to display `It is too cold!`.

Further suppose that you are able to assign the temperature, measured by some sort of temperature sensor, to a variable named `temperature`.

One solution is to write a program that uses an `if` statement in which the embedded statements are output statements:

```
#include <iostream.h>
main ( ) {
  int temperature;
  cin >> temperature;
  if (temperature < 25) cout << "It is too cold!" << endl;
  if (temperature > 50) cout << "It is too warm!" << endl;
}
```
———————————————— Sample Data ————————————————
```
55
```
———————————————————— Result ————————————————————
```
It is too warm!
```

277   The `if-else` statement is like the `if` statement, except that there is a second embedded statement, one that follows `else`:

```
if ( Boolean expression )
   if-true statement
else
   if-false statement
```

The if-false statement is executed if the Boolean expression evaluates to 0 or, said another way, if the Boolean expression is false.

278 Either the if-true statement or the if-false statement or both may be embedded if statements. Accordingly, another solution to the temperature-testing problem looks like this:

```
#include <iostream.h>
main ( ) {
  int temperature;
  cin >> temperature;
  if (temperature < 25)
    cout << "It is too cold!" << endl;
  else
    if (temperature > 50)
      cout << "It is too warm!" << endl;
}
```

———————————— Sample Data ————————————
55
———————————— Result ————————————
It is too warm!

Note that the first if statement's if-false statement is, itself, an embedded if statement. This embedded if statement is executed only if the temperature is *not* less than 25°F. If the temperature is between 25°F and 50°F, nothing is displayed.

279 The layout of nested if statements is a matter of convention. Here is another common arrangement:

```
#include <iostream.h>
main ( ) {
  int temperature;
  cin >> temperature;
  if (temperature < 25)
    cout << "It is too cold!" << endl;
  else if (temperature > 50)
    cout << "It is too warm!" << endl;
}
```

———————————— Sample Data ————————————
55
———————————— Result ————————————
It is too warm!

92

Whatever convention you use, you should be able to defend it on the ground that you think it contributes to program clarity.

280 Suppose that you want to execute more than one statement when an `if` or `if-else` statement's Boolean expression is true or not true. You need only to combine the multiple statements, using braces, into a single **compound statement**.

```
{
statement 1
...
statement n
}
```

In the following `if-else` statement, for example, you not only want to display a message when the value of `temperature` is above 50°F, but also want to assign 1 to a suitable variable so as to record that the temperature has gone above the threshold of 50°F:

```
if (temperature > 50) {
  high_temperature_switch = 1;
  cout << "It is too warm!  High temperature switch set to "
      << high_temperature_switch << endl;
}
```

281 Note the ambiguity in the following nested `if` statement:

```
if (temperature > 25)
   if (temperature < 50)
     cout << "It is normal." << endl;
     else cout << "It is too ?." << endl;
```

With what should you replace the question mark: warm or cold? As laid out on the page, it seems that warm is the right answer. Laid out another way, however, you might have the impression that cold is the right answer:

```
if (temperature > 25)
   if (temperature < 50)
     cout << "It is normal." << endl;
   else cout << "It is too ?." << endl;
```

Because C++ pays no attention to layout, you need to know that C++ assumes that each `else` belongs to the nearest `if` that is not already matched with an `else`. Thus, the question mark should be replaced by warm.

282 Although you can rely on the rule that if-false statements belong to the nearest unmatched `if` statement, it is better programming practice to use braces to avoid potential misreading.

In the following example, it is clear that the question mark should be replaced by warm, for the braces clearly group the if-false statement with the second `if` statement.

```
if (temperature > 25) {
  if (temperature < 50)
    cout << "It is normal." << endl;
  else cout << "It is too ?." << endl;
}
```

On the other hand, in the following example, it is clear that the question mark should be replaced by `cold`, for this time the braces clearly group the if-false statement with the first `if` statement.

```
if (temperature > 25) {
  if (temperature < 50)
    cout << "It is normal." << endl;
  }
else cout << "It is too ?." << endl;
```

283 Many C++ programmers use braces in every `if` statement they write, even though the braces often surround just one statement. Such programmers argue that the habitual use of braces reduces errors later on when a program is modified. When braces are not used, it is easy to add a second embedded statement to the `if` statement, yet forget that the modification requires the addition of braces.

284 Recall that C++'s `if` statement executes its embedded statement if the value of the Boolean expression is *not* 0. C++ has no complimentary statement, which might be called *unless*, if it existed, for which the embedded statement is executed when the value of the Boolean expression is 0.

One way to get the effect of the nonexistent *unless* statement by prefacing the Boolean expression with the not operator, `!`. Thus, the following tests are equivalent:

```
if (temperature < 25) cout << "It is too cold!" << endl;
if (!(temperature >= 25)) cout << "It is too cold!" << endl;
```

Another way to get the effect of the nonexistent `unless` statement is via an `if-else` statement with an **empty statement**—one that consists of a semicolon only—in the if-true position. Thus, the following tests are equivalent:

```
if (temperature < 25) cout << "It is too cold!" << endl;
if (temperature >= 25)
  ;
else cout << "It is too cold!" << endl;
```

285 So far, you have learned how to use `if-else` statements to execute one of two embedded computation-performing *statements*. You should also know about C++'s **conditional operator**, which enables you to compute a value from one of two embedded, value-producing *expressions*.

The conditional operator sees frequent service in output statements, where it helps you to produce the proper singular–plural distinctions. Consider, for example, the following program, which displays a temperature change:

```
#include <iostream.h>
main ( ) {
  int change;
  cin >> change;
  if (change == 1)
    cout << "The temperature has changed by "
         << change << " degree." << endl;
  else
    cout << "The temperature has changed by "
         << change << " degrees." << endl;
}
```
———————————— Sample Data ————————————
1
———————————————— Result ————————————————
The temperature has changed by 1 degree.

The program works, but most C++ programmers would be unhappy because there are two separate output statements that are almost identical. Such duplication makes programs longer, and the longer a program is, the greater the chance that a bug will creep in.

Accordingly, it would be better to move the variation—the part that produces either the word *degree* or the word *degrees*—into a value-producing expression inside a single output statement.

286 The following is the general pattern for C++'s value-producing conditional-operator expression:

`Boolean expression` ? `if-true expression` : `if-false expression`

Note that, in contrast to the operators you have seen so far, the conditional operator consists of a combination of distributed symbols, ? and :, separating three operands—the Boolean expression, the if-true expression, and the if-false expression. Thus, the conditional operator combination is said to be a **ternary operator** with **distributed operator symbols**.

Note also the similarity to the `if-else` statement—it is as though the `if` became a question mark, and moved between the first two expressions, and the `else` became a colon.

Finally, note that either the if-true expression or the if-false expression is evaluated, but both are not. Thus, any variable assignments or other side effects in the unevaluated expression do not occur.

287 The value of the following conditional-operator expression is the character string "degree" if the temperature change is 1 degree; otherwise, the value is the character string "degrees":

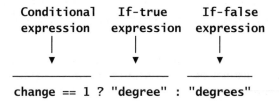

```
change == 1 ? "degree" : "degrees"
```

You can, if you wish, employ parentheses to delineate the Boolean expression, but parentheses are not needed in the example, because the equality operator has precedence higher than that of the conditional operator, as shown in Appendix A.

288   Because a conditional-operator expression, unlike an `if` statement, produces a value, you can place it inside another expression. In the following, for example, a conditional-operator expression appears inside an output expression, solving the duplication problem encountered in Segment 285:

```
#include <iostream.h>
main ( ) {
  int change;
  cin >> change;
  cout << "The temperature has changed by "
       << change
       << (change == 1 ? " degree" : " degrees")
       << endl;
}
```
———————————————— Sample Data ————————————————
```
1
```
———————————————— Result ————————————————
```
The temperature has changed by 1 degree
```

If the change is 1 degree, the value returned by the Boolean expression, and displayed, is "degree"; otherwise, the value returned, and displayed, is "degrees".

Note that the parentheses surrounding the Boolean expression are absolutely necessary, because the output operator has precedence higher than that of the conditional operator.

289   You can, if you wish, use conditional-operator expressions in place of `if` statements, as in
SIDE TRIP   the following example, in which one of the two output expressions is evaluated:

```
#include <iostream.h>
main ( ) {
  int change;
  cin >> change;
  change == 1 ? cout << "The temperature has changed by "
                     << change << " degree." << endl
              : cout << "The temperature has changed by "
                     << change << " degrees." << endl;
}
```
———————————————— Sample Data ————————————————
```
1
```
———————————————— Result ————————————————
```
The temperature has changed by 1 degree.
```

This program not only reintroduces needless duplication, but also introduces a conditional-operator expression that is not inside any other expression that can make use of the value produced. Instead, the conditional-operator expression forms a complete statement. Such use of the conditional operator is considered poor programming practice, and your C++ compiler should issue a warning.

290
PRACTICE Write a program that transforms a patient's weight and height into one of three messages: "The patient appears to be underweight," "The patient appears to be of normal weight," or "The patient appears to be overweight." Your program's input is three numbers: the first is the patient's weight in kilograms, the second is the patient's height in meters, and the third is a gender code—0 for men and 1 for women. You may assume that a patient's "perfect" weight is proportional to height, and that the overweight and underweight messages should not appear unless the patient's weight differs from the perfect weight by more than 10 percent.

291
PRACTICE Write a program that displays a message indicating the deviation from the patient's perfect weight, truncated to the nearest integer, of the form The patient is kilograms . Your program's input is three numbers: weight in kilograms, height in meters, and a gender code. Be sure that, if the deviation is just 1 kilogram, the word *kilogram* appears, rather than *kilograms*.

292
HIGHLIGHTS

- If you want to execute a statement only when an expression produces a value other than 0, **then** use an if statement:

  ```
  if (Boolean expression) statement
  ```

- If you want to execute one statement when an expression evaluates to any integer other than 0, and another when the expression evaluates to 0, **then** use an if-else statement:

  ```
  if (Boolean expression)
     if-true statement
  else
     if-false statement
  ```

- If you want to execute a group of statements in an if or if-else statement, **then** use braces to combine those statements into a single compound statement.

- If you want to use nested if-else statements, **then** use braces to clarify your grouping intention.

- If you want the value of an expression to be the value of one of two embedded expressions, **and** you want the choice to be determined by the value of a Boolean expression, **then** instantiate the following pattern:

  ```
  Boolean expression
     ?
     if-true expression : if-false expression
  ```

19 HOW TO COMBINE BOOLEAN EXPRESSIONS

293   In this section, you learn how to combine Boolean expressions to form larger Boolean expressions.

294   Roughly, the **and operator, &&**, and the **or operator**, ¦¦, do what they sound like they should do. The **and** operator returns 1 if *both* of its operands evaluate to any integer other than 0. The **or** operator returns 1 if *either* of its operands evaluates to an integer other than 0.

295   Recall that C++ treats 0 as false and any integer other than 0 as true. That is why you see the contorted expression, *any integer other than* 0, instead of just 1.

296   The following expression, for example, evaluates to 1 only if the value of the `temperature` variable is between 25 and 50:

```
25 < temperature && temperature < 50
```

Accordingly, the output statement embedded in the following `if` statement is evaluated only if the value of the `temperature` variable is inside the 25-to-50 range.

```
if (25 < temperature && temperature < 50)
   cout << "The temperature is normal." << endl;
```

297   The evaluation of **&&** and ¦¦ expressions is complicated by the fact that certain subexpressions may not be evaluated at all.

In **&&** expressions, the left-side operand is evaluated first: If the value of the left-side operand is 0, the right-side operand is ignored completely, and the value of the **&&** expression is 0.

If both operands evaluate to some integer other than 0, the value of the **&&** expression is 1.

In ¦¦ expressions, the left-side operand also is evaluated first: If the left-side operand evaluates to some integer other than 0, nothing else is done, and the value of the ¦¦ expression is 1; if both operands evaluate to 0, the value of the ¦¦ expression is 0.

298   Two ampersands, **&&**, and two vertical bars, ¦¦, are used for *and* and *or* because & and ¦
SIDE TRIP   are reserved for operations on bits, rather than on integers. Neither & nor ¦ is discussed in this book, because understanding bit manipulation is not a prerequisite to understanding either basic C++ programs or the special strengths of the language.

299   C++, as a rule, does not specify the order of operand evaluation. Thus, && and ¦¦ are
SIDE TRIP   exceptions to the general rule. The other exceptions are the conditional operator, which you learned about in Segment 286, and the comma operator, which you learn about in Segment 321.

It is possible to use && instead of an if statement by exploiting the property that the right-side operand of an && expression is evaluated only if the value of the left-side operand is not 0. Thus, the following two expressions are equivalent:

```
if (temperature > 50) cout << "It is too hot!" << endl;
(temperature > 50) && cout << "It is too hot!" << endl;
```

Similarly, it is possible to use || instead of an if-else statement by exploiting the property that the right-side operand of an || expression is evaluated only if the left-side operand evaluates to 0. Thus, the following two expressions are equivalent:

```
if (temperature > 50) ; else cout << "It is NOT too hot!" << endl;
(temperature > 50) || cout << "It is NOT too hot!" << endl;
```

Note, however, that many programmers object to the use of && and || operators to allow or block evaluation. They argue that, when an && or || operator is included in an expression, anyone who looks at the expression—other than the original programmer—naturally expects the value produced by the expression to be used. If the value is not used, the person who looks at the program might wonder whether the original programmer left out a portion of the program unintentionally.

Accordingly, some C++ compilers complain about using an && or || expression whenever the value of the expression is not actually put to use.

Write a function that transforms an athlete's pulse rate into one of three integers: if the rate is less than 60, the value returned by the function is to be -1; if the rate is more than 80, the value returned is to be 1; otherwise, the value returned is to be 0. Then, write another function that transforms an athlete's body fat as a percentage of weight into one of three integers: if the athlete's body-fat percentage is less than 10, the value returned is to be -1; if it is more than 20, the value returned is to be +1; otherwise, the value returned is to be 0.

Write a program that accepts two numbers—a pulse rate and a body-fat percentage—and displays "The athlete appears to be in great shape," if both the athlete's pulse rate and body fat are low.

- If you want to combine two predicate expressions, **and** the result is to be 1 if the values of *both* expressions are other than 0, **then** use &&.

- If you want to combine two predicate expressions, **and** the result is to be 1 if the value of *either* expression is other than 0, **then** use ||.

- Both && and || evaluate their left operand before they evaluate their right operand. The right operand is not evaluated if the value of the left operand of an && expression is 0 or if the value of the left operand of a || expression is not 0.

20 HOW TO WRITE ITERATION STATEMENTS

304   In this section, you learn how to tell C++ to repeat a computation by using C++'s most common iteration statements, the `while` and `for` statements.

305   C++'s **iteration statements** enable functions to do computations over and over until a test has been satisfied. C++'s `while` statement, for example, consists of a Boolean expression, in parentheses, followed by an embedded statement:

```
while ( Boolean expression )
  embedded statement
```

The Boolean expression is evaluated, and if the Boolean expression evaluates to *any integer* other than 0, the embedded statement is evaluated as well; otherwise, C++ skips the embedded statement. In contrast to an `if` statement, however, the evaluate-Boolean-expression–evaluate-embedded-statement cycle continues as long as the Boolean expression evaluates to some integer other than 0.

306   For example, the following function fragment repeatedly decrements n by 1 until n is 0:

```
while (n != 0)
  n = n - 1;
```

Replacement of the single embedded statement, n = n - 1;, by a compound statement enables the `while` statement to do useful computation while counting down n to 0.

307   Suppose, for example, that you are asked to figure out the number of customers that your railroad will have at a given time if the number of customers doubles each month starting now. Plainly, the number after n months is proportional to 2^n, thus requiring you to develop a function that computes the nth power of 2.

One way to do the computation is to count down the parameter, n, to 0, multiplying a variable, `result`, whose initial value is 1, by 2 each time that you decrement n:

```
int power_of_2 (int n) {
  int result = 1;              // Initial value is 1
  while (n != 0) {
    result = 2 * result;       // Multiplied by 2 n times
    n = n - 1;
  }
  return result;
}
```

308   Note that the value of the Boolean expression, n != 0, is 0, meaning false, if and only if the value of n is 0. Accordingly, the following `while` statements are equivalent:

```
while (n != 0)
    ...

while (n)
    ...
```

Thus, testing n to see whether it is not 0 is viewed by some C++ programmers as a form of lily gilding; such programmers use n rather than n != 0.

Other C++ programmers much prefer n != 0 because they believe that it is important to maintain a visible distinction between 0 viewed as a number and 0 viewed as a truth value.

309 The defect of many while loops is that the details that govern the looping appear in three places: the place where the counting variable is initialized, the place where it is tested, and the place where it is reassigned. Such distribution makes the looping difficult to understand. Accordingly, you also need to know about the for statement:

```
for ( entry expression ;
      Boolean expression ;
      continuation expression )
   embedded statement
```

The entry expression is evaluated only once, when the for statement is entered. Once the entry expression is evaluated, the Boolean expression is evaluated, and if the result is not 0, the embedded statement is evaluated, followed by the continuation expression. Then, the Boolean-expression–embedded-statement–continuation-expression evaluation cycle continues until the Boolean expression eventually evaluates to 0.

310 Specialized to counting down a counter variable, the for statement becomes the counting for loop:

```
variable declaration
for ( counter initialization expression ;
      counter testing expression ;
      counter reassignment expression )
   embedded statement
```

311 Now you can define the power_of_2 function using a for loop instead of a while loop. The initialization expression, counter = n, assigns the value of the parameter n to counter. Then, as long as the value of counter is not 0, the value of result, whose initial value is 1, is multiplied by 2 and the value of counter is decremented by 1.

```
int power_of_2 (int n) {
  int counter, result = 1;
  for (counter = n; counter; counter = counter - 1)
    result = 2 * result;
  return result;
}
```

312 **Augmented assignment operators** reassign a variable to a value obtained by combining the variable's current value with an expression's value via addition, subtraction, multiplication, or division. The following diagram illustrates how assignment using an augmented assignment operator differs from ordinary assignment:

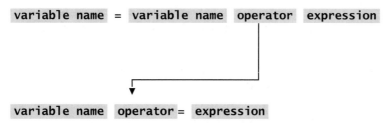

For example, you can rewrite `result = result * 2` in this way:

`result *= 2`

Even though this shorthand gives you a perfectly valid way to multiply and reassign, you may choose to write `result = result * 2`, which you see throughout this book, on the ground that `result = result * 2` stands out more clearly as a reassignment operation.

313 Although augmented assignment operators are not used in this book, there are situations

SIDE TRIP in which an expression written with an augmented assignment operator is arguably better than the corresponding expression without the augmented assignment operator. In Section 24, for example, you learn about C++ arrays: in particular, you learn that you can reassign an array element to twice its former value as follows:

`array name` [`index-producing expression`]
  = `array name` [`index-producing expression`] * 2

Alternatively, using an augmented assignment operator, you can write the reassignment expression as follows:

`array name` [`index-producing expression`] *= 2

Plainly, if the index-producing expression is complex, the augmented assignment operator offers one way to keep size down and to avoid a maintenance headache should the expression require modification.

314 In principle, you could rewrite `count = count - 1`, using an augmented assignment operator, as `count -= 1`. You are not likely to see such expressions, however, because C++ offers a still more concise shorthand for adding 1 to, or subtracting 1 from, a variable. To use the shorthand, you drop the equal sign altogether, along with the 1, and prefix the variable with the **increment operator**, ++, or the **decrement operator**, --. Thus, you replace `count = count - 1` by the following expression:

`--count`

Similarly, `++count` means increment the value of `count` by 1.

315 Using C++'s shorthand notations for variable reassignment, you can write the `power_of_2` function this way:

```
int power_of_2 (int n) {
  int counter, result = 1;
  for (counter = n; counter; --counter)
   result = result * 2;
  return result;
}
```

316   You can, in principle, embed expressions involving the increment operator, ++, or the decrement operator, --, in larger expressions, such as the following:

++x + x   // Bad: never do this

In such an expression, the increment operator, ++, is said not only to produce a value, but also to have the **side effect** of incrementing x.

Importantly, however, the C++ language does not prescribe the order in which operands are evaluation in arithmetic expressions. Thus, in the expression ++x + x, the left-side operand, ++x, may be evaluated either before or after the right-side operand, x, depending on the implementation.

Suppose, for example, that the initial value of x is 0. In an implementation that evaluates left-side first, the value of ++x + x will be 2; on the other hand, in an implementation that evaluates right-side first, the value of ++x + x will be 1.

Thus, the use of side-effect operators, such as ++ and --, can lead to mysterious portability problems.

Worse yet, a C++ compiler is free to compile some expressions for left-side-first evaluation and others for right-side-first evaluation. Thus, side-effect operands can cause plenty of trouble.

317   You can, in principle, position two plus signs or two minus signs as suffixes, rather than as
SIDE TRIP   prefixes. In either position, the plus signs or minus signs cause a variable's value to change, but if the incremented or decremented variable is embedded in a larger expression, the value handed over differs. If a variable is prefixed, the value handed over is the new, incremented value; if a variable is suffixed, the value handed over is the old, original value.

Suppose that the value of count is 3. Then, the value of the expression --count is 2, and the new value of count is 2. On the other hand, again supposing that the value of count is 3, the value of the expression count-- is 3, even though the new value of count is 2.

318   Consider, for example, the following oddball version of power_of_2, in which the decre-
SIDE TRIP   menting of the counter variable occurs in the Boolean expression, rather than in the normal continuation expression, which is rendered empty. The suffix form, counter--, must be used, rather than the prefix form, --counter, because decrementing is to be done after your program decides whether to go around the loop. Were you to use the prefix form, your program would fail to go around the loop enough times.

```
int power_of_2 (int n) {
  int counter, result = 1;
  for (counter = n; counter--;)
   result = 2 * result;
  return result;
}
```

319   There are many other ways to define power_of_2 using a for loop. Here is one in which the initialization of the result variable is included within the for statement, along with the initialization of the counter variable, the two being separated with a comma:

```
int power_of_2 (int n) {
  int counter, result;
  for (counter = n, result = 1; counter; --counter)
   result = result * 2;
  return result;
}
```

320   You can even, if you wish, bring the reassignment of the result variable within the reassignment part of the for loop, joining it to the reassignment of the counter variable. The result is a for loop with an empty embedded statement, which, as you may recall from Segment 284, consists of a semicolon only:

```
int power_of_2 (int n) {
  int counter, result;
  for (counter = n, result = 1;       // Initialization
       counter;                       // Test
       --counter, result = result * 2)   // Reassignment
   ;                                  // Empty statement
  return result;
}
```

321
SIDE TRIP   The initialization and reassignment portions of the for statement in Segment 320 both appear to consist of two separate expressions:

```
counter = n, result = 1
--counter, result = result * 2
```

However, both consist of just one expression, because the comma is viewed as just another operator—one on the lowest precedence level. The operands are evaluated left to right, and the value is the value of the right-hand operand.

322   The definition of power_of_2 that appears in Segment 319 is the best of the lot in many respects: All initialization is done in the initialization part of the for statement, a simple test of a counter variable occurs in the testing part of the for statement, the counter variable is reassigned in the reassignment part of the for statement, and the computation of the result is separated from the reassignment part. The for statement is deployed straightforwardly; there are no parlor tricks.

323   Write an iterative program that accepts two positive integers, m and n, and computes m^n.
PRACTICE

324
PRACTICE   Write an iterative program that accepts a positive integer, n, and computes the factorial of n, written $n!$, where $n! = n \times n - 1 \times \ldots \times 1$.

325
HIGHLIGHTS

- If you want to repeat a calculation for as long as a Boolean expression's value is not 0, **then** use a `while` loop:

  ```
  while ( Boolean expression )
     embedded statement
  ```

- If you want to repeat a calculation involving entry, Boolean, and continuation expressions, **then** use a `for` loop:

  ```
  for ( entry expression ;
       Boolean expression ;
       continuation expression )
     embedded statement
  ```

- If you want to repeat a calculation until a variable is counted down to 0, **then** use a counting `for` loop:

  ```
  variable declaration
  for ( counter initialization expression ;
       counter testing expression ;
       counter reassignment expression )
     embedded statement
  ```

- If you want to increment or decrement the value of a variable by 1, **then** instantiate one of the following patterns:

  ```
  ++ variable name
  -- variable name
  ```

- If you want to change a variable's value by combining it with the value of an expression via addition, subtraction, multiplication, or division, **then** consider instantiating the following pattern:

  ```
  variable name  operator = expression
  ```

21 HOW TO PROCESS DATA IN FILES

326   In this section, you learn how to use `while` loops and `for` loops to read data from files, processing each data item as it is encountered.

327   In Section 20, you learned about the `while` statement:

`while (` `Boolean expression` `)`
  `embedded statement`

The `while` reading pattern consists of a `while` statement with an input expression in the place reserved for a Boolean expression:

`while (` `input expression` `)`
  `embedded statement`

The idea is to process data until the input expression stops the loop.

328   Recall that the value of an input expression, such as `cin >> height`, is normally the same as the value of `cin` itself. Accordingly, an input expression is a suitable left argument for another input expression.

Thus, the following `while` statement will continue looping, as long as you keep typing numbers, because the value of `cin` is not 0:

`while (cin >> height >> width >> depth)`
  `...`

329   When you decide to stop the loop, assuming that you are working with a typical version of the UNIX or DOS operating systems, you can arrange for the input operator to return 0, instead of the value of `cin`, thus stopping the `while` loop, by typing the appropriate *keychord*.

You are said to type a **keychord** whenever you hold down one key while you press another. For example, if you are working with a typical version of UNIX, you tell the input operator to return 0 by holding down the `control` key and pressing the `d` key, thereby typing the `control-d` keychord.

330   Unfortunately, the effects of various keychords vary with the operating system and with the way the parameters of the operating system are set. The keychords listed in the following table thus are only typical:

	UNIX	DOS
To stop a program	`control-c`	`control-c`
To force an input expression to return 0	`control-d`	`control-z`

331 Thus, the following program computes box-car volumes as long as you type numbers; it stops when you type the control-d keychord.

```
#include <iostream.h>
double box_volume (double h, double w, double l) {return h * w * l;}
main ( ) {
  double height, width, depth;
  while (cin >> height >> width >> depth)
    cout << "The volume of a "
         << height << " by " << width << " by " << depth
         << " box car is " << box_volume (height, width, depth)
         << endl;
  cout << "You appear to have finished." << endl;
}
```
———————————— Sample Data ————————————
10.5 9.5 40.0
10.5 9.5 50.0
———————————— Result ————————————
The volume of a 10.5 by 9.5 by 40 box car is 3990
The volume of a 10.5 by 9.5 by 50 box car is 4987.5
You appear to have finished.

332 Recall that, if you are using UNIX or DOS, you can redirect input from your keyboard to a file, enabling you to use the program in Segment 331 to find the volumes of box cars that you have described in a file. The only new fact that you need to know is that input expressions evaluate to 0 when the end of a file is encountered.

Thus, to find the volumes of some boxes described in a file, you need only to type the following to your operating system, assuming that you have called your box-analyzing program box_car and that you have prepared a test file named test_data:

```
box_car < test_data
```

333 Just as there is a while reading pattern, there is also a for reading pattern. The following is the for reading pattern:

```
for ( initialization expression ;
      input expression ;
      reassignment expression )
  embedded statement
```

334 The for reading pattern is particularly useful when you want to count the data items as you read them, as in the following amended version of the program in Segment 331:

```
#include <iostream.h>
double box_volume (double h, double w, double l) {return h * w * l;}
main ( ) {
  double height, width, depth;
  int count;
  for (count = 0; cin >> height >> width >> depth; ++count)
    cout << "The volume of a "
         << height << " by " << width << " by " << depth
         << " box car is "
         << box_volume (height, width, depth) << endl;
  cout << "You have computed the volumes of "
       << count << " box cars." << endl;
}
```
───────────────── Sample Data ─────────────────
```
10.5 9.5 40.0
10.5 9.5 50.0
```
─────────────────── Result ───────────────────
The volume of a 10.5 by 9.5 by 40 box car is 3990
The volume of a 10.5 by 9.5 by 50 box car is 4987.5
You have computed the volumes of 2 box cars.

335
PRACTICE

Consider the program in Segment 331. What will happen if it encounters the end of a file after reading only two numbers? What will happen if you type control-d after providing only two numbers?

336
PRACTICE

An **iterative filter** is a program that transforms a sequence of inputs into a modified sequence of outputs. Write an iterative filter that transforms input characters into upper-case output characters. To do so, you need to know that the value of an expression consisting of a character, such as a, surrounded by single-quotation marks, such as 'a', is the integer character code for the letter *a*. The character codes for the lower-case letters are consecutive, as are the character codes for the upper-case characters.

337
HIGHLIGHTS

- If you want to read data until you reach the end of a file, **then** instantiate a while reading pattern:

  while (input expression)
     embedded statement

- If you want to read data until you reach the end of a file, **and** you want to keep track of how many data you read, **then** instantiate a for reading pattern:

  for (initialization expression ;
        input expression ;
        reassignment expression)
     embedded statement

22 HOW TO WRITE RECURSIVE FUNCTIONS

338   In Section 20, you learned how to repeat a computation by using iteration statements. In this section, you learn how to perform a computation over and over by using recursive function calls.

The reason for introducing recursion at this point is to create a natural context for discussing function prototypes, which are introduced in Section 23. If you are already comfortable with recursive programs, you can skip ahead to that section.

339   If you are not yet familiar with recursion, it is best to see how recursion works through an example involving a simple mathematical computation that you already know how to perform using iteration. Suppose, for example, that you want to write a function, recursive_power_of_2, that computes the *n*th power of 2 recursively.

340   To define recursive_power_of_2, you can take advantage of the power_of_2 function already provided in Section 20.

Given that power_of_2 exists, one way to define recursive_power_of_2 is to hand over the real work to power_of_2 as follows:

```
int recursive_power_of_2 (int n) {
  return power_of_2 (n);
}
```

Once you see that you can define recursive_power_of_2 in terms of power_of_2, you are ready to learn how gradually to turn recursive_power_of_2 into a recursive function that does not rely on power_of_2.

341   First, note that you can eliminate the need to call power_of_2 in the simple case in which the value of recursive_power_of_2's parameter is 0:

```
int recursive_power_of_2 (int n) {
  if (n == 0)
    return 1;
  else
    return power_of_2 (n);
}
```

342   Next, note that you can arrange for recursive_power_of_2 to hand over a little less work to power_of_2 by performing one of the multiplications by 2 in recursive_power_of_2 itself, and subtracting 1 from power_of_2's argument:

```
int recursive_power_of_2 (int n) {
  if (n == 0)
    return 1;
    else
    return 2 * power_of_2 (n - 1);
}
```

111

Clearly, `recursive_power_of_2` must work as long as one of the following two situations holds:

- The value of the parameter, n, is 0; in this situation, `recursive_power_of_2` returns 1.

- The value of n is not 0, but `power_of_2` is able to compute the power of 2 that is 1 less than the value of n.

343 Now for the recursion trick: You replace `power_of_2` in `recursive_power_of_2` by `recursive_power_of_2` itself:

```
int recursive_power_of_2 (int n) {
  if (n == 0)
    return 1;
    else return 2 * power_of_2 (n - 1);
}

int recursive_power_of_2 (int n) {
  if (n == 0)
    return 1;
    else return 2 * recursive_power_of_2 (n - 1);
}
```

The new version works for two reasons:

- If the value of the parameter, n, is 0, `recursive_power_of_2` returns 1.

- If the value of n is not 0, `recursive_power_of_2` asks itself to compute the power of 2 for a number that is 1 less than the value of n. Then, `recursive_power_of_2` may ask itself to compute the power of 2 for a number that is 2 less than the original value of n, and so on, until the `recursive_power_of_2` needs to deal with only 0.

344 When a function, such as `recursive_power_of_2`, is used in its own definition, the function is said to be **recursive**. When a function calls itself, the function is said to **recurse**.

Given a positive, integer argument, there is no danger that `recursive_power_of_2` will recurse forever—calling itself an infinite number of times—because eventually the argument is counted down to 0, which `recursive_power_of_2` handles directly, without further recursion.

345 There is also no danger that the values taken on by the parameter n will get in each other's way. Each time `recursive_power_of_2` is entered, C++ sets aside a private storage spot to hold the value of n for that entry:

112

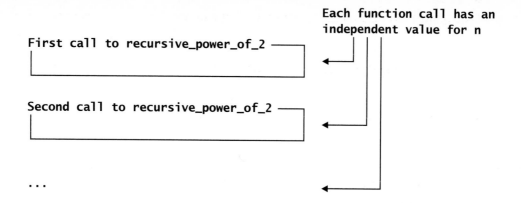

Each function call has an
independent value for n

First call to recursive_power_of_2 ⎯

Second call to recursive_power_of_2 ⎯

. . .

346   Note that the simple case—the one for which the result is computed directly—is handled by the **base** part of the definition.

The harder case—the one in which the result is computed indirectly, by another problem being solved first—is handled by the **recursive** part of the definition.

347   You can experiment with recursive_power_of_2 in a program such as this:

```
#include <iostream.h>
// Define recursive_power_of_2 function:
int recursive_power_of_2 (int n) {
  if (n == 0)
    return 1;
  else
    return 2 * recursive_power_of_2 (n - 1);
}
// Test recursive_power_of_2 function in main:
main ( ) {
  cout << "2 to the 0th power is " << recursive_power_of_2 (0) << endl
       << "2 to the 1st power is " << recursive_power_of_2 (1) << endl
       << "2 to the 2nd power is " << recursive_power_of_2 (2) << endl
       << "2 to the 3rd power is " << recursive_power_of_2 (3) << endl;
}
```
———————————————— Result ————————————————
```
2 to the 0th power is 1
2 to the 1st power is 2
2 to the 2nd power is 4
2 to the 3rd power is 8
```

348   Here is a look at the four calls involved when the recursive_power_of_2 function is set to work on 3:

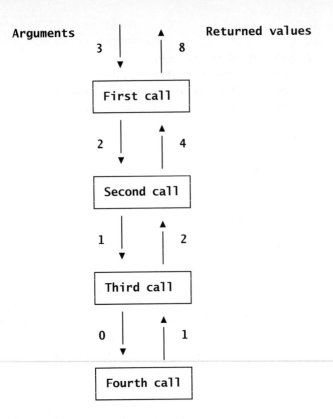

Arguments   Returned values

349 Now, for another, more interesting illustration of recursion, suppose that your railroad hauls rabbits. You are asked to predict the number of cars that you will need to get the rabbits to market when they are shipped a few months from now.

Fortunately, Fibonacci figured out long ago how fast rabbits multiply, deriving a formula that gives the number of female rabbits after n months, under the following assumptions:

- Female rabbits mature 1 month after birth.

- Once they mature, female rabbits have one female child each month.

- At the beginning of the first month, there is one immature female rabbit.

- Rabbits live forever.

- There are always enough males on hand to mate with all the mature females.

350 The following diagram shows the number of female rabbits at the end of every month for 6 months:

114

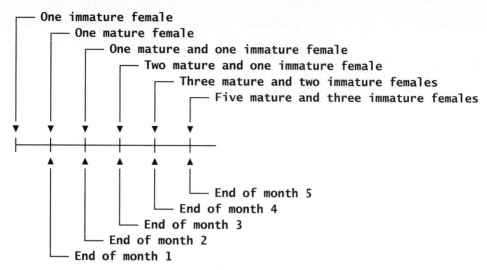

One immature female
One mature female
One mature and one immature female
Two mature and one immature female
Three mature and two immature females
Five mature and three immature females

End of month 5
End of month 4
End of month 3
End of month 2
End of month 1

Clearly, the number of female rabbits there are at the end of the *n*th month is the number of females there were at the end of the previous month plus the number of females that gave birth during the current month. But, of course, the number of females that gave birth during the current month is the number of mature female rabbits at the end of the previous month, which is same as the number of females there were all together at the end of the month before that. Thus, the following formula holds:

$$\text{Rabbits}(n) = \text{Rabbits}(n - 1) + \text{Rabbits}(n - 2)$$

351 Capturing the rabbit formula in the form of a C++ function, you have the following:

```cpp
#include <iostream.h>
// Define rabbits function:
int rabbits (int n) {
  if (n == 0 || n == 1)
    return 1;
  else return rabbits (n - 1) + rabbits (n - 2);
}
// Test rabbits function:
main ( ) {
  cout << "At the end of month 1, there is "  << rabbits (1) << endl
       << "At the end of month 2, there are " << rabbits (2) << endl
       << "At the end of month 3, there are " << rabbits (3) << endl
       << "At the end of month 4, there are " << rabbits (4) << endl
       << "At the end of month 5, there are " << rabbits (5) << endl;
}
```

——————————————————— Result ———————————————————
```
At the end of month 1, there is 1
At the end of month 2, there are 2
At the end of month 3, there are 3
At the end of month 4, there are 5
At the end of month 5, there are 8
```

352   Here is a look at the function `rabbits` at work on 3, the same argument previously used with `recursive_power_of_2`. The value returned is the number of rabbits at the end of the third month.

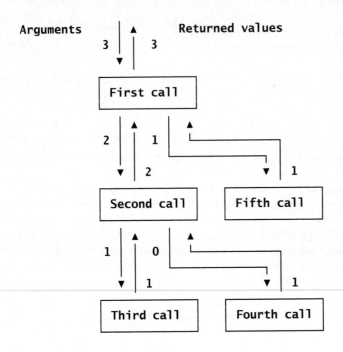

353   Now you have seen two recursive definitions, one for `power_of_2` and one for `rabbits`.

SIDE TRIP   Many mathematically oriented programmers prefer such recursive definitions to iterative definitions, when both are possible, believing that there is inherent elegance in defining a function partly in terms of itself.

Other, practically oriented programmers dislike recursive definitions for one or both of two reasons: first, the recursive approach usually produces much slower programs, because each function call takes time; and second, the recursive approach may have problems with large arguments, because the number of function calls in a recursive chain of calls is usually limited to a few hundred. Recursion aficionados counter by creating compilers that handle certain recursive functions in sophisticated ways that avoid such limits. These aficionados generally do not work on C++ compilers, however.

354   Write a recursive program that accepts two positive integers, m and n, and computes m^n.

PRACTICE

355   Write a recursive program that accepts a positive integer, n, and computes the factorial of

PRACTICE n, written $n!$, where $n! = n \times n-1 \times \ldots \times 1$.

356

HIGHLIGHTS

    • Recursive functions work by calling themselves to solve subproblems until the subproblems are simple enough for them to solve directly.

- The portion of a recursive function that handles the simplest cases is called the base part; the portion that transforms more complex cases is called the recursion part.

- If you want to solve a difficult problem, **then** try to break it up into simpler subproblems.

- If you are writing a recursive function, **then** your function must handle the simplest cases, **and** must break down every other case into the simplest cases.

- If your recursive function is to count down a number, **then** you may be able to instantiate the following pattern:

```
int  function name  (int n) {
  if (n == 0)
    return  result for n equal 0 ;
  else
    return  combination operand
            combination operator
            function name  (n - 1);
}
```

23 HOW TO SOLVE DEFINITION ORDERING PROBLEMS WITH FUNCTION PROTOTYPES

357   You know that C++ ordinarily requires you to define functions before you use them. Sometimes, however, functions refer to each other, which means you must learn to use C++'s function prototype mechanism to solve ordering problems.

So that you see the need for function prototypes, you learn about a set of three cooperating functions that provide an alternative to the rabbit-computing function that was introduced in Section 22.

358   In Segment 349, you learned that the number of rabbits after more than 1 month is the sum of the number at the end of the previous month and the month before that. With only this information, you can rewrite the `rabbits` function in terms of two auxiliary functions, `previous_month` and `penultimate_month`:

```
int rabbits (int n) {
  if (n == 0 || n == 1)
    return 1;
  else return previous_month (n) + penultimate_month (n);
}
```

Then, realizing that `previous_month` must return the number of rabbits at the end of the previous month, you can see that you can define `previous_month` as follows:

```
int previous_month (int n) {return rabbits (n - 1);}
```

Analogous reasoning leads you to the following definition for `penultimate_month`:

```
int penultimate_month (int n) {return rabbits (n - 2);}
```

359   Although the `rabbits`, `previous_month`, and `penultimate_month` functions capture one line of reasoning about rabbits, the `previous_month` and `penultimate_month` functions are so short, that most programmers would incorporate the expressions in those functions into the definition of `rabbits`, as shown in Segment 351. In this section, however, all three functions are retained, because, as separate functions, they provide a simple example of a situation for which you must use one or more function prototypes.

360   In principle, `rabbits`, `previous_month`, and `penultimate_month` should work fine together. However, if you just put them as is into a program, you soon discover that, no matter how you arrange the functions, at least one function is referred to before it is defined. In the following arrangement, for example, `rabbits` is referred to before it is defined.

```
int previous_month (int n) {return rabbits (n - 1);}
int penultimate_month (int n) {return rabbits (n - 2);}
int rabbits (int n) {
  if (n == 0 || n == 1)
    return 1;
  else return previous_month (n) + penultimate_month (n);}
```

The C++ compiler cannot compile a program that includes these three functions defined in this order, because the C++ compiler does not know how to prepare calls to the `rabbits` function before the `rabbits` function is defined. Yet calls to the `rabbits` function occur in both `previous_month` and `penultimate_month`, both of which are defined before `rabbits` is defined.

361 In Segment 167, you learned about function prototypes for member functions; here you learn about function prototypes for ordinary functions. As you learned in Segment 167, a function prototype is like a function definition without parameter names or a body.

By supplying a function prototype, you supply only what the C++ compiler needs to know about a function's parameter types and return type in order to prepare calls to the function. In the function prototype of `rabbits`, for example, the parameter name and the entire body disappear, leaving only the data-type declarations for the return value and the parameter:

```
int rabbits (int);
```

Because the body of the function is supplied later, a function prototype cannot refer to other functions, be they defined or not yet defined. Other definitions can refer to the function once its function prototype has been seen, however.

362 Accordingly, you can solve the `rabbits`, `previous_month`, and `penultimate_month` ordering problem this way:

- First, supply a function prototype for `rabbits`. Because the function prototype has no body, there are no references to `previous_month` or to `penultimate_month`.

- Next, supply definitions for `previous_month` and `penultimate_month`. Both refer to `rabbits`, but those references are now harmless, because the `rabbits` function prototype is in place.

- Finally, supply a definition for `rabbits`. This definition includes calls to other functions, `previous_month` and `penultimate_month`, but those calls are harmless, because both functions have been defined.

363 Thus, you can compile and run the following program:

```
#include <iostream.h>
// Function prototype for rabbits function:
int rabbits (int);
// Function definitions requiring rabbits function prototype:
int previous_month (int n) {return rabbits (n - 1);}
int penultimate_month (int n) {return rabbits (n - 2);}
// Function definition for rabbits function:
int rabbits (int n) {
  if (n == 0 || n == 1)
    return 1;
  else return previous_month (n) + penultimate_month (n);
}
```

120

```
// Test rabbits function:
main ( ) {
  cout << "At the end of month 1, there is "  << rabbits (1) << endl
       << "At the end of month 2, there are " << rabbits (2) << endl
       << "At the end of month 3, there are " << rabbits (3) << endl
       << "At the end of month 4, there are " << rabbits (4) << endl
       << "At the end of month 5, there are " << rabbits (5) << endl;
}
```

——————————————————— Result ———————————————————

```
At the end of month 1, there is 1
At the end of month 2, there are 2
At the end of month 3, there are 3
At the end of month 4, there are 5
At the end of month 5, there are 8
```

364 The following diagram shows rabbits and its two auxiliaries working to determine how
many rabbits there are at the end of 3 months.

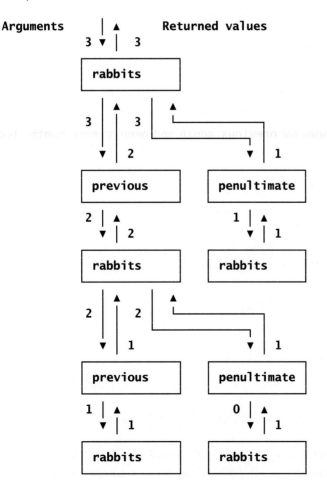

Each of the three cooperating functions can initiate a chain of calls that ends in a call to itself. Thus, the cooperating functions exhibit indirect, rather than direct, recursion.

The recursion bottoms out in calls to `rabbits` when the value of n is either 0 or 1. Thus, `rabbits` is not a particularly efficient function, because it twice computes the value of `rabbits (1)`.

365
SIDE TRIP You may, if you wish, include parameter names in function prototypes. For example, instead of `int rabbits (int);` you can write the following:

```
int rabbits (int n);
```

Although parameter names are optional, there are two advantages to including them. First, parameter names often provide a form of documentation; second, if you include parameter names in function prototypes, you can write the function prototype by copying from the function definition, without any error-prone removal of the parameter names.

366
SIDE TRIP In Section 10, you learned about function prototypes in connection with the definition of complex classes. In that context, the purpose of a function prototype is to transplant the function body out of a class definition, not to solve ordering problems.

367
PRACTICE Temporarily suspending disbelief, convert the program that you wrote in Segment 355 into a program consisting of three cooperating functions, `factorial`, `base`, and `recurse`. The factorial function is to look like this:

```
int factorial (n) {
  if (n == 0)
    return base ();
  else
    return recurse (n);
}
```

The `recurse` function is to call the `factorial` function, thus requiring you to use at least one function prototype.

368
HIGHLIGHTS

- C++ generally requires you to define functions before you refer to them in other functions.

- You can, however, provide a function prototype, instead of a full definition. Once you have provided a function prototype, you can refer to the function.

- If you want to define cooperative, indirectly recursive functions, **then** you must provide at least one function prototype.

- If you need a function prototype, **then** instantiate the following pattern:

```
return data type  function name ( data type of parameter 1 ,
                                  ...
                                  data type of parameter n )
```

24 HOW TO WORK WITH ARRAYS OF NUMBERS

369 In this section, you learn how to store numbers in arrays, and you learn how to retrieve those numbers.

370 A one-dimensional **array** is a collection of places where objects are stored and retrieved using an integer **index**. Each object in an array is called an **element** of that array. In C++, the first element is indexed by zero; hence, C++ is said to have zero-based arrays.

The following, for example, is a one-dimensional array with integer elements:

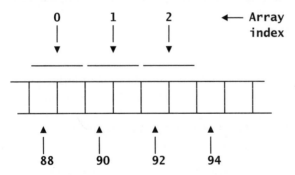

371 The number of bytes allocated for each place in an array is determined by the type of the objects to be stored. If an array is to hold integers of type short, for example, most implementations of C++ would allocate 2 bytes per integer:

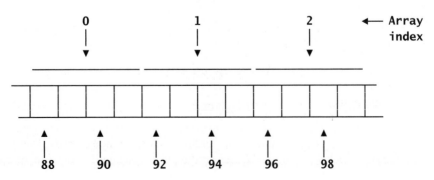

In this example, the first element of the array appears at memory address 88, the second appears at 90, and the third appears at 92.

372 On the other hand, if an array is to hold integers of type int, most implementations of C++ would allocate 4 bytes per integer:

In this example, the first element in the array appears at memory address 88, the second appears at 92, and the third appears at 96.

373 Note that a C++ array cannot hold elements of one type in some locations and elements of another type in other locations. All the objects in a C++ array must belong to the same data type.

374 To define a **global array**—one introduced outside of the definition of any function—you need to supply an array definition that tells C++ the name of the array, the type of objects that the array is to contain, the number of dimensions the array has, and the size of each dimension. The C++ compiler uses array definitions to calculate how much storage to allocate for the array.

The following array definition, for example, tells the C++ compiler to allocate memory for a one-dimensional array containing five integers of type `int`, each of which represents a distance to be traveled by a train:

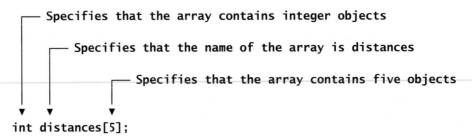

375 Thus, a one-dimensional global array definition looks like an ordinary global variable definition augmented by a bracketed number that specifies the array's size.

376 To use an array, once it is created, you need to know how to write into and read from the various locations in the array, each of which is identified by its numerical indexes.

Consider `distances`, the one-dimensional array of integers. To write data into `distances`, you use assignment statements in which the array name and a bracketed integer index appear on the left side of an assignment statement, the place where you are accustomed to seeing variable names. The following expression, for example, inserts an integer into the place indexed by the value of `counter`.

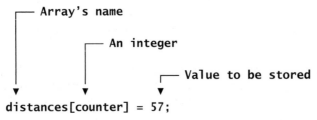

To read data from the `distances` array, once the data have been written, you write an expression containing the array name and a bracketed integer index. The following expression, for example, yields the integer stored in the place indexed by the value of `counter`:

```
distances[counter]
```

377 The following is a program in which an array of five integers is defined, data are wired in via five assignment statements, and the data are accessed in an output statement:

```cpp
#include <iostream.h>
// Define global integer array:
int distances[5];
main ( ) {
  // Wire in sample data:
  distances[0] = 57;  distances[1] = 72;
  distances[2] = 94;  distances[3] = 22;
  distances[4] = 35;
  // Display:
  cout << "The total distance traveled is "
       << distances[0]
          + distances[1]
          + distances[2]
          + distances[3]
          + distances[4]
       << endl;
}
```
——————————————— Result ———————————
```
The total distance traveled is 280
```

378 You know that you can use an input statement to assign a value to a variable:

```cpp
cin >> variable name
```

You can also use an input statement to assign a value to an array location:

```cpp
cin >> array name [ index ]
```

379 Now suppose that you want to fill an array using data in a file. You probably do not know exactly how many objects you need to store. Accordingly, you need an approach to dealing with uncertainty.

The simplest approach, albeit one not as elegant as the list-oriented approach you learn about in Section 47, is to define an array that is sure to be large enough to hold all the objects you can possibly encounter. Then, you can proceed to fill that array using a while reading pattern or a for reading pattern.

In the following program, for example, you create an array that can hold up to 100 integers representing distances. Then, you fill part or all of that array with integer distances using a for reading pattern. Then, you use another for loop to add up the integer distances, producing the total length of a trip.

Of course, the program could be written with just one for loop, and no array, but introducing the array makes it easy to perform other computations without rereading the file.

```
#include <iostream.h>
// Define global integer array:
int distances[100];
main ( ) {
  // Declare various integer variables:
  int limit, counter, sum = 0;
  // Read numbers and write them into array:
  for (limit = 0; cin >> distances[limit]; ++limit)
    ;
  // Display the sum of all integers in the array:
  for (counter = 0; counter < limit; ++counter)
    sum = sum + distances[counter];
  cout << "The sum of the "
       << limit << " distances traveled is "
       << sum << endl;
}
```

─────────────────── Sample Data ───────────────────
57   72   94   22   35
─────────────────────── Result ───────────────────────
The sum of the 5 distances traveled is 280

<table>
<tr><td>380</td></tr>
<tr><td>PRACTICE</td></tr>
</table>

380
PRACTICE

You easily can define arrays with more than one dimension: You simply add more bracketed dimension sizes. For example, to define a double array with 2 rows and 100 columns, you proceed as follows:

```
int 2_d_array[2][100];
```

Write writer functions to write the lengths and radii of cylinders in such an array. Use your writers to store cylinder radius–length pairs provided in a file. Then, write readers to help you determine the average radius, length, and volume of the cylinders.

381
HIGHLIGHTS

- If you want to create a one-dimensional array, **then** instantiate the following pattern:

  data type array name [maximum number of items];

- If you have an array, **and** you want to write values into the array, **then** instantiate an assignment-statement pattern or a input-statement pattern:

  array name [index] = expression ;
  cin >> array name [index];

- If you have a value stored in an array, **and** you want to read that value, **then** instantiate the following pattern:

  array name [index]

25 HOW TO WORK WITH ARRAYS OF CLASS OBJECTS

382   You can use arrays to store not only numbers, but also class objects. In this section, you learn how to create, write into, and read from an array of cylinder objects.

383   The following is a one-dimensional array with three places for storing cylinder objects, each of which includes, say, a radius and a length:

0	1	2	← Index
cylinder object	cylinder object	cylinder object	

384   The number of bytes allocated for each place in an array is determined by the objects to be stored. Suppose, for example, that you define the cylinder class like this:

```
class cylinder {public: double radius, length;};
```

Then, if an array is to hold cylinders, each of which contains floating-point numbers of type double for the cylinder's radius and length, each place will consist of 16 bytes in most implementations:

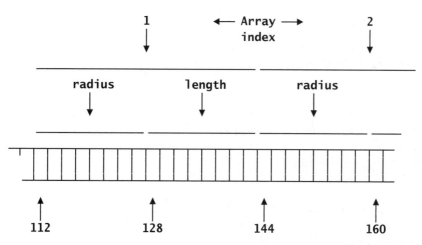

In this example, the first cylinder is described by the 16 bytes at memory addresses 112 through 227. Of these 16 bytes, the first 8 bytes contain a floating-point number that represents the cylinder's radius, and the second 8 bytes contain a floating-point number that represents the cylinder's length. The second cylinder is described by the 16 bytes starting at memory address 128.

385   To define a one-dimensional cylinder array, you must define the cylinder class first; then, you can write an array definition, as you would to define any array.

The following statement, for example, is an array definition that tells C++ to allocate memory for a one-dimensional array, named oil_tanks, containing three cylinders:

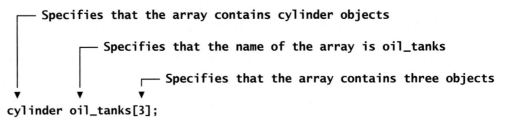

```
cylinder oil_tanks[3];
```

Thus, an array definition for class objects looks like an ordinary array definition, except that a class name, such as cylinder, appears, instead of the name of a language-defined type, such as int.

386 To write into the oil_tanks array in the first place, you can use assignment statements in which the array name, a bracketed integer index, and the member-variable name appear on the left side:

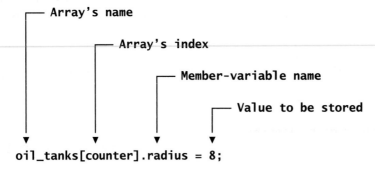

```
oil_tanks[counter].radius = 8;
```

To read data from the oil_tanks array, once the data have been inserted, you simply write an expression containing the array name, a bracketed integer index, and the member-variable name. The following expression, for example, yields the radius of the cylinder stored in the place indexed by the value of counter:

```
oil_tanks[counter].radius
```

387 The following program creates an array of three cylinder objects, wires in data via assignment statements, and accesses the data in a output statement:

```
#include <iostream.h>
const double pi = 3.14159;
// Define the cylinder class:
class cylinder {
  public: double radius, length;
          double volume ( ) {return pi * radius * radius * length;}
};
// Define cylinder array:
cylinder oil_tanks[3];
```

```
main ( ) {
  // Wire in sample data:
  oil_tanks[0].radius = 4.7; oil_tanks[0].length = 40.0;
  oil_tanks[1].radius = 3.5; oil_tanks[1].length = 35.5;
  oil_tanks[2].radius = 3.5; oil_tanks[2].length = 45.0;
  // Display volumes:
  cout << "The volumes of the cylinders in the oil-tank array are"
      << endl
      << oil_tanks[0].volume ( ) << ", "
      << oil_tanks[1].volume ( ) << ", and "
      << oil_tanks[2].volume ( ) << endl;
}
```

————————————————— Result —————————————————

The volumes of the cylinders in the oil-tank array are
2775.91, 1366.2, and 1731.8

388 Similarly, in the following program, you create an array that can hold up to 100 cylinders. Then, you fill part or all of it using a for reading pattern, and you use another for loop to add up the volumes, producing the total volume of the oil storage tanks:

```
#include <iostream.h>
const double pi = 3.14159;
// Define the cylinder class:
class cylinder {
  public: double radius, length;
          double volume ( ) {return pi * radius * radius * length;}
};
// Define cylinder array:
cylinder oil_tanks[100];
main ( ) {
  // Declare various variables:
  int limit, counter;
  double radius, length, sum = 0.0;
  // Read numbers and write them into array:
  for (limit = 0; cin >> radius >> length; ++limit) {
    oil_tanks[limit].radius = radius;
    oil_tanks[limit].length = length;
  }
  // Compute volumes:
  for (counter = 0; counter < limit; ++counter)
    sum = sum + oil_tanks[counter].volume ( );
  // Display sum:
  cout << "The total volume in the "
      << limit << " storage tanks is "
      << sum << endl;
}
```

―――――――――――――― Sample Data ――――――――――――――
4.7   40.0
3.5   35.5
3.5   45.0
―――――――――――――――― Result ――――――――――――――――
The total volume in the 3 storage tanks is 5873.91

389   Alternatively, you can have the input expression place numbers directly in the cylinder member variables, rather than indirectly through radius and length variables:

```cpp
#include <iostream.h>
const double pi = 3.14159;
// Define the cylinder class:
class cylinder {
  public: double radius, length;
          double volume ( ) {return pi * radius * radius * length;}
};
// Define cylinder array:
cylinder oil_tanks[100];
main ( ) {
  // Declare various variables:
  int limit, counter;
  double sum = 0.0;
  // Read numbers and write them into array:
  for (limit = 0;
       cin >> oil_tanks[limit].radius
           >> oil_tanks[limit].length;
       ++limit)
    ;
  // Compute volumes:
  for (counter = 0; counter < limit; ++counter)
    sum = sum + oil_tanks[counter].volume ( );
  // Display sum:
  cout << "The total volume in the "
       << limit << " storage tanks is "
       << sum << endl;
}
```

―――――――――――――― Sample Data ――――――――――――――
4.7   40.0
3.5   35.5
3.5   45.0
―――――――――――――――― Result ――――――――――――――――
The total volume in the 3 storage tanks is 5873.91

390   All the programs in this section define global arrays of cylinder objects. None of them
SIDE TRIP   happen to define a default constructor for cylinder objects, but as you learned in Segment 180, the C++ compiler defines a default constructor if you do not.

When, you might ask, do your C++ programs run the default constructors for objects in arrays? Here are the answers:

- The constructors for global arrays of class objects are activated at run time, just before C++ runs the `main` function.

- The constructors for local arrays of class objects are activated at run time, when the corresponding function is entered.

391
PRACTICE

Add reader and writer member functions to read and write cylinder information that is stored in a cylinder array. Use your writers to store cylinder radius–length pairs provided in a file. Then, use your readers to determine the average radius, length, and volume of the cylinders.

392
PRACTICE

Write a test program to determine when constructors are run for class objects that initialize global and local variables.

393
HIGHLIGHTS

- If you want to create a one-dimensional array of class objects, **then** instantiate the following pattern:

  `class name` `array name` [`maximum number of items`];

- If you have an array of class objects, **and** you want to write values into the array, **then** instantiate an assignment-statement pattern or a input-statement pattern:

  `array name` [`index`]. `member variable name` = `expression`;
  `cin >>` `array name` [`index`]. `member variable name`;

- If you have a value stored in a member variable in an array of class objects, **and** you want to read that value, **then** instantiate the following pattern:

  `array name` [`index`]. `member variable name`

26 HOW TO CREATE FILE STREAMS FOR INPUT AND OUTPUT

394   In this section, you learn how to access information in files directly, so that you do not have to depend on input–output redirection to get information in and out of files.

395   A **stream** is a sequence of data objects. In the context of file input and output, `cout` is the name of a stream that flows from your program to your screen, and `cin` is the name of a stream that flows from your keyboard to your program.

```
              cin stream                    cout stream
Keyboard ─────────────────────► Your program ─────────────────────► Screen
```

To read data from a file, you create an input stream that flows from an input file to your program. Similarly, to write data into a file, you create an output stream that flows from your program to the output file.

396   To create an input stream or an output stream, you must inform the C++ compiler that you plan to use C++'s file-handling library by including the following line in your program:

```
#include<fstream.h>
```

397   To create an input stream, you use a **file-opening statement** that sets up an input stream, names the stream, and specifies the file:

```
ifstream  stream name ( file specification , ios::in);
```

The following is an example in which the stream happens to be named `cylinder_stream` and the file specification happens to be `"test.data"`:

```
ifstream cylinder_stream ("test.data", ios::in);
```

Thus, input file-opening statements include `ifstream`, an acronym for *input file stream*, followed by a stream name such as `cylinder_stream`. Then, surrounded by parentheses, come a file specification, such as `"test.data"`, and `ios::in`, which tells C++ that the file named `test.data` is an input file.

Of course, the file specification may include a file directory path, as in the following example:

```
ifstream cylinder_stream ("/usr/phw/cpp/test.data", ios::in);
```

398   Once you have opened a file for input, you can substitute the corresponding stream name for `cin` in input statements. For example, the following statement tells C++ to read a radius and a length from the file connected to the stream named `cylinder_stream`:

```
cylinder_stream >> radius >> length;
```

399   Just as `ifstream` creates a stream that enables you to read from a file, `ofstream`, an acronym for *output file stream*, creates a stream that enables you to write into a file:

```
ofstream stream name (file specification, ios::out);
```

The following file-opening statement is an example for which the stream name happens to be `volume_stream` and the file specification happens to be provided by the character string `"test.result"`:

```
ofstream volume_stream ("test.result", ios::out);
```

In general, `ofstream` statements include a **stream name**, `volume_stream` in the example. Then, surrounded by parentheses, come a file specification, such as `"test.result"`, and `ios::out`, which tells the C++ compiler that the file named `test.result` is to be opened for output.

400   Once you have opened a file for output, you can substitute its stream name instead of `cout` in output statements. For example, the following output statement writes the volume of one of `cylinder` objects in the `oil_tanks` array into the file connected to the stream named `volume_stream`:

```
volume_stream << oil_tanks[counter].volume ( ) << endl;
```

401   From the implementation perspective, stream names are variables assigned to class objects. For example, `cin` is an object belonging to the `istream` class, and `cout` is an object belonging to the `ostream` class.

Similarly, input-file streams are objects that belong to the `ifstream` class, and output-file streams are objects that belong to the `ofstream` class.

402   Collecting what you have just learned about file input and output, you easily can amend programs that read from your keyboard and display on your screen such that they read from a file and write to a file.

The following program, for example, fills an array with cylinder radii and lengths from a file named `test.data`, and then writes the sum of the cylinders' volumes into a file named `test.result`:

```
#include <iostream.h>
#include<fstream.h>
const double pi = 3.14159;
// Define the cylinder class:
class cylinder {
  public: double radius, length;
          double volume ( ) {return pi * radius * radius * length;}
};
// Define cylinder array:
cylinder oil_tanks[100];
```

```
main ( ) {
  // Declare various variables:
  int limit, counter;
  double sum = 0.0;
  // Connect an input stream to the file named test.data:
  ifstream cylinder_stream ("test.data", ios::in);
  // Connect an output stream to the file named test.result:
  ofstream volume_stream ("test.result", ios::out);
  // Read numbers from the test.data file:
  for (limit = 0;
       cylinder_stream >> oil_tanks[limit].radius
                       >> oil_tanks[limit].length;
       ++limit)
    ;
  // Compute volume:
  for (counter = 0; counter < limit; ++counter)
    sum = sum + oil_tanks[counter].volume ( );
  // Write sum into the test.result file:
  volume_stream << "The total volume in the "
                << limit << " storage tanks is "
                << sum << endl;
}
```

———————————— Sample Data ————————————

```
4.7      40.0
3.5      35.5
3.5      45.0
```

———————————— Result ————————————

```
The total volume in the 3 storage tanks is 5873.91
```

Once you have finished writing information into a file, you must **close** the file before you can open it for reading and further processing. The do-nothing, somewhat dangerous way to close your files is to wait until your program stops executing: At that point, your operating system is supposed to close all open files automatically. The safer way to close your files is to include an explicit **file-closing** statement:

```
stream name .close ( );
```

The following, for example, closes the output-file stream named `volume_stream`:

```
volume_stream.close ( );
```

The notation reflects the fact that streams are actually class objects. Evidently, `close` is a member function of the `output-file-stream` class or a superclass of that class.

403 It is good programming practice to close input streams when you are finished reading from them. You close input streams with the same sort of statement that you use to close output streams:

```
cylinder_stream.close ( );
```

404   For now, it is enough to know how to open files for reading and writing and how to close such files when you are finished with them. As you might expect, however, there is a great deal more that you can learn about input and output.

405
PRACTICE   Write a program that transforms all the alphabetic characters in an input file into uppercase characters in an output file. Call the input file `lower.source`, and call the output file `upper.sink`. Base your program on the program you wrote for the problem given in Segment 336.

406
HIGHLIGHTS

- **If** you want to tell C++ that you intend to work with input or output streams, **then** include the following line in your program:

  `#include<fstream.h>`

- **If** you want to open an input file, **then** instantiate the following pattern:

  `ifstream` `stream name` `(file specification`, `ios::in);`

- **If** you want to open an output file, **then** instantiate the following pattern:

  `ofstream` `stream name` `(file specification`, `ios::out);`

- **If** you want to read data from an open input file, **then** substitute the stream name for `cin` in input statements.

- **If** you want to write data into an open output file, **then** substitute the stream name for `cout` in output statements.

- **If** you are finished with an input or output stream, **then** you should close it by instantiating the following pattern:

  `stream name` `.close ( );`

27 HOW TO CREATE NEW CLASS OBJECTS AT RUN TIME

407 Ordinarily, whenever you define a global variable, the C++ compiler allocates the memory required to hold an object corresponding to the variable's type, be it a built-in type, such as `int`, or a user-defined class, such as `cylinder`. In this section, you learn about an alternative whereby C++ allocates only a small amount of memory for a **pointer** at compile time, deferring until run time the allocation of memory for an object.

In Section 28, you learn that run-time allocation enables you to reduce the memory consumed by your program when the number of objects that your program encounters is less than your worst-case estimate of that number.

408 A global variable of type `cylinder` identifies the address in memory where the allocated memory begins for a `cylinder` object:

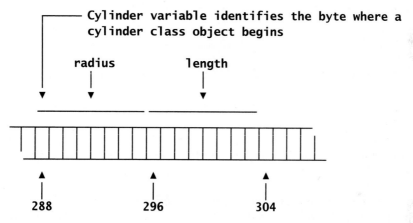

In the illustration, the radius and length are assumed to be floating-point numbers of type `double`.

409 A **pointer** is a chunk of memory that holds the address of an object. A **pointer name** identifies a chunk of memory containing the address of an object.

In general, the amount of memory consumed by a pointer is determined by the designers of your C++ compiler. I tested the programs in this book using an implementation in which all pointers consist of 4 bytes, enabling the addressing of 2^{32} memory locations.

You need not know how much memory is consumed by a pointer, however, because the correct amount is determined by the C++ compiler.

410 Although pointers are usually longer, short, two-byte pointers are used in the illustrations in this book so as to keep the size of the illustrations manageable.

In the following, for example, a two-byte pointer variable identifies a chunk of memory that contains the address of an object of type `cylinder`:

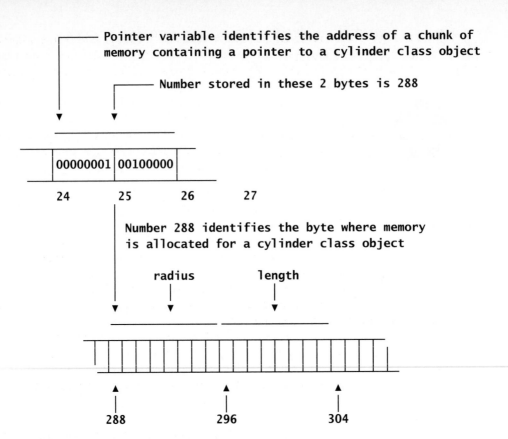

Pointer variable identifies the address of a chunk of memory containing a pointer to a cylinder class object

Number stored in these 2 bytes is 288

| 00000001 | 00100000 | |

24   25   26   27

Number 288 identifies the byte where memory is allocated for a cylinder class object

radius   length

288   296   304

411 You define global pointer variables just as you define other global variables, except that an asterisk appears in the definition when you define a global pointer variable:

```
double d;        // Allocate space for a double variable
double *dptr;    // Allocate space for a pointer to a double variable
cylinder c;      // Allocate space for a cylinder
cylinder *cptr;  // Allocate space for a pointer to a cylinder
```

The definition `double *dptr;` makes `dptr` a pointer variable, and the chunk of memory allocated for `dptr` is expected to contain the address of a chunk of memory allocated for a floating-point number of type `double`.

Thereafter, `dptr`, without an asterisk, identifies the location of an address; `*dptr`, with an asterisk, identifies the location of the floating-point number identified by the address.

412 Thus, `dptr` identifies *a location that contains an address that refers to* a location in memory that contains an integer, whereas *`*dptr`* identifies a location in memory that contains an integer. Thus, the asterisk has the effect of removing the italicized part of the preceding sentence—the part containing the words *refers to*. Accordingly, the asterisk is often called the **dereferencing** operator.

413 The definition, `cylinder *cptr;` makes `cptr` a pointer variable, and the chunk of memory allocated for `cptr` contains the address of a chunk of memory allocated for a `cylinder` object.

Thereafter, `cptr`, without a dereferencing asterisk, refers to the location of the address; `*cptr`, with a dereferencing asterisk, refers to the location of the `cylinder` object identified by the address. Said more concisely, `cptr`'s value is an address, whereas `*cptr`'s value is a `cylinder` object.

414   Note that, when you define a pointer variable in your program, the C++ compiler allocates only the small amount of memory required to hold an address. Then, later on, you can arrange for that address to be the address of a chunk of memory that is allocated for an object at run time.

```
cylinder c;     // Allocate space for a cylinder;
                // in the implementation on which the programs
                // in this book were tested, the space allocated
                // happens to be 16 bytes for a basic definition
                // in which there are two member variables,
                // of type  double , in the cylinder class
cylinder *cptr; // Allocate space for a pointer to a cylinder;
                // in the implementation on which the programs
                // in this book were tested, the space allocated
                // happens to be 4 bytes, no matter what the
                // nature of the definition of the cylinder class
```

415   Each C++ program has access to a large chunk of memory called the **free store**. The new operator allocates memory for a specified object at run time by treating the free store as a reservoir. Thus, the expression new `double` allocates the memory required to hold a floating-point object, and new `cylinder` allocates the memory required to hold a `cylinder` object.

416   Crucially, the value of a new expression is the address of the memory that new has allocated. Consequently, you can tie a pointer variable to a run-time–allocated chunk of memory for a floating-point number using an assignment statement:

```
           ┌──── Refers to a memory location that can hold the address
           │     of a chunk of memory allocated for a floating-point number
           │
           │       ┌──── Returns the address of a chunk of memory allocated
           │       │     for a floating-point number at run time
           ▼       ▼
          dptr = new double;
```

417   Similarly, you can tie a pointer variable to a run-time–allocated chunk of memory for a `cylinder` object using an assignment statement:

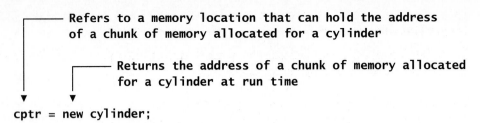

Refers to a memory location that can hold the address
of a chunk of memory allocated for a cylinder

Returns the address of a chunk of memory allocated
for a cylinder at run time

```
cptr = new cylinder;
```

When you use such a statement to allocate memory for a class object, your program automatically calls the default constructor function.

Note that the definition of the `cylinder` pointer, `cptr`, does not cause your program to call a `cylinder` constructor. A `cylinder` constructor is called only when space for the `cylinder` object is allocated by `new`.

Later, in Section 42, you see that you can also arrange to have `new` statements call constructors with arguments instead of the default constructor.

418 Given that `*cptr`'s value is a `cylinder` object, you can embed `*cptr` in larger expressions, involving the class-member operator, that retrieve member-variable values. The following, for example, retrieves the radius of a cylinder:

```
(*cptr).radius
```

Note that you must enclose `*cptr` in parentheses to refer the radius of the `cylinder` object to which `cptr` points, because the class-member operator, the period, has precedence higher than that of the dereferencing operator, the asterisk. Accordingly, a version without parentheses, `*cptr.radius`, is equivalent to `*(cptr.radius)`, which means *produce the object pointed to by a pointer stored, peculiarly, in the radius member variable of a pointer to a cylinder object.* What you want, of course, is the version that means *produce the value stored in the radius member variable of the dereferenced pointer to a cylinder object.*

419 Just as you can retrieve member-variable values through dereferenced pointers, you also can execute functions. The following, for example, executes the volume function on the cylinder pointed to by `*cptr`:

```
(*cptr).volume ( )
```

Note that, again, you must enclose `*cptr` in parentheses to defeat C++ normal precedence assumptions.

420 Actually, few C++ programmers would write `(*cptr).radius` or `(*cptr).volume (`
`)`. Instead, most would take advantage of the **class-pointer operator**, `->`, which you can think of as a shorthand that takes the place of both the dereferencing operator and the class-member operator. Thus, the following are equivalent:

Equivalent

```
(*cptr).radius           cptr -> radius
```

The following are also equivalent:

```
(*cptr).volume ( )  ←——————→  cptr -> volume ( )
```

Thus, the class-pointer operator takes the place of two other operators and eliminates the need for precedence-defeating parentheses.

421   You can use the class-pointer operator not only to read the value in a member variable, but also to write a value into the memory reserved for a member variable. Thus, the following writes into the radius member variable of a `cylinder` object:

```
cptr -> radius = 3.9
```

422   From the data-type perspective, `new` internally generates a pointer which is said to be of type `void*`. Such pointers have the property that they can be cast into pointers of any type.

Then, if the `new` expression is `new double`, the `void*` pointer is cast automatically into a object of type `double*`, which is a pointer a `double` object. Analogously, if the `new` expression is `new cylinder`, the `void*` pointer is cast automatically into a pointer to an object of type `cylinder*`, which is a pointer to a `cylinder` object.

423   Another way to tie a pointer to an object is to use the **address-of** operator, &, which obtains
SIDE TRIP   the address of an object in memory. For example, if `c` is an object of type `cylinder`, then the value of the expression &c is the address of that `cylinder` object, and, inasmuch as the value of &c is a `cylinder` object's address, you can assign that value to a cylinder pointer:

```
cptr = &c;
```

The address-of operator is not used as much in C++ as in C, because C++'s reference parameter feature, introduced in Section 37, reduces the need to pass pointers as function arguments.

424   What will happen if you run the following program? Why?
PRACTICE

```
#include <iostream.h>
const double pi = 3.14159;
class cylinder {
  public:
    double radius, length;
    double volume ( ) {return pi * radius * radius * length;}
};
main ( ) {
  cylinder *cptr;
  while (1) cptr = new cylinder;
}
```

425
HIGHLIGHTS

- An ordinary variable refers to the location of an object. A pointer variable refers to the address of the location of an object.

- Pointers generally take far less memory than do class objects.

- If you want to define a pointer variable, **then** instantiate the following pattern:

  `data type` `* pointer name`

- If you want to allocate a chunk of memory at run time, **and** you want to assign the address of that chunk of memory to a pointer variable, **then** instantiate the following pattern:

  `pointer name` = new `data type` ;

- If you want to access a member variable in a class object, **and** you have a pointer to that class object, **then** instantiate one of the following patterns:

  ```
  (* pointer name ). member variable name     // OK
  pointer name -> member variable name     // Better
  ```

- If you want to write a value into the memory reserved for a member variable in a class object, **and** you have a pointer to that class object, **then** instantiate one of the following patterns:

  ```
  // OK:
  (* pointer name ). member variable name = expression
  // Better:
  pointer name -> member variable name = expression
  ```

28 HOW TO STORE POINTERS TO CLASS OBJECTS

426 Frequently, it is difficult to predict exactly how many data you will encounter at run time. Hence, you may find yourself creating ridiculously large global arrays just to be sure that you do not run out of space. Such arrays can waste a lot of memory, particularly if they hold large class objects.

Fortunately, you now know that you can arrange for the C++ compiler to allocate only pointers at compile time, deferring the allocation of memory for objects until run time.

In this section, you learn that arrays of pointers waste much less space on excess array capacity than arrays of objects do.

427 Recall that you define an array of `cylinder` objects with a definition that looks like a variable definition with a bracketed number added:

```
cylinder oil_tanks[100];
```

And you can define an array of pointers to `cylinder` objects by adding an asterisk before the array name:

```
cylinder *oil_tank_pointers[100];
```

428 Note that the pointer-declaring asterisk, `*`, takes precedence over the array-declaring brackets, `[ ]`, in declarations. Thus, `*oil_tank_pointers[100]` means *an array of 100 pointers to cylinders*, not *a pointer to an array of 100 cylinders*.

429 Note that `oil_tanks[7]` refers to the eighth `cylinder` object in the `oil_tanks` array (the first being indexed by 0). Similarly, `oil_tank_pointers[7]` refers to the eighth pointer in the `oil_tank_pointers` array.

To refer to the `cylinder` object indexed by the value of a variable, `limit`, in the `oil_tanks` array, you write `oil_tanks[limit]`; to refer to the radius of that `cylinder` object, you write `oil_tanks[limit].radius`.

When you work with an array of pointers to `cylinder` objects, you need to dereference a pointer when you want to refer to a `cylinder` object. Hence, `*oil_tank_pointers[7]` refers to the `cylinder` object pointed to by the eighth pointer in an array. To refer to the eighth `cylinder` object's radius, you can add `.radius`, producing the following expression, which is baroque looking, inasmuch as it has parentheses, an asterisk, brackets, and a period:

```
(*oil_tank_pointers[7]).radius
```

Alternatively, and preferably, you can combine dereferencing and member selection using the class-pointer operator, `->`:

```
oil_tank_pointers[7] -> radius
```

430 Now it is time to develop a program that uses an array of pointers to class objects. The program is a modification of the program in Segment 388 that reads cylinder radii and lengths, puts them into an array of `cylinder` objects, and displays their total volume.

The modified program does the same work, but differs in that memory is allocated for the pointers at compile time, leaving memory for the `cylinder` objects to be allocated at run time.

431 First, the original version defines an array of `cylinder` objects:

```
cylinder oil_tanks[100];
```

The modified version defines an array of pointers to `cylinder` objects:

```
cylinder *oil_tank_pointers[100];
```

432 Next, the version of the original program contains a `for` statement that does reading and writing:

```
for (limit = 0; cin >> radius >> length; ++limit) {
  oil_tanks[limit].radius = radius;
  oil_tanks[limit].length = length;
}
```

You need to add a statement that allocates new space for a `cylinder` object and deposits the address of the newly allocated space into the appropriate array location:

```
oil_tank_pointers[limit] = new cylinder;
```

Also, you need to modify existing statements to dereference cylinder pointers:

```
oil_tank_pointers[limit] -> radius = radius;
oil_tank_pointers[limit] -> length = length;
```

The class-pointer operators appear in the assignment statements, because you are working with an array of `cylinder` pointers, rather than of `cylinder` objects.

433 Finally, the original program contains a `for` loop that computes the sum of the volumes of the `cylinder` objects:

```
for (counter = 0; counter < limit; ++counter)
  sum = sum + oil_tanks[counter].volume ( );
```

The `for` loop in the modified program has to dereference pointers to `cylinder` objects:

```
for (counter = 0; counter < limit; ++counter)
  sum = sum + oil_tank_pointers[counter] -> volume ( );
```

434 Combining the pieces, you have the following program:

```
#include <iostream.h>
const double pi = 3.14159;
// Define the cylinder class:
class cylinder {
  public: double radius, length;
          double volume ( ) {return pi * radius * radius * length;}
};
// Define cylinder array:
cylinder *oil_tank_pointers[100];
main ( ) {
  // Declare various variables:
  int limit, counter;
  double radius, length, sum = 0.0;
  // Read numbers and write them into pointer array:
  for (limit = 0; cin >> radius >> length; ++limit) {
    oil_tank_pointers[limit] = new cylinder;
    oil_tank_pointers[limit] -> radius = radius;
    oil_tank_pointers[limit] -> length = length;
  }
  // Compute volumes:
  for (counter = 0; counter < limit; ++counter)
    sum = sum + oil_tank_pointers[counter] -> volume ( );
  // Display sum:
  cout << "The total volume in the "
       << limit << " storage tanks is "
       << sum << endl;
}
```

——————————————— Sample Data ———————————————

4.7	40.0
3.5	35.5
3.5	45.0

——————————————— Result ———————————————

The total volume in the 3 storage tanks is 5873.91

435   Now consider the memory consumed by the old and new versions of the volume-computing programs. The old version, using an array of 100 cylinders—each of which consumes, say, 16 bytes—uses 1600 bytes, no matter how many cylinders are read from a file. The new version, using an array of 100 pointers—each of which consumes, say, 4 bytes—uses 400 bytes for pointers plus 16 bytes for each cylinder read from a file.

If 100 cylinders are read from a file—the worst case—the total memory consumed by the new version, the one that uses pointers, is 2000 bytes, which is more than the 1600 required by the old version. On the other hand, if only 10 cylinders are read, the total memory consumed by the new version is only $400 + 10 \times 16 = 560$, which is much less than the 1600 required by the old version. Thus, you can save a great deal of memory if the expected number of class objects is much less than the worst-case number of class objects you need. Your saving increases as the size of each class object grows relative to the size of each pointer.

436 Later, in Section 43, you learn about `delete`, an operator that does the opposite of `new`:
SIDE TRIP Instead of allocating a chunk of memory from the free store for an object, `delete` returns the memory allocated to an object to the free store. You will see that you need to use `delete` whenever you write a program that repeatedly reassign one or more pointers to objects created at run time using `new`.

437 Adapt the program shown in Segment 434 so that it works on `box` class objects, rather
PRACTICE than on `cylinder` class objects.

438 The `sizeof` operator computes the number of bytes required by an object. For example,
PRACTICE `sizeof(char)`, produces the number of bytes required by a character object.

Use the `sizeof` operator to determine the number of bytes occupied on your computer by a `box` object and by a pointer to `box` object.

439 Suppose, that you want to be able to store information, on average, about 10 `box` objects,
PRACTICE but you must be prepared, in the worst case, to handle 1000. In the average case, how much memory will you save by using an array of pointers to `box` objects, created at run time, rather than using an array of `box` objects.

440
HIGHLIGHTS

- If you must be prepared to store a large number of class objects in the worst case, **and** the expected number of class objects is much smaller, **and** you want to conserve memory, **then** define an array of pointers to class objects, instead of an array of class objects.

- If you want to create a one-dimensional array of class-object pointers, **then** instantiate the following pattern:

```
class name * array name [ maximum number of objects ];
```

- If you want to allocate a chunk of memory at run time, **and** you want to refer to the address of that chunk of memory in a pointer array, **then** use the `new` operator and instantiate the following pattern:

```
array name [ index ] = new class name ;
```

- If you want to write a value into the memory reserved for a member variable in a class object, **and** you have an array that contains a pointer to that class object, **then** instantiate one of the following patterns:

```
// Ok:
(* array name [ index ]). member variable name = expression ;
// Better:
array name [ index ] -> member variable name = expression ;
```

- If you want to access a member variable in a class object, **and** you have an array that contains a pointer to that class object, **then** instantiate one of the following patterns:

```
(* array name [ index ]). member variable name      // OK

array name [ index ] -> member variable name        // Better
```

441   You have already learned about programs that work with arrays of integers, of integer pointers, of cylinders, and of cylinder pointers. Now, you learn about `analyze_train`, a program that works with an array of railroad-car pointers. The basic `analyze_train` program introduced in this section reads railroad-car–type numbers and displays a report listing railroad-car–type names.

The `analyze_train` program is a keystone program, because it brings together many concepts, including C++'s mechanisms for reading, displaying, testing, conditional execution, iteration, and pointer dereferencing.

Once you have learned about the basic `analyze_train` program introduced in this section, you will be ready to tackle many other C++ mechanisms, each of which is introduced in subsequent sections through modifications to the `analyze_train` program. Some modifications expose more sophisticated ideas, such as inheritance through a class hierarchy and run-time function selection using virtual functions. Other modifications introduce commonplace mechanisms that have been skipped over so as to expose you to C++'s strengths more quickly.

442   Imagine that your railroad company has installed a device that classifies each car as that car rumbles into the company's central switching yard. A program written by your predecessors at the company uses that sensor's output to create a file in which each railroad car is represented by a number that encodes that car's type. Here, for example, is the file for a certain short train:

0 1 1 2 3

Further imagine that you want to use those numbers to display a list of short, three-character names:

eng
box
box
tnk
cab

443   You could write a simple program to translate the numbers:

```
#include <iostream.h>
main ( ) {
  int type_code;
  while (cin >> type_code)
    if (type_code == 0)        cout << "eng" << endl;
    else if (type_code == 1)   cout << "box" << endl;
    else if (type_code == 2)   cout << "tnk" << endl;
    else if (type_code == 3)   cout << "cab" << endl;
}
```

Such a program is called an **iterative filter**, because it can be used to transform a data stream into a new data stream.

444 Although the program in Segment 443 is simple, you are likely to want to do a great deal more analysis on the input file. Accordingly, you decide to create an array of pointers to railroad-car objects.

445 To get started, you decide to revive part of the railroad-car class hierarchy that you learned about in Section 15:

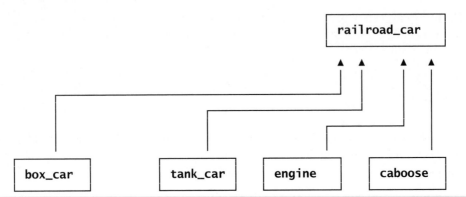

446 Definitions of the railroad_car class and that class's subclasses can contain all sorts of member variables, default constructors, constructors with arguments, and other member functions. For the moment, for the sake of simplicity, suppose that you strip out all that detail, leaving only default, do-nothing constructors:

```
class railroad_car {
  public: railroad_car ( ) { }
};
class box_car : public railroad_car {
  public: box_car ( ) { }
};
class tank_car : public railroad_car {
  public: tank_car ( ) { }
};
class engine : public railroad_car {
  public: engine ( ) { }
};
class caboose : public railroad_car {
  public: caboose ( ) { }
};
```

447 At first, you might think you could define some sort of an array to hold a train full of engine, box-car, tank-car, and caboose objects. You cannot, however, because the objects stored in any one array must be of the same type. You could have an array of engines, another array of box cars, another of tank cars, and still another of cabooses, but you cannot have an array with some of each.

448   One reason why C++ requires the objects in arrays to be of the same type is that such a requirement ensures that each object occupies exactly the same amount of memory as every other object. This requirement makes it easy to compile efficient object code for locating each array object, given that object's array index.

From the perspective of software engineering, many expert programmers argue that objects in any given array should all be of the same type even in the absence of efficiency considerations. Their rationale is that associating data types with arrays ensures that you can see what sort of objects are allowed in a given array without looking inside a programmer's head.

449   Importantly, however, if you define an array of pointers to objects in a certain class, the actual pointers can point not only to any object in that class, but also to any object in its subclasses.

The following, for example, defines `train` to be an array of pointers to objects in the `railroad_car` class:

```
// Define railroad car pointer array:
railroad_car *train[100];
```

Once you have created such an array of pointers to objects in the `railroad_car` class, you can arrange for particular pointers to point to `railroad_car` objects that also happen to be in the `engine`, `box_car`, `tank_car`, or `caboose` classes.

The following, for example, arranges for the first pointer in the `train` array to point to a `railroad_car` object that also happens to be an `engine` object created at run time by the new operator:

```
// Allocate memory for an engine, and
// cast engine* pointer into a railroad_car* pointer:
train[0] = new engine;
```

450   From the perspective of casting, `new engine` produces a pointer of type `engine*`, a pointer to an `engine` object. Then, because `train` is an array of pointers to `railroad_car` objects, the pointer of type `engine*` is cast automatically into a pointer of type `railroad_car*`. The pointer still points, however, to a chunk of memory holding an `engine` object.

451   Thus, you can write a program to create an entire array of pointers to objects, with the memory chunk for each object allocated at run time according to the type number observed in the sensor file:

```
#include <iostream.h>
// Define classes:
class railroad_car {
  public: railroad_car ( ) { }
};
class box_car : public railroad_car {
  public: box_car ( ) { }
};
// ... Similar definitions of tank_car, engine, and caboose go here ...
// Define railroad car array:
railroad_car *train[100];
main ( ) {
  // Declare various integer variables:
  int car_count, type_code;
  // Read type number and create corresponding objects:
  for (car_count = 0; cin >> type_code; ++car_count)
    if (type_code == 0)        train[car_count] = new engine;
    else if (type_code == 1)   train[car_count] = new box_car;
    else if (type_code == 2)   train[car_count] = new tank_car;
    else if (type_code == 3)   train[car_count] = new caboose;
  // Display car count:
  cout << "There are " << car_count << " cars in the array." << endl;
}
```

———————————————— Sample Data ————————————————

```
0 1 1 2 3
```

———————————————— Result ————————————————

```
There are 5 cars in the array.
```

452 Having created an array full of objects, you are almost ready to iterate through that array, displaying lines containing the cars' short names. First, however, you must choose how you want to store and display short names.

One approach is to include a member variable for short names in the railroad_car class. Next, you arrange for constructors in each railroad-car subclass to write into that member variable the appropriate character string—eng, box, tnk, or cab. Finally, you can display the value of the member variable using the output operator.

In Section 36, you learn how to declare member variables for character strings. In this section, you learn to include, in each railroad-car class, a member function that knows how to display that class's short name. Although not as simple as the member-variable–declaration approach, the function-definition approach has a pedagogical benefit, because that approach exposes you to the need for C++'s soon-to-be-explained virtual functions.

453 The following is a definition of the box_car class augmented to include the definition of a member function that displays the short name associated with that class:

```
class box_car : public railroad_car, public box {
  public: // Constructor:
          box_car ( ) { }
          // Displayer:
          void display_short_name ( ) {cout << "box";}
};
```

454 You might think that similar amendments to the engine, tank_car, and caboose classes would enable you to display car names using a for loop such as the following:

```
for (n = 0; n < car_count; ++n) {
  train[n] -> display_short_name ( );
  cout << endl;
}
```

After all, train[n] picks a particular pointer out of the array, and the class-pointer operator, ->, tells C++ to go through the pointer to get at display_short_name, a member function defined in the definitions of all four car types.

Your C++ compiler rejects the program, nevertheless. The reason is that the train array is supposed to contain pointers to railroad_car objects, and you have defined no display_short_name function for railroad_car objects. At compile time, the compiler has no clue that the pointers in the train array may actually point to objects that belong to subclasses for which the display_short_name function is defined.

455 Of course, you could define a display_short_name function for railroad_car in which rrc is an acronym for *railroad cars*:

```
class railroad_car {
  public: railroad_car ( ) { }
          void display_short_name ( ) {cout << "rrc";}
};
```

Including such a definition gets you past the C++ compiler, but then, you find the result peculiar:

```
rrc
rrc
rrc
rrc
rrc
```

The reason you get nothing but lines containing rrc is that C++ ordinarily decides which display_short_name function to use at compile time, and at compile time, all C++ knows is that it is looking at an array that is supposed to contain railroad_car objects.

456 Accordingly, you must somehow arrange for your compiled program to determine which display_short_name function to use, rather than having the C++ compiler decide, in advance, at compile time.

You could easily imagine many ways to convey such a message to C++. The way the designers of C++ decided to convey the message is to place a special symbol, `virtual`, in front of the definition of `display_short_name` in the `railroad_car` class:

```
class railroad_car {
  public: // Constructor:
          railroad_car ( ) { }
          // Virtual display function:
          virtual void display_short_name ( ) { };}
};
```

Thus, to mark a member function for selection at run time, rather than at compile time, you preface its definition with `virtual`. Such a function is said to be a **virtual member function**.

Virtual member functions are called *virtual* because the information required to determine which function to use is not available—hence is only virtual—at compile time.

457 More generally, you define a virtual member function under the following circumstances:

- You have a pointer defined to point to an object belonging to a certain class. Suppose the class is named `superclass`.

- You assign the pointer to an object, introduced at run time, that belongs to a subclass of `superclass`. Suppose that the subclass is named `subclass`.

- You want C++ to pick a member function, say `member_function`, on the basis of the object's class, `subclass`.

Then, you must define a version of `member_function` in `superclass`, and you must mark that function with `virtual`. That member function and all versions defined in classes that are subclasses of `superclass` are said to be virtual member functions.

458 Until you are completely comfortable with virtual functions, you may find it helpful to think the phrase *multiversion function for which the version to be called is determined by object class at run time* whenever you see the phrase *virtual function*.

459 Once a function is marked virtual in one class, it is automatically virtual in every subclass of that class. Nevertheless, it does no harm, and it does increases clarity, to mark as virtual every instance of every virtual function.

460 Bringing together both the modified class definitions and the modified definition of `main`, you have the following:

```
#include <iostream.h>
class railroad_car {
  public: railroad_car ( ) { }
          virtual void display_short_name ( ) {cout << "rrc";}
};
class box_car : public railroad_car {
  public: box_car ( ) { }
          virtual void display_short_name ( ) {cout << "box";}
};
// ... Similar definitions of tank_car, engine, and caboose go here ...
// Define railroad car pointer array:
railroad_car *train[100];
main ( ) {
  // Declare various integer variables:
  int n, car_count, type_code;
  // Read car-type number and create car class objects:
  for (car_count = 0; cin >> type_code; ++car_count)
    if (type_code == 0)        train[car_count] = new engine;
    else if (type_code == 1)   train[car_count] = new box_car;
    else if (type_code == 2)   train[car_count] = new tank_car;
    else if (type_code == 3)   train[car_count] = new caboose;
  // Display classes using display_short_name virtual function:
  for (n = 0; n < car_count; ++n)
    {train[n] -> display_short_name ( ); cout << endl;}
}
```

———————————— Sample Data ————————————

0 1 1 2 3

———————————————— Result ————————————————

eng
box
box
tnk
cab

461 One virtual function can shadow another, just as an ordinary member function can shadow
     another. Thus, the display_short_name virtual functions in the engine, box_car,
     tank_car, and caboose classes shadow the display_short_name virtual member func-
     tion in the railroad_car class.

     Assuming that you never intend to create any individual class objects at the railroad_car
     level, the only reason to define the display_short_name function in the railroad_car
     class definition is to inform C++ that lower-level display_short_name virtual functions
     are defined.

     On the other hand, if you fail to define a display_short_name function, either deliberately
     or accidentally, in, say, the engine class definition, then there will be nothing to shadow the
     display_short_name function defined in the railroad_car class definition when you

attempt to display the short name of an engine. Accordingly, your program will display
`rrc`.

462 Given that the `display_short_name` virtual function defined in the `railroad_car` class should be shadowed in every situation, you do not expect that version ever to be executed. You can signal this expectation by replacing the existing virtual function by what is called a **pure virtual function**. Such functions signal an error whenever called.

Syntactically, pure virtual functions are like ordinary virtual functions, except that the body is replaced, by convention, with = 0;. Hence, the `railroad_car` class could be defined this way:

```
class railroad_car {
  public: railroad_car ( ) { }
          virtual void display_short_name ( ) = 0;
}
```

463 In Section 32, you learn more about virtual functions. First, in Section 30 and Section 31, you learn about more basic mechanisms that make the `analyze_train` program look more like the product of an experienced programmer.

464 Add virtual member functions to the program shown in Segment 460 such that it displays
not only the short name of each car, but also the number of axles for that railroad car type, as in the following example:

```
eng     6
box     4
box     4
tnk     4
cab     4
```

- A pointer defined to point to an object belonging to a particular class may also point to an object belonging to any of that class's subclasses.

- If you have an array defined to contain pointers to class objects, **and** those pointers actually point to objects belonging to subclasses, **and** you want to call member functions defined in those subclasses, **then** you must include a virtual-function definition in the class.

- If you want to define a virtual function, **then** instantiate the following pattern:

  virtual `ordinary member function definition`

- A virtual function defined in one class is automatically virtual in all that class's subclasses.

30 HOW TO WRITE MULTIWAY CONDITIONAL STATEMENTS

466   You know how to use `if` statements when you want a program to decide which of two alternative statements to execute. In this section, you learn how to use `switch` statements when you want your program to decide which of many alternative statements to execute.

467   The purpose of a `switch` statement is to execute a particular sequence of statements according to the value of an expression that produces an integer. In most `switch` statements, each anticipated value of the integer-producing expression and the corresponding sequence of statements is sandwiched between a `case` symbol on one end and a `break` statement on the other, with a colon separating the anticipated value and the statement sequence:

```
switch ( integer-producing expression ) {
  case integer constant 1: statements for integer 1 break;
  case integer constant 2: statements for integer 2 break;
  ...
  default: default statements
}
```

When such a switch statement is encountered, the expression is evaluated, producing an integer. That value is compared with the integer constants found following the `case` symbols. As soon as there is a match, evaluation of the following statements begins; it continues up to the first `break` statement encountered.

The line beginning with the `default` symbol is optional. If the expression produces an integer that fails to match any of the `case` integer constants, the statements following the `default` symbol are executed.

If there is no match and no `default` symbol, no statements are executed.

468   The version of the `analyze_train` shown in the program in Segment 460 contains a sequence of `if-else` statements that determines what to do for any given value of the `type_code` variable:

```
if (type_code == 0)      train[n] = new engine;
else if (type_code == 1) train[n] = new box_car;
else if (type_code == 2) train[n] = new tank_car;
else if (type_code == 3) train[n] = new caboose;
```

Most C++ programmers use a `switch` statement instead:

```
switch (type_code) {
  case 0: train[n] = new engine;   break;
  case 1: train[n] = new box_car;  break;
  case 2: train[n] = new tank_car; break;
  case 3: train[n] = new caboose;  break;
}
```

469 The following `switch` statement pattern contains no `break` statements. Thus, once execution begins, all subsequent statements up to the end of the `switch` statement are executed.

```
switch ( integer-producing expression ) {
  case integer constant 1: statements for integer 1
  case integer constant 2: statements for integer 2
  ...
  default: default statements
}
```

In general, when there is no `break` statement to terminate the execution of a sequence of statements, execution is said to **fall through** to the next sequence of statements, where execution continues, once again, in search of a `break` statement.

The reason for the fall-through feature is that you occasionally want to perform the same action in response to any of several conditions. Note carefully, however, that inadvertently forgetting a `break` is a common error.

470 Suppose that you want to collect neither `engine` nor `caboose` objects in the `train` array. Instead, you want to display a message, `Nonrevenue car type encountered`. The following switch statement does the work with no duplication of the output statement:

```
switch (type_code) {
  case 0: case 3:
    cout << "Nonrevenue car type encountered" << endl;
    break;
  case 1: train[n] = new box_car;  break;
  case 2: train[n] = new tank_car; break;
}
```

471 Now suppose that your data contains an unknown car-type number. If you like, you can handle such unknown car-type numbers using the `default` part of the `switch` statement. In the following example, you choose to have unknown railroad-car–type numbers displayed on your screen:

```
switch (type_code) {
  case 0: train[n] = new engine;   break;
  case 1: train[n] = new box_car;  break;
  case 2: train[n] = new tank_car; break;
  case 3: train[n] = new caboose;  break;
  default: cout << "Car-type number " << type_code
               << " is unknown!" << endl;
}
```

472 When you are displaying information about evident errors, however, it is better programming practice to use the `cerr` stream, rather than the `cout` stream. One reason is that characters sent to your screen via the `cout` stream are **buffered**, which means that they may not appear on your screen until an end-of-line symbol, `endl`, is encountered. In contrast, characters sent to your screen via the `cerr` stream are *not* buffered; they appear immediately.

473 Now suppose that you want to take more drastic action, terminating your program whenever it encounters an unknown car-type number. To arrange for an orderly termination, you need to inform C++ that you intend to make use of the `exit` function by including the following line in your program:

```
#include <stdlib.h>
```

Then, you can insert a call to the `exit` function after a output statement that displays data via the `cerr` stream:

```
switch (type_code) {
  case 0: train[n] = new engine;    break;
  case 1: train[n] = new box_car;   break;
  case 2: train[n] = new tank_car;  break;
  case 3: train[n] = new caboose;   break;
  default: cerr << "Car code " << type_code
                << " is unknown!" << endl;
            exit (0);
}
```

Note that `exit` expects an integer argument. That integer argument generally should be 0, thereby indicating that your program's termination is not to evoke a special reaction from your operating system.

474
SIDE TRIP
If your program is activated by another program, rather than by your typing of a command line to the operating-system, then `exit`'s argument is returned to the calling program. It is up to you and the author of that calling program to negotiate what the calling program is to do with the returned value.

475
SIDE TRIP
Whenever you use the `return` function inside `main`, the effect is as though you had used `exit` with the same argument supplied to `return`. If `main` has neither a `return` statement nor an `exit` statement, `main` statement is compiled as though the final statement were `return 0`, which is equivalent to `exit 0`.

476
PRACTICE
Write a program that accepts two numbers, representing a year and a month, and displays the number of days in that month. Use a `switch` statement, and be sure to exploit the fall-through feature. Note that leap years occur in years divisible by 4, except for centenary years that are not divisible by 400.

477
PRACTICE
Amend the `analyze_train` program such that it announces an error if you supply it with a train containing more than 100 cars.

478
HIGHLIGHTS

- If you want a program to decide which of many alternative statements to evaluate, **then** instantiate the following pattern:

```
switch ( integer-producing expression ) {
  case integer constant 1 : statements for integer 1 break;
  case integer constant 2 : statements for integer 2 break;
  ...
  default: default statements
}
```

159

- In switch statements, you may omit the symbol default: and the default statements.

- In switch statements, the integer-producing expression can produce a value belonging to any of the integral data types, including the char data type.

- In switch statements, once embedded statement execution begins, execution continues up to the first embedded break statement or to the end of the switch statement, whichever comes first. Bugs emerge when you forget to pair case symbols with break statements.

- If you want to display information describing an error, **then** use cerr as the target of an output statement, rather than cout.

- If you want a program to stop, because an error has occurred, **then** tell C++ you intend to make use of the appropriate library **and then** insert an exit statement:

```
#include <stdlib.h>
...
exit (0);
```

31 HOW TO USE ENUMERATIONS TO IMPROVE READABILITY

479   In this section, you learn how to make your programs easier to understand by replacing integer codes by mnemonic symbols.

480   At this point, you have seen a `switch` statement that analyzes type codes found in a sensor file and that creates appropriate objects:

```
switch (type_code) {
  case 0: train[n] = new engine;   break;
  case 1: train[n] = new box_car;  break;
  case 2: train[n] = new tank_car; break;
  case 3: train[n] = new caboose;  break;
}
```

Although this `switch` statement works fine, it is difficult to remember which number goes with which car type. In general, it is difficult to maintain a program that is littered with such nonmnemonic encoding.

481   In principle, you could replace integers with named integer constants. Then, you would need to maintain the correct correspondence between the sensor code for car types and the corresponding car type in just one place. Elsewhere, you have the mnemonic power of the integer-constant's name working for you.

For example, you could define integer constants as follows near the beginning of your program:

```
const int eng_code = 0;
const int box_code = 1;
const int tnk_code = 2;
const int cab_code = 3;
```

482   Although there is nothing wrong with defining integer constants using `const int`, most experienced C++ programmers would be more likely to use an **enumeration statement**, as in the following example:

```
enum {eng_code, box_code, tnk_code, cab_code};
```

Such a statement declares all the symbols in braces to be enumeration constants and assigns integer values to those constants. By default, the value of the first enumeration constant is 0; also by default, the value of each succeeding enumeration constant is 1 more than the previous value. Hence, the value of `eng_code` is 0, that of `box_code` is 1, that of `tnk_code` is 2, and that of `cab_code` is 3.

483   Once you have introduced enumeration constants, you can improve the clarity of the `switch` statement by replacing the integers with those enumeration constants:

```
switch (type_code) {
  case eng_code: train[n] = new engine;    break;
  case box_code: train[n] = new box_car;   break;
  case tnk_code: train[n] = new tank_car;  break;
  case cab_code: train[n] = new caboose;   break;
}
```

484   The following revised version of the analyze_train program replaces if-else statements with a switch statement, includes error handling, and exploits enumeration constants:

```
#include <iostream.h>
#include <stdlib.h>
// ... Railroad car class definitions go here ...
// Define railroad car pointer array:
railroad_car *train[100];
// Declare enumeration constants, needed in switch statement:
enum {eng_code, box_code, tnk_code, cab_code};
main ( ) {
  // Declare various integer variables:
  int n, car_count, type_code;
  // Read car-type number and create car class objects:
  for (car_count = 0; cin >> type_code; ++car_count)
    switch (type_code) {
      case eng_code: train[car_count] = new engine;    break;
      case box_code: train[car_count] = new box_car;   break;
      case tnk_code: train[car_count] = new tank_car;  break;
      case cab_code: train[car_count] = new caboose;    break;
      default: cerr << "Car code " << type_code
                    << " is unknown!" << endl;
              exit (0);
    }
  // Display classes using display_short_name virtual function:
  for (n = 0; n < car_count; ++n) {
    train[n] -> display_short_name ( );
    cout << endl;
  }
}
```
———————————————— Sample Data ————————————————

0 1 1 2 3
———————————————— Result ————————————————

eng
box
box
tnk
cab

485 If you like, you can provide values for particular enumeration constants by including integers in the enumeration statement. In the following example, the value of the additional hop_code constant is 5, and because the value of each succeeding constant lacking an expressed value is 1 more than that of the previous constant, the value of ref_code is 6:

```
enum {eng_code, box_code, tnk_code, cab_code, hop_code = 5, ref_code};
```

Note the contrast with the following, alternative declaration, for which the value assigned to hop_code is 4 and the value assigned to ref_code is 5:

```
enum {eng_code, box_code, tnk_code, cab_code, hop_code, ref_code};
```

486
SIDE TRIP
A more general form of the enumeration statement allows you to create **enumeration data types**. These new data types allow you, in turn, to create **enumeration variables**.

The following statement, for example, makes car_code an enumeration data type and assigns values to four enumeration constants:

```
enum car_code {eng_code, box_code, tnk_code, cab_code};
```

Subsequently, you can declare particular variables to be car_code variables by using the two symbols enum car_code as a data type. The following, for example, makes c a car_code variable:

```
enum car_code c;
```

487
PRACTICE
Amend the program you were asked to write in Segment 476 by using the names of the months as enumeration constants in the switch statement.

488
HIGHLIGHTS

- If you wish to make your programs easier to read, **then** replace integer constants with enumeration constants.

- If you wish to create a set of enumeration constants, **and** you want those constants to have consecutive values beginning with 0, **then** instantiate the following pattern:

```
enum { first constant ,  second constant ,  ···};
```

- If you wish to create a set of enumeration constants, **and** you want those constants to have specified values, **then** instantiate the following pattern:

```
enum { first constant  =  first value ,
       second constant  =  second value ,
       ...
};
```

32 HOW TO WRITE CONSTRUCTORS THAT CALL OTHER CONSTRUCTORS

489 In Section 11, you learned that constructors are member functions that you use to construct class objects. In this section, you learn how to arrange for one class's constructor to call another class's constructor explicitly. This connection of constructors is useful, for example, when you want a `box_car` default constructor to make use of argument-bearing constructors found in the higher-level `box` and `railroad_car` classes.

490 At this point, the `analyze_train` program displays a report listing each car's type. Now suppose that you want to display not only each car's type, but also each car's load-bearing capacity, if any, in cubic feet. Accordingly, you must first reinstate the dimension member variables—`height`, `width`, `radius`, and `length`—and `volume` member functions that have been missing from the class definitions in recent sections.

491 In Section 15, you learned about `box` and `box_car` classes defined such that the `box` class contains the `height`, `width`, and `length` member variables that are initialized by the default constructor contained in the `box_car` class:

```
class box : public container {
  public: double height, width, length;
          // Default constructor:
          box ( ) { }
          // Other member function:
          double volume ( ) {return height * width * length;}
};
...
class box_car : public railroad_car, public box {
  public: // Default constructor:
          box_car ( ) {
             height = 10.5; width = 9.2; length = 40.0;}
};
```

The `box` class, however, can have its own constructor for initializing its own member variables:

```
class box : public container {
  public: double height, width, length;
          // Default constructor:
          box ( ) { }
          // Argument-bearing constructor:
          box (double h, double w, double l) {
             height = h; width = w; length = l;
          }
          // Other member function:
          double volume ( ) {return height * width * length;}
};
```

Given such an argument-bearing constructor in the box class, naturally you would like to have a way to make use of it in the definition of the default constructor defined in the box_car class.

492   When you want a constructor in a derived class to hand arguments to an argument-bearing constructor in a base class, you modify the derived-class constructor's definition by sandwiching base-class constructor calls between its argument list and its body, and you signal your intention to do this sandwiching with a colon.

For example, if you want the default box_car constructor to supply arguments for the three-argument box constructor, you modify the box_car default constructor as follows:

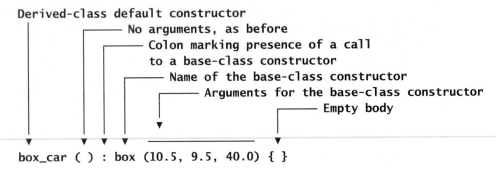

```
box_car ( ) : box (10.5, 9.5, 40.0) { }
```

You should compare this constructor-calling default constructor with the previous member-variable-assigning version:

```
box_car ( ) {
  height = 10.5; width = 9.2; length = 40.0;
}
```

493   You can, if you wish, arrange for explicit calls to more than one constructor. You simply separate the calls by commas, as in the following example, in which two calls appear to argument-bearing constructors, one of which is a hypothetical, argument-bearing, railroad_car constructor:

```
box_car ( ) : box (10.5, 9.5, 40.0),
              railroad_car ( arguments )
              { }
```

494   The syntax for linking constructors together has a somewhat arbitrary flavor, but such arbitrariness is, regrettably, not uncommon in computer languages in general.

495   There are other ways to pitch information from a derived-class constructor to a base-class
SIDE TRIP constructor, such as by specifying a class object to be copied. Such mechanisms are not described in this book, because you do not need to know about them until you are ready for the transition from a C++ novice to a C++ Olympian.

You have seen, in this section, how you can have a default constructor call an argument-bearing constructor. You can also have an argument-bearing constructor call another argument-bearing constructor.

Suppose, for example, that all box cars have the same height and width—they vary only in length. Write a one-argument constructor for the box_car class that does all its work by calling the appropriate box class constructor.

Next, rewrite the default box_car constructor such that it makes use of the one-argument box_car constructor.

- **If** you want one constructor to call another explicitly, **then** instantiate the following pattern:

```
calling constructor's name
  ( calling constructor's parameters )
  : called constructor's name
      ( called constructor's arguments ) {
  calling constructor's body
}
```

33 HOW TO WRITE MEMBER FUNCTIONS THAT CALL OTHER MEMBER FUNCTIONS

498   Ordinarily, you supply a member function with a class object by writing the name of the class object, followed by the class-member operator, followed by the name of the member function. In this section, you learn how to pass along such a class object from a directly called member function in one class to an indirectly called member function.

499   Your current objective, in refining the train-analysis program, is to display a report containing each car's type and load-bearing capacity.

At this point, the default constructors in the box_car and tank_car class definitions work together with the argument-bearing constructors in the box and cylinder class definitions to ensure that box cars and tank cars are created with the proper default dimensions.

You also have volume member functions in both the box and cylinder class definitions. These functions soon prove useful in computing load-bearing capacity.

500   The analyze_train program shown in Segment 484 produces an array of pointers to engine, box_car, tank_car, and caboose objects. Subsequently, the analyze_train program uses a for loop to display short names:

```
// Display classes using display_short_name virtual function:
for (n = 0; n < car_count; ++n) {
  train[n] -> display_short_name ( );
  cout << endl;
}
```

501   Accordingly, you might decide to display load capacities by defining display_capacity member functions in the box_car and tank_car classes.

You now know, however, that the decision about which of those functions to use must be determined at run time. Accordingly, you have to plant a virtual display_capacity function in the railroad_car class:

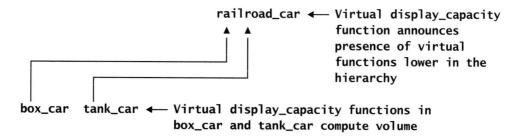

502   Once display_capacity is defined in the railroad_car, box_car, and tank_car classes, you can add it to the for loop:

```
// Display classes using display_short_name virtual function:
for (n = 0; n < car_count; ++n) {
  train[n] -> display_short_name ( );
  cout << "      ";
  train[n] -> display_capacity ( );
  cout << endl;
}
```

503 You could, of course, define a display_capacity member function as follows, in the box_car class, relying on values for the height, width, and length member variables inherited from the box class:

```
virtual void display_capacity ( ) {cout << height * width * length;}
```

The blatant defect of this approach is that you already have a perfectly good function for computing box volumes defined as a box class member function. You should make use of that function, rather than duplicating its innards.

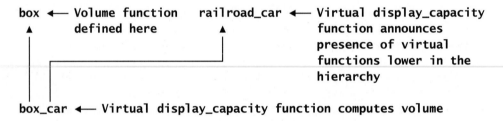

504 But now you have to face a problem: How do you call the volume function from inside a display_capacity function? Ordinarily, you call the volume function by writing down an expression that evaluates to a box_car object, then the class-member operator, and finally the symbol volume and an empty argument list:

box_car object .volume ( )

You call the yet-to-be-defined display_capacity function the same way:

box_car object .display_capacity ( )

Hence, the class object acts like an argument; however, unlike an ordinary argument, the class object has no corresponding parameter inside either display_capacity or volume. How then do you specify that you want the volume function to work on the same class object that was handed over to display_capacity?

505 The answer is that you use the volume function without an explicit class argument, as in the following definition of display_capacity:

```
virtual void display_capacity ( ) {cout << volume ( );}
```

By convention, because the class object argument and the class-member operator are absent, the volume function is handed the same class-object argument that was handed to display_capacity. Thus, volume has an **implicit argument**.

The implicit-argument mechanism makes use of what is called the this pointer. Every member function has an implied parameter, named this, whose value is a pointer to the member function's class-object argument.

When you want to refer to the class argument of a member function, you could write down this along with a dereferencing asterisk. Thus, you could define the display_capacity function inside the box_car class definition as follows:

**Argument is the same as the
argument handed to display_capacity**

|
▼
―――――

```
virtual void display_capacity ( ) {cout << (*this).volume ( );}
```

Alternatively, you can use the class-pointer operator to go through the pointer:

```
virtual void display_capacity ( ) {cout << this -> volume ( );}
```

Fortunately, C++ allows you to leave out the first argument entirely:

```
virtual void display_capacity ( ) {cout << volume ( );}
```

Thus, the real result of leaving out an explicit class-object argument is that the dereferenced this pointer is used to supply a default class-object argument.

507   At last, you have the following definitions for the box_car and tank_car classes:

```
class box_car : public railroad_car, public box {
  public: // Default constructor:
          box_car ( ) : box (10.5, 9.5, 40.0) { }
          // Displayers:
          virtual void display_short_name ( ) {cout << "box";}
          virtual void display_capacity ( ) {cout << volume ( );}
};
class tank_car : public railroad_car, public cylinder {
  public: // Default constructor:
          tank_car ( ) : cylinder (3.5, 40.0) { }
          // Displayers:
          virtual void display_short_name ( ) {cout << "tnk";}
          virtual void display_capacity ( ) {cout << volume ( );}
};
```

The volume function mentioned in the definition of the box_car display_capacity function must be the volume function inherited from the box class. Similarly, the volume function mentioned in the tank_car display_capacity function must be the volume function inherited from the cylinder class.

508   Next, to ensure access to those display_capacity functions, you need to install a virtual version of display_capacity in the railroad_car class:

```
class railroad_car {
  public: railroad_car ( ) { }
          virtual void display_short_name ( ) { }
          virtual void display_capacity ( ) { }
};
```

Although this version of the display_capacity does no displaying, you accomplish two objectives by defining it. First, because this version is marked virtual, C++ knows that railroad_car pointers may be directed at run time to class objects that require versions of display_capacity found in railroad_car subclasses.

Second, assuming that there are no definitions for display_capacity in the engine and caboose classes, inheritance ensures that the version found in the railroad_car class is the version used when engines or cabooses are encountered. Thus, the do-nothing version of display_capacity found in the railroad_car class acts as a safety net for class objects that otherwise would not have a display_capacity member function.

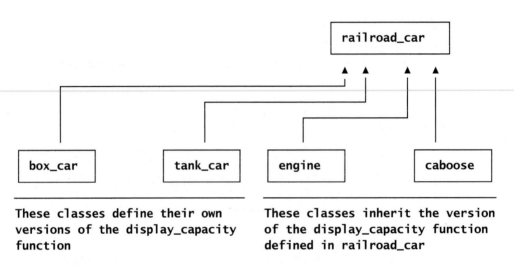

These classes define their own versions of the display_capacity function

These classes inherit the version of the display_capacity function defined in railroad_car

509 The following is the analyze_train program, revised to include the volume-displaying augmentations:

```
#include <iostream.h>
const double pi = 3.14159;
class box {
  public: double height, width, length;
    // Default constructor:
    box ( ) { }
    // Argument-bearing constructor:
    box (double h, double w, double l) {
      height = h; width = w; length = l;
    }
    // Volume member function:
    double volume ( ) {return height * width * length;}
};
```

```
// ... Cylinder definition goes here ...
class railroad_car {
  public: railroad_car ( ) { }
          virtual void display_short_name ( ) { }
          virtual void display_capacity ( ) { }
};
class box_car : public railroad_car, public box {
  public: box_car ( ) : box (10.5, 9.5, 40.0) { }
          virtual void display_short_name ( ) {cout << "box";}
          virtual void display_capacity ( ) {cout << volume ( );}
};
// ... Tank car definition goes here ...
class engine : public railroad_car {
  public: engine ( ) { }
          virtual void display_short_name ( ) {cout << "eng";}
};
// ... Caboose definition goes here ...
// Define railroad car pointer array:
railroad_car *train[100];
// Declare enumeration constants, needed in switch statement:
enum {eng_code, box_code, tnk_code, cab_code};
main ( ) {
  int n, car_count, type_code;
  for (car_count = 0; cin >> type_code; ++car_count)
    switch (type_code) {
      case eng_code: train[car_count] = new engine;    break;
      case box_code: train[car_count] = new box_car;   break;
      case tnk_code: train[car_count] = new tank_car;  break;
      case cab_code: train[car_count] = new caboose;   break;
    }
  for (n = 0; n < car_count; ++n) {
    train[n] -> display_short_name ( );
    cout << "      ";
    train[n] -> display_capacity ( );
    cout << endl;
  }
}
```

――――――――――――――― Sample Data ―――――――――――――――

```
0 1 1 2 3
```

――――――――――――――― Result ―――――――――――――――

```
eng
box      3990
box      3990
tnk      1539.38
cab
```

Adapt the program shown in Segment 509 such that it displays floor areas rather than volumes. First, write an appropriate member function for the box class. Then, make use of that box class member function by defining virtual functions in the railroad_car class hierarchy. Assume that engines, cabooses, and tank cars have no floor area.

- If you want a member function to work on a specific class object, **then** instantiate the following pattern:

  `class object` . `member function` (`ordinary arguments`)

- If you want to call a member function from inside another member function, **and** the called member function is to work on the same object that you handed to the calling function, **then** drop the class object argument and the class-member operator, instantiating the following pattern:

  `member function` (`ordinary arguments`)

512   One principle of software engineering is that you should try to protect both data and functions from misuse. In this section, you learn how to protect member variables and member functions from misuse using C++'s private, protected, and public categories.

513   Recall that the box_car and box class definitions, as developed so far, are as follows:

```cpp
class box {
  public: double height, width, length;
    // Default constructor:
    box ( ) { }
    // Argument-bearing constructor:
    box (double h, double w, double l) {
        height = h; width = w; length = l;
    }
    // Volume member function:
    double volume ( ) {
      return height * width * length;
    }
};
class box_car : public railroad_car, public box {
  public:
    // Default constructor:
    box_car ( ) : box (10.5, 9.5, 40.0) { }
    // Displayers:
    virtual void display_short_name ( ) {
      cout << "box";
    }
    virtual void display_capacity ( ) {
      cout << volume ( );
    }
};
```

Although these class definitions work, you can improve them in a variety of ways using the C++ protection mechanisms described in this section.

514   In Section 14, you learned that class definitions can have a private part as well as a public part. More specifically, you learned that you can access a class's private member variables only through member functions that belong to the same class.

If, for example, you decide that a cylinder's dimensions never change once the cylinder is built, you can reflect that constraint in the cylinder class definition by moving the dimensions out of the public interface into the private part of the definition:

```
class box {
  public:
    // Default constructor:
    box ( ) { }
    // Argument-bearing constructor:
    box (double h, double w, double l) {
      height = h; width = w; length = l;
    }
    // Volume member function:
    double volume ( ) {return height * width * length;}
  private: double height, width, length;
};
```

Given this box class definition, only the argument-bearing constructor defined in the box class can write values into the three dimension member variables. Similarly, only the volume member function can reference values in those member variables.

Because no other access to the member variables is allowed, no member function of box_car can write directly into or read directly from the dimension member variables; all writing and reading must go through the argument-bearing constructor and volume functions defined in the box class's public interface.

515   Plainly, movement of the dimension member variables into the private part of the box class definition is an extreme step. If you want to take a slightly less extreme step, allowing you to read the dimensions elsewhere, but not to write them, you can add readers to the public interface:

```
class box {
  public:
    // Define readers:
    double read_height ( ) {return height;}
    double read_width ( ) {return width;}
    double read_length ( ) {return length;}
    // Default constructor:
    box ( ) { }
    // Argument-bearing constructor:
    box (double h, double w, double l) {
      height = h; width = w; length = l;
    }
    // Volume member function:
    double volume ( ) {return height * width * length;}
  private: double height, width, length;
};
```

Because the readers are defined in the box class, they have access to the dimension member variables declared in the private part of the box class. Because the readers themselves are defined in the public part of the definition, they are accessible everywhere. Thus, if you use the publicly defined readers, any member function or ordinary function can read a box car's dimension member variables, but only those member functions defined in the box-car class can write into those dimension member variables.

516 Alternatively, instead of defining readers to expand access to the dimension member variables, you can expand access by moving the dimension declarations into what is called the **protected** part of the class definition:

```
class box {
  public:
    // Default constructor:
    box ( ) { }
    // Argument-bearing constructor:
    box (double h, double w, double l) {
      height = h; width = w; length = l;
    }
    // Volume member function:
    double volume ( ) {return height * width * length;}
  protected: double height, width, length;
};
```

Member variables and member functions in the protected part of a class definition are accessible only from member functions that are defined in the same class or in subclasses of that class. No access from any other function is allowed.

517 Having moved the dimension member variables to the protected part of the definition, you make their values available not only in the `volume` function defined in the `box` class definition, but also in any function you might choose to define in the `box_car` subclass. You could, for example, define a `display_height` member function in the `box_car` class:

```
class box_car : public railroad_car, public box {
  public:
    // Default constructor:
    box_car ( ) : box (10.5, 9.5, 40.0) { }
    // Displayers:
    virtual void display_height ( ) {cout << height;}
    virtual void display_short_name ( ) {cout << "box";}
    virtual void display_capacity ( ) {cout << volume ( );}
};
```

Note that, once you move the dimension member variables into the protected part of the `box` class definition, a member function defined in the `box_car` class definition can write values into those member variables, as well as read from them.

518 Now suppose that you want information about a **box** object's dimensions to be accessible to member functions defined in the `box_car` class, but you do not want that information to be generally accessible, and you do not want functions defined outside the `box` class to be able to change any of those dimensions.

You need to combine the virtues of private and public placement. First, you return the dimension member variables to the private part of the `box` class definition, to prevent accidental writing by member functions defined in the `box_car` class definition. Second, you provide access to the dimension member-variable values through readers defined in the protected part of the `box` class definition:

```
class box {
  public:
    // Default constructor:
    box ( ) { }
    // Argument-bearing constructor:
    box (double h, double w, double 1) {
      height = h; width = w; length = 1;
    }
    // Volume member function:
    double volume ( ) {return height * width * length;}
  protected:
    // Define readers:
    double read_height ( ) {return height;}
    double read_width ( ) {return width;}
    double read_length ( ) {return length;}
  private: double height, width, length;
};
```

Because the member variables are in the private part of the box class definition, they are
accessible only to member functions defined in the box class. Because the readers are in
the protected part of the box class definition, they are accessible only to member functions
defined in either the box or box_car class definitions.

519 To improve your understanding of the public, protected, and private parts of a class definition, contemplate the following diagram. Note that you can think of the private–protected–
public distinction as a means for establishing three rings, each of which corresponds to a
particular degree of member-variable and member-function protection.

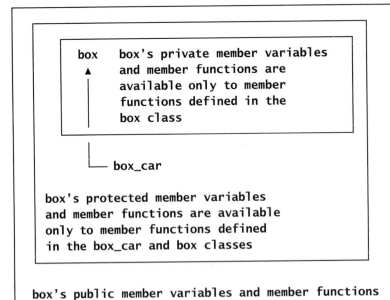

The inner ring—the one corresponding to private member variables and functions—is the most constrained. The outer ring—the one corresponding to public member variables and functions—is the least constrained, inasmuch as there is no protection whatever.

- If you want to limit access to a member variable or member function to member functions defined in the same class, **then** place that member variable or member function in the private part of the class definition.

- If you want to limit access to a member variable or member function to member functions defined in the same class or in subclasses of that class, **then** place that member variable or member function in the protected part of the class definition.

- If you do not wish to limit access to a member variable or member function, **then** place that member variable or member function in the public part of the class definition.

- If you wish to prevent member variable reassignment, **and** you wish to reference those member variables, **then** place the member variables in the private part of the class definition, **and** define member variable readers in the public or protected part of the class definition.

35 HOW TO USE PROTECTED
AND PRIVATE CLASS DERIVATIONS

521   You have seen that you can control access to member variables and member functions *at the point where they are declared and defined* by distributing them to the private, protected, and public parts of the class in which you declare and define them.

In this section, you learn that you can further limit access to member variables and member functions *at the point where they are inherited* by using private, protected, or public class derivation.

522   So far, you have seen only instances of **public derivation**, marked by the symbol `public`.

If you change a derivation from public to protected, every public member variable or member function in the base class acts as though it were part of the protected part of the definition of the derived class.

Suppose, for example, that you define the `box` and `box_car` classes as follows, with a **protected derivation** of the `box_car` class from the `box` class:

```
class box {
  public: double height, width, length;
    // Default constructor:
    box ( ) { }
    // Argument-bearing constructor:
    box (double h, double w, double l) {
      height = h; width = w; length = l;
    }
    // Volume member function:
    double volume ( ) {return height * width * length;}
};
class box_car : public railroad_car, protected box {
  public:
    // Default constructor:
    box_car ( ) : box (10.5, 9.5, 40.0) { }
    // Displayers:
    virtual void display_height ( ) {cout << height;}
    virtual void display_short_name ( ) {cout << "box";}
    virtual void display_capacity ( ) {cout << volume ( );}
};
```

Because the derivation of `box_car`, relative to the `box` class, is a protected derivation, all public member variables and member functions defined in the `box` base class act as though they are protected member variables and member functions in the derived `box_car` class. Because they act as though they are protected, they are still accessible to member functions defined in the `box_car` class and to member functions defined in any subclasses that may be derived from the `box_car` class. For example, the `display_height` function defined in the `box_car` class can read from the `height` member variable.

523　To see that the member-variable protection imposed by a protected derivation persists in classes derived from the subclass, suppose that you define a `refrigerator_car` class to be a class derived from the `box_car` class. Further suppose that the derivation is public or protected. Then, if you define a `display_height` function in the `refrigerator_car` class definition, that `display_height` function can get at the `height` member variable declared in the `box` class definition:

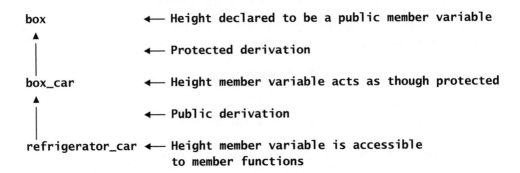

524　On the other hand, you cannot access the `height` member variable of a `refrigerator_car` or `box_car` object other than in a member function. For example, if you declare a `box_car` or `refrigerator_car` variable, you cannot read the `height` member variable using the class-member operator, because access to that member variable is limited as though the member variable were in the protected part of a class definition:

```
box_car box_car_variable;
cout << box_car_variable.height;              // DEFECTIVE!
refrigerator_car refrigerator_car_variable;
cout << refrigerator_car_variable.height;     // DEFECTIVE!
```

Note, however, that you can still read the `height` member variable of a `box` using the class-member operator:

```
box box_variable;
cout << box_variable.height;                  // OK
```

Thus, access via `box_car` objects to the `height` member variable declared in the `box` base class definition is limited by the protected nature of the derivation, but for only those class objects belonging to the derived `box_car` class and its subclasses.

525　The most extreme way to limit access to member variables and member functions at the point where they are inherited is to use **private derivation**.

When you make a derivation private, each public and protected member variable or member function in the base class acts as though it were part of the private part of the definition of the derived class.

Suppose, for example, that you derive the `box_car` class from the `box` class privately:

```
class box {
  public: double height, width, length;
    // Default constructor:
    box ( ) { }
    // Argument-bearing constructor:
    box (double h, double w, double l) {
      height = h; width = w; length = l;
    }
    // Volume member function:
    double volume ( ) {return height * width * length;}
};
class box_car : public railroad_car, private box {
  public:
    // Default constructor:
    box_car ( ) : box (10.5, 9.5, 40.0) { }
    // Displayers:
    virtual void display_height ( ) {cout << height;}
    virtual void display_short_name ( ) {cout << "box";}
    virtual void display_capacity ( ) {cout << volume ( );}
};
```

Because the derivation of box_car, relative to the box classes, is a private derivation, all public and protected member variables and member functions defined in the box base class act as though they were private member variables and member functions of the derived box_car class. Because they act as though they were private, they are still accessible, but only to member functions defined in the box_car class, and *not* to member functions defined in any subclasses that may be derived from the box_car class. The display_height function, for example, can read from the height member variable.

526 To see that the member-variable privatization imposed by a private derivation blocks access in classes derived from the subclass, you can suppose that you define a refrigerator_car class to be a class derived from the box_car class. Once again, suppose that the derivation is public or protected. This time, however, if you define a display_height function in the refrigerator_car class definition, that display_height function *cannot* get at the height member variable declared in the box class definition:

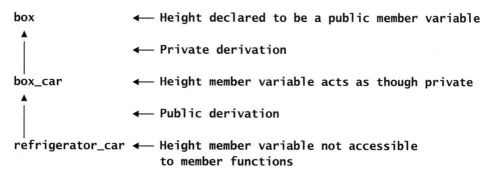

Evidently, access to the height member variable is blocked by the private nature of the way the box_car class is derived from the box class.

527 In summary, the effect of protected and private derivation is to elevate the effective status of member variables and member functions of the base class as viewed from the derived class:

- A protected derivation makes all the public member variables and member functions of the base class appear to be protected member variables and member functions.

- A private derivation makes all the public and protected member variables and member functions of the base class appear to be private member variables and member functions.

The following table reflects the same points:

	Public derivation	Protected derivation	Private derivation
Public member function	remains public	becomes protected	becomes private
Protected member function	remains protected	remains protected	becomes private
Private member function	remains private	remains private	remains private

528 At this point, you have seen several ways to control access to member variables and member functions:

- You can limit access to member variables and member functions at the point where they are declared.

- You can limit access to member variables and member functions at the point where one class is derived from another.

- You can gain access to otherwise private or protected member variables through protected or public readers or writers.

529

- If you want all member variables and member functions of a base class to retain their status in a derived class, **then** make the derivation public by instantiating the following pattern:

  ```
  class derived-class name : public base-class name { ··· }
  ```

- If you want to elevate all public member variables and member functions in a base class to protected status in a derived class, **then** make the derivation protected by instantiating the following pattern:

  ```
  class derived-class name : protected base-class name { ··· }
  ```

- If you want to elevate all public and protected member variables and member functions in a base class to private status in a derived class, **then** make the derivation private by instantiating the following pattern:

  ```
  class derived-class name : private base-class name { ··· }
  ```

36 HOW TO WRITE FUNCTIONS THAT RETURN CHARACTER STRINGS

530   In this section, you learn how to return character strings from functions.

531   At this point, you have a working train-describing program, but you may decide to take another look at the `for` loop where displaying is done:

```
for (n = 0; n < car_count; ++n) {
  // Display short name, such as eng, box, tnk, or cab:
  train[n] -> display_short_name ( );
  // Display spaces:
  cout << "     ";
  // Display load capacities:
  train[n] -> display_capacity ( );
  // Terminate the line:
  cout << endl;
}
```

This `for` loop works, but you may not like to have the actual displaying distributed all over the place in functions such as `display_short_name` and `display_capacity`. By bringing to one place all the output statements, you make them easier to control.

532   One step that is easy to take is to convert the `display_capacity` function, which displays but returns nothing, into `capacity`, a function that displays nothing but returns a capacity. Recall that `display_capacity` is defined as follows in the `railroad_car` class definition:

```
virtual void display_capacity ( ) { }
```

Further recall that `display_capacity` is defined as follows in the `box_car` and `tank_car` class definitions:

```
virtual void display_capacity ( ) {cout << volume ( );}
```

Using those definitions as a model, you might define `capacity` in the `railroad_car` class definition as follows:

```
virtual double capacity ( ) {return 0.0;}
```

And you might define `capacity` this way in the `box_car` and `tank_car` class definitions:

```
virtual double capacity ( ) {return volume ( );}
```

533   Because you have told C++ that the `capacity` function returns a floating-point number, C++ can determine how to handle `capacity` in output statements. Accordingly, you can rewrite the `for` loop as follows:

```
for (n = 0; n < car_count; ++n) {
  // Display short name, such as eng, box, tnk, or cab:
  train[n] -> display_short_name ( );
  // Display spaces:
  cout << "     ";
  // Display load capacity, and terminate the line:
  cout << train[n] -> capacity ( ) << endl;
}
```

534 Having rid yourself of display_capacity, you might like to take the next natural step: to rid yourself of display_short_name as well. Then, you could construct a for loop in which all the displaying is done explicitly:

```
for (n = 0; n < car_count; ++n) {
  // Display short name and capacity and terminate the line:
  cout << train[n] -> short_name ( )
       << "     "
       << train[n] -> capacity ( )
       << endl;
}
```

To define short_name, using display_short_name as a model, you need to know what the return type should be:

```
// Definition in railroad_car
virtual what type here? short_name ( ) {return "rrc";}
// Definition in box_car
virtual what type here? short_name ( ) {return "box";}
...
```

535 When you delimit a sequence of characters by double quotation marks, you are really telling C++ to create an array in which the elements are the particular characters between the double quotation marks. The following, for example, is what C++ stores on encountering "box".

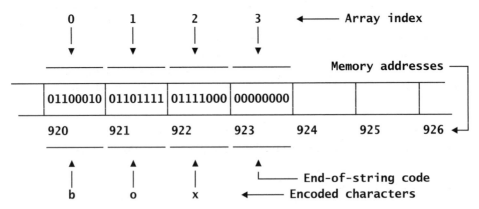

Note that the three characters in box are actually stored in a four-element array in which the last element is filled by the **null character**, rather than by an actual character's code.

Character arrays terminated by null characters are called **character strings**, or, more succinctly, **strings**. Thus, "box" is a notation for a string. Somewhat colloquially, most programmers say that "box" is a string.

536   You frequently see the null character written as \0 in string-manipulation programs. By using \0 instead of 0 identifies the places where 0 is used as the special null character, rather than as an ordinary integer, you increase program clarity.

537   The reason strings are terminated by null characters is that string-manipulation functions—both those that are built in and those you may choose to define—generally have no way to know, in advance, how many characters there are in any given string. Those functions rely, instead, on null characters—serving as end-of-string markers—to tell them when to stop as they work their way through the characters.

In particular, the output operator, <<, relies on null characters when it deals with strings.

538   Whenever a string appears in an expression, the value of that string is a pointer to the first element in the corresponding character array:

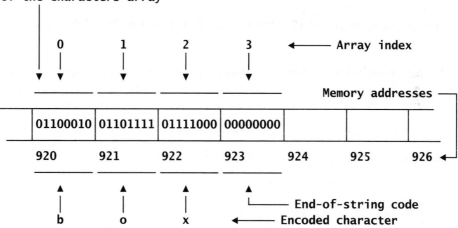

539   The following declaration creates a character-pointer variable and arranges for the initial value of that variable to point to the first character in the "box" string:

```
char *character_pointer = "box";
```

Thus, a character-pointer declaration, with a string provided as the initial value, produces an arrangement of memory such as the following:

187

character_pointer

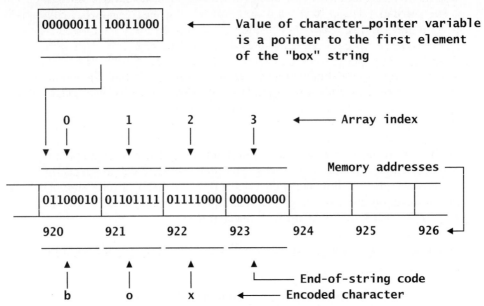

00000011	10011000

⟵ Value of character_pointer variable is a pointer to the first element of the "box" string

| 0 | 1 | 2 | 3 | ⟵ Array index |

Memory addresses

01100010	01101111	01111000	00000000			
920	921	922	923	924	925	926 ⟵

b o x ⟵ Encoded character
└── End-of-string code

540   Thus, there is no such data type as a string. When you hand over a string to a function, you supply a character pointer that points to the first character in that string. When you want to return a string from a function, you really ask for a pointer to the first character in that string.

For example, when you define the short_name function in the railroad_car class, you declare that it is to return a character pointer as follows:

```
virtual char* short_name ( ) {return "rrc";}     // For railroad_car
```

Similarly, the following defines a short_name function for the box_car class definition:

```
virtual char* short_name ( ) {return "box";}     // For box_car
```

Thus, both short_name functions return character pointers.

541   After installing these definitions, and appropriate definitions for engines, tank cars, and cabooses, you can use the following for loop:

```
for (n = 0; n < car_count; ++n) {
  // Display short name and capacity and terminate the line:
  cout << train[n] -> short_name ( );
       << "      "
       << train[n] -> capacity ( )
       << endl;
}
```

Using this for loop, the latest version of the analyze_train program is as follows:

```
#include <iostream.h>
const double pi = 3.14159;
// ... Box, cylinder, and railroad car definitions go here ...
class box_car : public railroad_car, public box {
  public: box_car ( ) : box (10.5, 9.5, 40.0) { }
          virtual char* short_name ( ) {return "box";}
          virtual double capacity ( ) {return volume ( );}
};
class tank_car : public railroad_car, public cylinder {
  public: tank_car ( ) : cylinder (3.5, 40.0) { }
          virtual char* short_name ( ) {return "tnk";}
          virtual double capacity ( ) {return volume ( );}
};
// ... Engine and caboose definitions go here ...
// Define railroad car pointer array:
railroad_car *train[100];
// Declare enumeration constants, needed in switch statement:
enum {eng_code, box_code, tnk_code, cab_code};
main ( ) {
  // Declare various integer variables:
  int n, car_count, type_code;
  // Read type number and create car class objects:
  for (car_count = 0; cin >> type_code; ++car_count)
    switch (type_code) {
      case eng_code: train[car_count] = new engine;    break;
      case box_code: train[car_count] = new box_car;   break;
      case tnk_code: train[car_count] = new tank_car; break;
      case cab_code: train[car_count] = new caboose;   break;
    }
  // Display report:
  for (n = 0; n < car_count; ++n)
    // Display short name and capacity and terminate the line:
    cout << train[n] -> short_name ( )
         << "      "
         << train[n] -> capacity ( )
         << endl;
}
```

———————————————— Sample Data ————————————————

0 1 1 2 3

———————————————— Result ————————————————

eng	0
box	3990
box	3990
tnk	1539.38
cab	0

Note that there is one small difference between this report and the one produced in Segment 509: zeros are displayed, rather than nothing, for the capacities of engines and cabooses.

542
PRACTICE Suppose that you modify the short_name function appearing in the box_car class in the program shown in Segment 541 as follows:

```
virtual char* short_name ( ) {
  char *character_pointer = "box";
  return character_pointer;
}
```

What happens? Explain your answer.

543
PRACTICE Suppose that you modify the short_name function appearing in the box_car class in the program shown in Segment 541 as follows:

```
virtual char* short_name ( ) {
  char character_array = "box";
  return &character_pointer;
}
```

What happens? Explain your answer.

544
PRACTICE Suppose that you add the following member function definition to the box class definition in the program shown in Segment 541.

```
virtual char* short_name ( ) {
  return "box";
}
```

What happens? Explain your answer.

545
HIGHLIGHTS

- Character strings are stored as one-dimensional character arrays terminated by the null character.

- If you want to declare a variable whose value is a string, **then** instantiate the following pattern:

  char * `variable name` = `character string` ;

- If a function is to return a string, **then** declare that its return type is a character pointer by instantiating the following pattern:

  char* `function name` · · ·

37 HOW TO USE CALL-BY-REFERENCE PARAMETERS

546   In this section, you learn that ordinary functions that take class object arguments may have to take their arguments by reference, rather than by value, thus departing from the C++ call-by-value default.

547   There are occasions when you have to hand a class object to a member function as an ordinary argument, rather than via the class-pointer operator or the class-member operator.

For example, if you want to define a function that takes two class-object arguments, only one, at most, can be delivered via the class-pointer operator or the class-member operator.

Also, if you want to overload an operator, such as the output operator, you are restrained, because operator operands cannot be delivered via the class-pointer operator, ->, or via the class-member operator.

548   Suppose that you decide to define an ordinary function—not a member function—that takes an ordinary railroad-car argument and computes that car's volume. You might try to define `ordinary_capacity_function` as an ordinary function by having it give all the work to the already-defined `capacity` virtual member function:

```
// DEFECTIVE attempt to define ordinary_capacity_function!
double ordinary_capacity_function (railroad_car r) {
  return r.capacity ( );
}
```

You might think that this function would work properly in the `analyze_train` program if called as follows:

```
for (n = 0; n < car_count; ++n) {
// Display short name and capacity and terminate the line:
 cout << train[n] -> short_name ( )
      << "     "
      << ordinary_capacity_function (*train[n])
      << endl;                          ─────────
}                                         ▲
                                         │
Dereferenced array pointer identifies ──┘
a chunk of memory that holds a box car,
tank car, engine, or caboose
```

Perhaps unexpectedly, incorporating this version of `ordinary_capacity_function` into the `analyze_train` program leads to the following result:

```
eng    0
box    0
box    0
tnk    0
cab    0
```

549 To understand why the revised `analyze_train` program fails, you need to learn more about how the C++ compiler handles class-object arguments.

Recall that, because C++ is a call-by-value language, C++ programs ordinarily reserve a memory chunk for each parameter whenever a function is called. Then, C++ programs copy evaluated arguments into those chunks of memory:

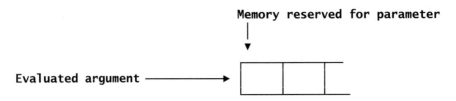

If an argument consists of a single variable, a C++ program copies the value of that variable into the reserved memory chunk:

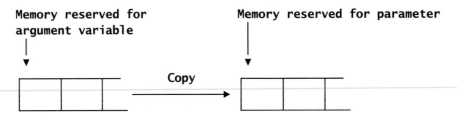

550 Now recall that in `ordinary_capacity_function`, the parameter, r is a `railroad_car` parameter. Accordingly, the argument is copied into a chunk of memory suited to a `railroad_car` object.

Suppose, however, that the argument is actually a `box_car` object, identified by a dereferenced railroad-car pointer. Unfortunately, at compile time, the C++ compiler cannot anticipate that your program will hand such an argument to `ordinary_capacity_function`. Accordingly, only the railroad-car portion of the `box_car` object is copied:

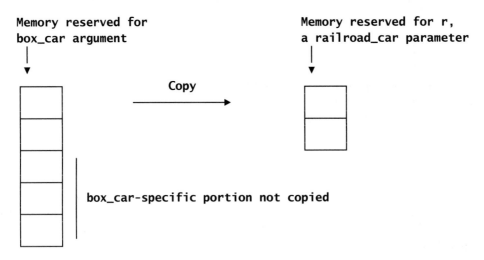

The net result is that only the chunk of memory that holds a `railroad_car` object is visible to the C++ mechanism that is supposed to figure out what version of the `capacity` virtual member function to use at run time. Because the railroad-car version of `capacity` returns `0.0`, you end up with `0.0` filling an entire column of the report displayed by the `analyze_train` program.

551   Although C++ programs normally adhere to the call-by-value convention, C++ allows you to stipulate that you want particular parameters to be **call-by-reference parameters**. Whenever a call-by-reference parameter is paired with an argument that is a single-variable expression, the parameter shares the memory chunk named by the variable; nothing is copied:

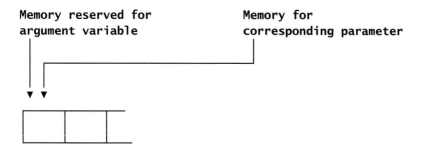

552   In particular, if you arrange for the `railroad_car` parameter, r, to be a call-by-reference parameter, the entire `box_car` object is visible to the C++ mechanism that determines which `capacity` virtual member function to use:

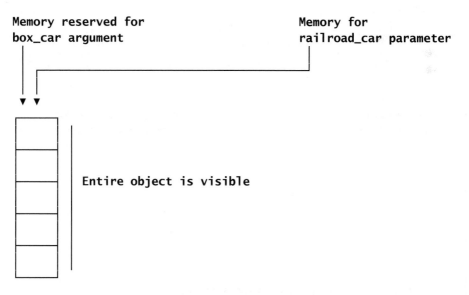

At this point, because the `capacity` function is a virtual function and because a version of `capacity` is defined in the `box_car` class, the `box_car` version is executed, causing the appropriate volume to be returned.

553   What you have just learned about arguments that consist of a single variable also holds for any argument that identifies an existing chunk of memory, such as a parameter, array element, or dereferenced array pointer.

554   To tell the C++ compiler that a parameter is to be a call-by-reference parameter, you add an ampersand, &, to the parameter's type indicator.

For example, in the `ordinary_capacity_function`, you tell the C++ compiler that r is to be a call-by-reference parameter as follows:

```
              Tell C++ that the parameter is to be ─┐
              a call-by-reference parameter          │
                                                     ▼
double ordinary_capacity_function (railroad_car& r) {
  return r.capacity ( );
}
```

With this one-character amendment, the `ordinary_capacity_function` works fine. The `analyze_train` program displays the following report, as it should:

```
eng    0
box    2880
box    2880
tnk    1130.97
cab    0
```

555   Here, by way of summary, is where you are:

- You know that you ordinarily use call-by-value parameters. C++ programs always allocate a chunk of memory for each call-by-value parameter and C++ programs always arrange for argument values to be copied into that chunk. The rationale is that you want to isolate each function's parameters from other parameters, local variables, and global variables that happen to have the same name.

- You know that you generally use call-by-reference parameters when a function's argument is to be an object that belongs to a subclass of the parameter's type. The rationale is that all of the object, rather than just the portion associated with the parameter's type, must be visible inside the function. Each call-by-reference parameter shares an existing memory chunk with a corresponding argument, rather than copying that argument into a newly allocated chunk; hence, all data in the existing memory chunk remains visible.

556   There are two other important reasons to use call-by-reference parameters.

- First, argument copying may take time that cannot be spared, particularly if the argument is a large class object.

- Second, you may wish to write a function that modifies one of its arguments, which it cannot do if it has only a copy with which to work.

Suppose that you have an array of `box_car` objects, rather than `railroad_car` objects. Then, you could define `floor_space_function` as follows:

```
double floor_space_function (box_car b) {
  return b.width * b.length;
}
```

Equipped with the floor_space_function, you could incorporate it into a program that uses your array of box_car objects:

```
box_car *box_car_array[100];
...
main ( ) {
...
  for (n = 0; n < car_count; ++n) {
    // Display floor space and terminate the line:
    cout << floor_space_function (*box_car_array[n])
        << endl;
  }
}
```

This program will run faster if you define floor_space_function with a call-by-reference parameter to avoid copying the box_car object:

```
double floor_space_function (box_car& b) {
  return b.width * b.length;
}
```

557   Note that a function with a call-by-reference parameter can alter the corresponding argument. The following, for example, would reset a box_car object's percentage_loaded member variable to 100:

```
void loading_function (box_car& b) {
  b.percentage_loaded = 100;
  return;
}
```

The following alternative would not work, because the change would alter only a copy of the argument, rather than the argument itself:

```
void loading_function (box_car b) {  // DEFECTIVE!
  b.percentage_loaded = 100;
  return;
}
```

558   The following program is stripped down to a few essentials so as to illustrate the speed-up and argument-altering properties of call-by-reference parameters without the complexity involved in reading information and producing a report:

```cpp
#include <iostream.h>
// ... Class definitions; container class includes percent_loaded ...
// Define ordinary functions:
double slow_floor_space_function (box_car b) {
  return b.width * b.length;
}
double fast_floor_space_function (box_car& b) {
  return b.width * b.length;
}
void defective_loading_function (box_car b) {
  b.percent_loaded = 100;
  return;
}
void working_loading_function (box_car& b) {
  b.percent_loaded = 100;
  return;
}
main ( ) {
  box_car typical_box_car;
  cout << "                        Slow    Fast" << endl
       << "Area computations:    "
       << slow_floor_space_function (typical_box_car)
       << "      "
       << fast_floor_space_function (typical_box_car)
       << endl;
  typical_box_car.percent_loaded = 0;
  cout << "                                    Percent Loaded"
       << endl;
  cout << "Before calling either loading function:   "
       << typical_box_car.percent_loaded
       << endl;
  defective_loading_function (typical_box_car);
  cout << "After calling defective_loading_function: "
       << typical_box_car.percent_loaded
       << endl;
  working_loading_function (typical_box_car);
  cout << "After calling working_loading_function:   "
       << typical_box_car.percent_loaded
       << endl;
}
```

--------------------------- Result ---------------------------

	Slow	Fast
Area computations:	380	380

	Percent Loaded
Before calling either loading function:	0
After calling defective_loading_function:	0
After calling working_loading_function:	100

The type of a call-by-reference parameter does not need to be a class. Call-by-reference parameters can be, for example, of type int or double. Predict the output obtained from the following program:

```cpp
#include <iostream.h>
int call_by_value_square (int m) {
  m = m * m;
  return m;
}
int call_by_reference_square (int& m) {
  m = m * m;
  return m;
}
main ( ) {
  int n = 5;
  cout << "n's value is " << n << endl;
  cout << "The call-by-value square of n is "
       << call_by_value_square (n) << endl;
  cout << "n's value is " << n << endl;
  cout << "The call-by-value square of n+1 is "
       << call_by_value_square (n + 1) << endl;
  cout << "n's value is " << n << endl;
  cout << "The call-by-reference square of n is "
       << call_by_reference_square (n) << endl;
  cout << "n's value is " << n << endl;
  cout << "The call-by-reference square of n+1 is "
       << call_by_reference_square (n + 1) << endl;
  cout << "n's value is " << n << endl;
}
```

Suppose that you try to fix the problem raised in Segment 548 by defining additional functions specialized to the various railroad_car subclasses:

```cpp
double ordinary_capacity_function (box_car b) {
  return b.capacity ( );
}
double ordinary_capacity_function (tank_car t) {
  return t.capacity ( );
}
double ordinary_capacity_function (engine e) {
  return e.capacity ( );
}
double ordinary_capacity_function (caboose c) {
  return c.capacity ( );
}
```

Does the program perform correctly with these additional functions? Explain your answer.

- C++ programs ordinarily use call-by-value parameters. Thus, the value of any parameter or variable that appears as an argument is copied into a memory chunk freshly reserved for the corresponding parameter. The effect of a parameter reassignment cannot propagate outside of the function in which the reassignment occurs.

- You can force the C++ compiler to treat a parameter as a call-by-reference parameter. Then, the memory chunk holding the value of any variable, parameter, array element, or dereferenced array pointer that appears as an argument is shared by the corresponding call-by-reference parameter. Therefore, the effect of a parameter reassignment can propagate outside of the function in which the reassignment occurs.

- One reason to force the C++ compiler to treat a parameter as a call-by-reference parameter is to ensure that the parameter provides access to all of a run-time–allocated object provided via a dereferenced pointer, rather than to only the superclass portion of that object.

- Another reason to force the C++ compiler to treat a parameter as a call-by-reference parameter is to save the time involved in copying an argument.

- Still another reason to force the C++ compiler to treat a parameter as a call-by-reference is to enable a function to modify an argument.

- If you want a parameter to be a call-by-reference parameter, rather than an ordinary call-by-value parameter, **then** add an ampersand to the parameter-type declaration in the parameter list:

```
data type  function name  (···,
                           data type & parameter name ,
                           ···)
```

38 HOW TO OVERLOAD THE OUTPUT OPERATOR

562   In this section, you learn about overloading the output operator. Also, you learn about situations in which you must tell the C++ compiler to put aside its habit of copying return values.

563   The memory set aside for each function's call-by-value parameters and local variables is set aside only temporarily. When a function is called, memory chunks are pushed onto the end of an area of memory called the **stack**; after a function returns, the memory in those chunks is overwritten as soon as subsequent function calls cause new memory chunks to be pushed onto the stack.

564   The following sequence shows how the stack grows and shrinks. The first diagram in the sequence shows the stack just before a function is called:

In use	In use	In use	Unused	Unused	Unused

Next, the stack grows to accommodate parameters and local variables as a function is called; in the diagram, two chunks are pushed on to the end of the stack, overwriting unused memory:

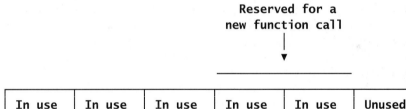

In use	In use	In use	In use	In use	Unused

Next, the stack shrinks when the function returns; memory previously used for parameters and local values becomes unused and ready for reuse:

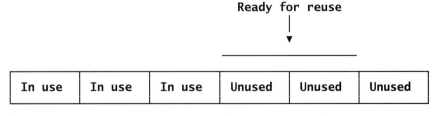

In use	In use	In use	Unused	Unused	Unused

Finally, the stack grows again to accommodate the next function call, and memory previously occupied is overwritten; the new function call happens to require three chunks of memory:

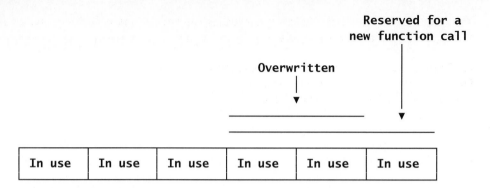

| In use | In use | In use | In use | In use | In use |

565   Now suppose that a function is to return the value of a call-by-value parameter or of a local variable. Normally, the C++ compiler arranges, by default, for such values to be copied before they are lost:

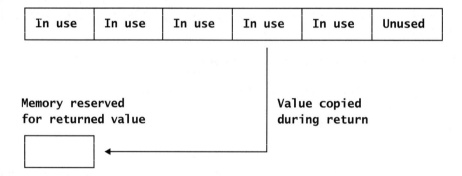

566   Note, however, that the C++ compiler's value-copying default is not always what you want. In particular, some functions involve a **pass-through object**: an object that is handed to the function via a call-by-reference parameter, without copying, and is to be returned as the function's value, also without copying.

567   In the remainder of this section, you learn how to overload the output operator using a definition that involves a pass-through object. Note, however, that you are not likely to define functions involving pass-through objects yourself until you are well beyond the novice stage.

568   Suppose that you decide that you want to decorate the capacity report—the one displayed by the analyze_train program—with a simple iconic train, such as the following:

[eng]-[box]-[box]-[tnk]-[cab]

You could arrange for this display by amending the `for` loop that does displaying. As it stands, the `for` loop looks like this:

```
// Display short names and capacities:
for (n = 0; n < car_count; ++n) {
  cout << train[n] -> short_name ( )
       << "      "
       << train[n] -> capacity ( )
       << endl;
}
```

As amended to display an iconic train representation, the `for` loop looks like this:

```
// Display icon for first car, no hyphen:
cout << "[" << train[0] -> short_name ( ) << "]";
// Display icons for other cars, hyphen included:
for (n = 1; n < car_count; ++n) {
  cout << "-[" << train[n] -> short_name ( ); << "]";
}
```

569 Although the amended `for` loop does the job, it is inelegant. You might wonder whether you can make the output operator, `<<`, display appropriate characters when given a dereferenced railroad-car pointer, just as it displays appropriate characters when given objects belonging to built-in data types, such as integers. Then, you could write the icon-displaying `for` loop this way:

```
// Display icon for first car, no hyphen:
cout << *train[0];
// Display icons for other cars, hyphen included:
for (n = 1; n < car_count; ++n) {
  cout << "-" << *train[n];
}
```

570 In C++, you can overload operators, such as the output operator, just as you can overload ordinary functions. To overload an operator, you proceed as though you were defining an ordinary function, except that you substitute the operator symbol for the function name, and you add the symbol `operator`.

The ordinary definition pattern follows:

```
data type  function name ( parameters ) {
  body
}
```

The operator-overloading definition pattern for a binary operator follows:

```
data type operator operator symbol
  ( left parameter type and name , right parameter type and name ) {
  body
}
```

201

571   You know that the output operator, <<, takes two operands: The operand on the left tells the output operator where to put data, and the operand on the right is an object of some sort—possibly a class object.

To overload the output operator, you need to know that the left-side operand, such as cout, is a class object belonging to the ostream class. Moreover, the object returned by the output operator is supposed to be the same object that is supplied as the left-side operand.

Accordingly, to overload the output operator, you use a specialized version of the general pattern for operator overloading:

```
ostream& operator<<
    (ostream& output_stream, right parameter type and name ) {
    statements
    return output_stream;
}
```

Note the ampersands in the pattern for overloading the output operator. These particular ampersands tell the C++ compiler that you do not want your program to make copies of the ostream object either at the time of call or at the time of return.

572   More specifically, the ampersand in the parameter declaration tells the C++ compiler that you want the output_stream parameter to be a call-by-reference parameter. The value of the left-side operand is handed to the operator function as is, without copying.

The other ampersand—the one in front of operator<<—tells the C++ compiler that you want to return the parameter value from the function without copying.

Because there is no copying, the output operators in nested output expressions all work with exactly the same ostream object.

573   Note that the ampersand in the return-value type declaration cannot appear without the ampersand in the parameter type declaration:

- The parameter whose value is the ostream object is a call-by-reference parameter. Thus, nothing is pushed onto the stack for that parameter.

- Because the memory reserved for a call-by-reference parameter does not go on the stack, that memory is not disturbed when the function returns. Thus, there is no need to copy the class object when the function returns. Hence, a copy-free return is possible.

574   Using the specialized pattern, you can overload the output operator so that output statements can handle railroad-car operands, surrounding each car's short name with brackets:

```
ostream& operator<< (ostream& output_stream, railroad_car& r) {
    output_stream << "[" << r.short_name ( ) << "]";
    return output_stream;}
```

Note that the parameter, r, declared to be a railroad_car must be a call-by-reference parameter, because you want the overloaded output operator to handle objects that belong to subclasses of the railroad_car class, such as box_car objects. As you learned in

Section 37, if r were a call-by-value parameter, and the argument were, say, a box_car object, then only that part of the object inherited from the railroad_car class would be copied, and there would be no way for the overloaded output operator to know that [box], rather than [rrc], is supposed to be displayed.

575 On the other hand, because r is a call-by-reference parameter, any kind of railroad car handed over, including a box car, is visible in full. In particular, the virtual member function, short_name, which is defined in all the subclasses of the railroad_car class, returns the appropriate short name, be it box, tnk, eng, or cab.

576 Now that you have overloaded the output operator, enabling it to handle railroad_car objects, you can use dereferenced railroad-car pointers as output-operator operands, as in the following version of the analyze_train program:

```cpp
#include <iostream.h>
const double pi = 3.14159;
// ... Class definitions go here ...
// Define railroad-car pointer array:
railroad_car *train[100];
// Declare enumeration constants, needed in switch statement:
enum {eng_code, box_code, tnk_code, cab_code};
// Overload <<:
ostream& operator<< (ostream& output_stream, railroad_car& r) {
  output_stream << "[" << r.short_name ( ) << "]";
  return output_stream;}
main ( ) {
  // Declare various integer variables:
  int n, car_count, type_code;
  // Read car-type number and create car class objects:
  for (car_count = 0; cin >> type_code; ++car_count)
    switch (type_code) {
      case eng_code: train[car_count] = new engine;    break;
      case box_code: train[car_count] = new box_car;   break;
      case tnk_code: train[car_count] = new tank_car;  break;
      case cab_code: train[car_count] = new caboose;   break;
    }
  // Display icons:
  cout << *train[0];
  for (n = 1; n < car_count; ++n) {
    cout << "-" << *train[n];
    }
  cout << endl;
}
```
———————————————————— Sample Data ————————————————————
0 1 1 2 3
—————————————————————— Result ——————————————————————
[eng]-[box]-[box]-[tnk]-[cab]

203

Thus, the overloaded output operator always displays the appropriate three-letter short name, surrounded by brackets. It also returns the same output stream that appeared as the left-side operand.

577
SIDE TRIP The ordinary output operator supplied by C++ is defined by a collection of overloading definitions with a pass-through parameter.

578
PRACTICE Further overload the output operator such that iconic train displayed by the program in Segment 576 looks like the following example:

```
<engine>-[box]-[box]-(tank)-[caboose]
```

579
HIGHLIGHTS
- If you want to overload a binary operator, **then** instantiate the following pattern:

  ```
  data type operator operator symbol
    (left parameter type and name,
     right parameter type and name) {
    body
  }
  ```

- If you want to overload the output operator, **then** instantiate the following pattern:

  ```
  ostream& operator<<
    (ostream& output_stream, right parameter type and name) {
    statements
    return output_stream;
  }
  ```

204

580   C++'s output operator, <<, provides you with a convenient, easy-to-use way to get information out of your programs, especially when you exploit C++'s overloading feature. The output operator is not so helpful, however, when you want to exercise a great deal of control over just how information is displayed. Read this section if you want to learn what to do when you want such control; skip it if you are interested only in C++'s distinguishing features, because the features described in this section come directly from C.

581   At this point, you have seen many examples in which C++'s output operator, <<, displays strings and numbers. Although convenient, the examples using the output operator have one conspicuous defect: You get ragged-looking display when the widths of the items displayed vary from line to line.

In principle, you can exert control over how the output operator does its job by using various library functions that manipulate stream objects, such as the `cout` stream and `ofstream` streams. Nevertheless, many programmers find the current generation of stream-manipulation functions to be insufficiently flexible.

582   Accordingly, C++ allows you to exploit certain input–output mechanisms originally devised for C. In particular, you can call C's `printf` function.

The general form for `printf` statements is as follows:

```
printf ( a character string ,
         argument 1 ,
         argument 2 ,
         ...
         argument n );
```

The character-string argument serves as a pattern into which the other evaluated arguments are inserted.

583   As usual, before you can use `printf` you need to announce your intention via an `#include` declaration that tells the C++ compiler in which library `printf` resides:

```
#include <stdio.h>
```

584   The simplest `printf` statements have only one argument—a string to be displayed—such as the following sentence from Vergil's **Aeneid**:

```
printf ("Forsan et haec olim meminisse iuvabit.\n");
```

585   Note that the character string contains the character pair \n. When such a character pair appears in a `printf` statement, the effect is to terminate the current line and to start a new one.

You can also use \n in character strings you display with the output operator, <<.

Most programmers prefer to use `endl` to terminate lines, rather than \n, because `endl` not only terminates lines, but also directs your computer to complete the delivery to your screen of all the characters that have accumulated in an **output buffer**. Thus, << is said to **flush** the output buffer.

586 In most `printf` statements, the string argument contains **print specifications**, marked by specification-introducing percent signs. Each print specification determines how a corresponding argument value is to be displayed. In the following example, the string contains two print specifications, %s and %i. The %s specification indicates that the next argument value is assumed to be a string, and marks where that string is to be placed. The %i specification indicates that the next argument value is assumed to be an integer, and marks where that integer is to be placed:

```
printf ("The capacity of the %s car is %i.\n",
        "box",
        4703);
```

When this `printf` statement is executed, the result is as follows:

The capacity of the box car is 4703.

Of course, you get the same result with the following C++ output statement:

```
cout << "The capacity of the " << "box" << " car is " << 4703 << "."
     << endl;
```

587 The power of the `printf` function, relative to the output operator, <<, is that you can control how much space each argument value occupies by adding a number to the print specification. The print specification %6s means *display at least six characters using the corresponding argument value, a string, along with extra spaces, if necessary, on the left.* Similarly, %8i means *display at least eight characters using the corresponding argument value, an integer, along with spaces, if necessary, on the left.*

Consider, for example, the following `printf` call:

```
printf ("%6s%8i\n", "box", 4703);
```

The result includes the argument values, along with the spaces required to meet the stipulated minimum number of characters:

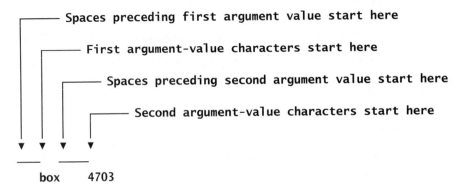

The stipulated minimum number of characters is called the **field width**. The spaces used to augment the space taken by the argument values are called **padding characters**.

588 If you like, you can tell the C++ compiler to put the padding characters on the right by adding a minus sign:

```
printf ("%-6s%-8i\n", "box", 4703);
```

The result is left justification, rather than right justification:

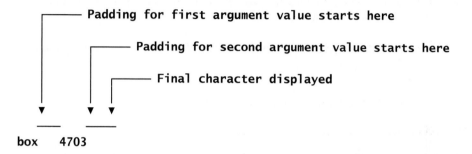

589 You can, if you wish, display a floating-point number without the fractional part by converting it to an integer using C++'s casting mechanism. As you learned in Section 17, all you need to do is to preface the number with (int), as in the following illustration:

```
printf ("%6s%8i\n", "box", (int) 4703.8);
```

The result is:

```
   box    4703
```

A better approach is to use the %f print specification, as in the following example:

```
                  field width
                      |
                      ▼
printf ("%6s%8.0f\n", "box", 4703.8);
                        ▲
                        |
            number of digits to appear in the number's fractional part
```

Again, the result is:

```
   box    4703
```

The %f print specification, along with those for integers, strings, and other data types, is explained more fully in Appendix B.

Using `printf`, amend the program in Segment 541 such that it displays reports such as the following:

```
engine        0
box car    3990
box car    3990
tank car   1539
caboose       0
```

- If you want to control display spacing, **then** use the `printf` function, rather than the output operator, **and** instantiate the following pattern:

  ```
  printf ( a string, with one print specification per argument ,
          argument 1 ,
          argument 2 ,
          ...
          argument n );
  ```

- If you want to include a string argument, **then** use the `%s` specification.

- If you want to include an integer argument, **then** use the `%i` specification.

- If you want to specify a field width, **and** you want the displayed characters to be to the right of the padding, **then** include an integer between the percent sign and the character.

- If you want to specify a field width, **and** you want the displayed characters to be to the left of the padding, **then** include a negative integer between the percent sign and the character.

40 HOW TO WRITE STATEMENTS THAT READ CHARACTER STRINGS FROM FILES

592   You have learned a little about character strings in Section 36—you know how to display them, and you know how to have them handed to a function and returned from a function. In this section, you learn how to obtain character strings from a file, and you learn how to deposit them into an array in preparation for analysis.

593   You have learned about a program that presumes that train files contain integers that encode car types. Now suppose that the file contains serial numbers, such as the following, in which the first three characters identify the car's owner, the next character after the hyphen identifies the car's type, and the digits identify particular cars.

```
TPW-E-783
PPU-B-422
NYC-B-988
NYC-T-988
TPW-C-271
```

You soon learn how to extract these serial numbers from a file, how to analyze them, and how to store them in class objects. Along the way, you need to learn about several subjects:

- How to read strings from a file

- How to extract characters from a string

- How to determine which character you have

- How to store strings in class objects

594   To read a string from a file, you must first create an array in which to store the string temporarily. You must be sure that the array that you create is long enough to hold all anticipated characters plus the required null character that serves as the end-of-string marker. For the information to be read by the `analyze_train` program, 100 characters is surely enough:

```
char input_buffer[100];
```

595   Next, you need to learn a little more about character arrays, previously introduced in Section 36. In particular, you need to know that, when you define any sort of array, the array name becomes a constant, and its value is a pointer to the first element of the array.

Thus, the `input_buffer` symbol is really a constant, and its value is a pointer to the first element of the `input_buffer` array:

input_buffer

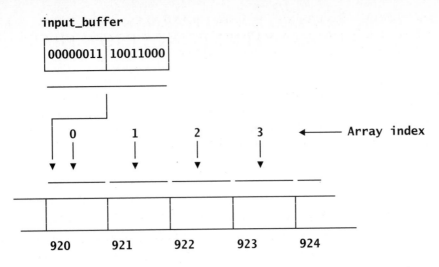

The input operator, >>, recognizes operands, such as input_buffer, that are pointers to character arrays. On seeing such a pointer, >> reads a string from the input stream up to the first **whitespace character**—space, tab, or carriage return. Then, the input operator deposits that string into the array identified by the pointer.

Suppose, for example, that the expression cin >> input_buffer is evaluated, given an input file in which the next unread characters are TPW-E-783. The evaluation causes the input_buffer array to look like this:

input_buffer

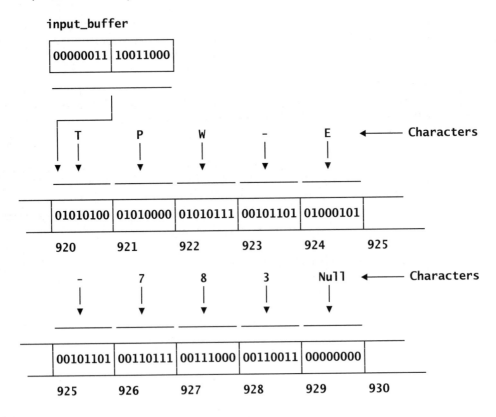

The input operator reads character sequences only up to the first whitespace character, which makes it awkward to deal with input data such as the following, in which the hyphens have been replaced by spaces and comments have been added:

```
TPW E 783
PPU B 422          ; Needs door repair.
NYC B 988
NYC T 988          ; Wheel going bad.
TPW C 271          ; Not to be confused with the Ritz Carlton.
```

Fortunately, C++ offers a variety of alternative ways to read data. One such alternative is to use the `getline` function:

cin.get(   )

`getline(` name of character array `,` maximum characters to be read `)`

Write a program, using `getline`, that reads lines such as those just shown and that displays only the serial numbers, without the comments, but with line numbers, as in the following example:

```
TPW E 783          1
PPU B 422          2
NYC B 988          3
NYC T 988          4
TPW C 271          5
```

- A character-array name is really the name of a constant that points to the first element in the character array. A variable of the character-pointer type can point to any character in a character array.

- Wherever you see the phrase *name of character array* in a pattern, the phrase *variable of the character-pointer type* usually works, and vice versa. You cannot, however, reassign the name of a character array, because array names are constants.

- If you wish to prepare to read a string from a file, **then** you must create a character array large enough to hold the string.

- If you wish to read a string from a file, **and** you have created a character array to hold the string, **then** instantiate the following pattern:

  `cin >>` name of character array

41 HOW TO TEST STRING CHARACTERS

599   In this section, you learn how to extract characters from strings, and you learn how to use such characters to determine what to do next.

600   In the `analyze_train` program shown in Segment 541, the following `for` loop reads integers from a file, assigning them successively to the integer variable, `type_code`:

```
for (n = 0; cin >> type_code; ++n)
  ...
```

Analogously, then, the following `for` loop reads strings from a file, depositing each, in turn, in the front part of the `input_buffer` array—the place where TPW-E-783 is located in the example.

```
for (n = 0; cin >> input_buffer; ++n)
  ...
```

601   The input operator, when reading a string, stops reading when it encounters a whitespace character. You must be sure to include a whitespace character at the end of every data file to ensure that the final string is read.

602   Of course, when the value of `type_code` was an integer, it was straightforward to build a `switch` statement around the value of `type_code` to pick out the right sort of class object to create:

```
switch (type_code) {
  case eng_code: train[n] = new engine;   break;
  ...
}
```

To deal with a string stored in `input_buffer`, your program has to do more work, because it has to extract a type-indicating character from the array holding the serial number. Then, it must decide what to do by noting which character it has extracted.

603   Obtaining the type-indicating character from the `input_buffer` character array is easy. You need only to access the `input_buffer` as follows:

```
input_buffer[4]
```

Good programming practice dictates that the access should be done via a reader function, however. That way, should the railroad's numbering convention change, you need to change only one reader function, rather than to change a million places where you need to dig type information out of a serial number. Suppose that you decide to call your function `extract_car_code`; then, you supply `extract_car_code` with `input_buffer` as the argument, remembering that an array name is really a constant that points to the array:

```
extract_car_code (input_buffer)
```

604　Evidently, `extract_car_code` must take an argument that is a pointer to a character array, and it must return a character. Hence, the definition of `extract_car_code` must declare a character-pointer argument and a character return value:

```
char extract_car_code (char *input_buffer) {···}
```

The body, of course, just needs to pick out the fourth element—the one carrying the car-type information:

```
char extract_car_code (char *input_buffer) {
  return input_buffer[4];
}
```

605　Once you have defined `extract_car_code`, you can incorporate `extract_car_code` into the `switch` statement that worked previously, in Segment 602, on an integer variable, rather than on a returned character:

```
switch (extract_car_code (input_buffer)) {···}
```

606　At this point, you need to recall that `switch` views the character data type as just another kind of integer. As long as you compare the value of a character-returning Boolean expression with various characters, viewed as integers, `switch` works just fine.

607　In C++, you obtain the integer corresponding to a specific character by surrounding that character with single quotation marks. For example, C++ translates `'A'` into 65; accordingly, 65 is said to be the **character code** for the character *A*.

608　Given a means to obtain specific character codes, you could replace type-denoting enumeration constants in the `switch` statement with character codes. For example, you could replace `eng_code` with `'E'`:

```
switch (extract_car_code (input_buffer)) {
  case 'E': train[n] = new engine;    break;
  ...
}
```

609　There is a better way to use character codes in switch statements, however. You can change the values of the type-defining enumeration constants. Previously, in Section 31, they were declared as follows, with C++ assigning `eng_code` to 0, `box_code` to 1, and so on:

```
enum {eng_code, box_code, tnk_code, cab_code};
```

Recall, however, that you can supply particular integers instead. Further recall that C++ views characters as an integer data type. Thus, you can declare the type-defining enumeration constants as follows:

```
enum {eng_code = 'E', box_code = 'B', tnk_code = 'T', cab_code = 'C'};
```

610　Having redeclared the type-defining enumeration constants, you need only to replace the conditional part of the `switch` statement; the rest remains as it was:

```
switch (extract_car_code (input_buffer)) {
  case eng_code: train[n] = new engine;    break;
  ...
}
```

Thus, enumeration constants provide a form of detail-hiding data abstraction, and, as is usual with data abstraction, the use of enumeration constants simplifies change.

611   Here, then, is the revised program:

```
#include <iostream.h>
const double pi = 3.14159;
// ... Class definitions, with short_name and capacity definitions ...
// Define railroad car pointer array:
railroad_car *train[100];
// Define input buffer:
char input_buffer[100];
// Declare enumeration constants, needed in switch statement:
enum {eng_code = 'E', box_code = 'B', tnk_code = 'T', cab_code = 'C'};
char extract_car_code (char *input_buffer) {return input_buffer[4];}
main ( ) {
  // Declare various integer variables:
  int n, car_count;
  // Read serial number and create car class objects:
  for (car_count = 0; cin >> input_buffer; ++car_count)
    switch (extract_car_code (input_buffer)) {
      case eng_code: train[car_count] = new engine;   break;
      case box_code: train[car_count] = new box_car;  break;
      case tnk_code: train[car_count] = new tank_car; break;
      case cab_code: train[car_count] = new caboose;  break;
    }
  // Display report:
  for (n = 0; n < car_count; ++n)
    cout << train[n] -> short_name ( ) << "      "
         << train[n] -> capacity ( ) << endl;
}
```

————————————— Sample Data —————————————

```
TPW-E-783
PPU-B-422
NYC-B-988
NYC-T-988
TPW-C-271
```

————————————————— Result —————————————————

```
eng    0
box    3990
box    3990
tnk    1539.38
cab    0
```

612
PRACTICE
Suppose that, incredibly, the railroad-car serial-numbering standard changes. Now the railroad name may occupy any number of characters, so you must find the type-encoding character behind the first hyphen. Also, instead of just a one-type–one-character relation, box cars are indicated by *b* or *B*, or by *x* or *X*, and tank cars are indicated by *T* or *L* or *G*. Modify the program in Segment 611 to accommodate the changes. Be sure to change only the `extract_car_code` function.

613
PRACTICE
Suppose that, incredibly, the railroad-car serial-numbering standard changes. Now the fifth and sixth characters are both numbers, with numbers from 10 to 19 indicating box cars, 20 to 29 indicating tank cars, 30 to 39 indicating box cars, 40 to 50 indicating cabooses, and 90 to 99 indicating engines. Modify the program in Segment 611 to accommodate the change. Be sure to change only the `extract_car_code` function.

614
HIGHLIGHTS

- If you wish to extract a character from a character array, **then** access that array as you would any other:

  `array name` [`character's index`]

- If you wish to obtain the character code for a specific character, **then** surround that character with single quotation marks.

- You can use character codes in switch statements.

- You can assign character codes to enumeration constants in enumeration statements.

42 HOW TO DEPOSIT CHARACTER STRINGS INTO CLASS OBJECTS

615　In the previous two sections, you learned how to obtain character strings from a file, how to extract characters from character strings, and how to test characters. In this section, you learn how to move a character string from a temporary buffer to a permanent location inside a class object using functions provided by C++'s string-handling library.

616　If you want to store the appropriate serial number with each new class object, you need to create a character array to store that number. You cannot just use the `input_buffer` array, because that array is reused repeatedly, once for each number read. Fortunately, you can create new arrays just as you can create new class objects. In fact, you use the same operator, `new`. Thus, the following creates a new array that is just long enough to hold the nine characters in a serial number plus a terminating null character:

```
new char[10]
```

617　You should, however, anticipate that serial numbers may get longer, or may become variable in length. Such anticipation requires you to measure the length of the serial number lying in the `input_buffer` array so that you can construct a new character array that is just the right size. To measure the length of a string, such as the serial number, you can use a function supplied by C++'s string-handling library, which you announce your intention to use through the following declaration:

```
#include <string.h>
```

The string-handling function that you need is `strlen`, for *string len*gth:

```
strlen(input_buffer)
```

Because `strlen` returns the number of characters in a string, you need to add 1, to account for the null character, when you create a new array:

```
new char[strlen(input_buffer) + 1]
```

618　You can keep a grip on the new character array using a member variable declared in the `railroad_car` class. That member variable must be a character pointer:

```
class railroad_car {
  public: char *serial_number;
          ...
};
```

619　The right place to create the new character buffer—and assign it to the `serial_number` pointer—is inside a one-argument constructor. The following `engine` class definition exhibits such a constructor:

```
class engine {
  public: engine ( ) { }
          // New constructor:
          engine (char *input_buffer) {
            // Create new array just long enough:
            serial_number = new char[strlen(input_buffer) + 1];
            ...
          }
          virtual char* short_name ( ) {return "eng";}
};
```

Thus, the new `engine` constructor arranges for the `serial_number` member variable, declared in the `railroad_car` class, to point to the first character in a new character array.

620 Next, you must arrange for the serial number to be copied into the new character array using `strcpy`, for *string copy*, another function from the string library. Note that the target array is the first argument, and the source array is the second:

strcpy (serial_number, input_buffer);

The effect of `strcpy` is to copy the serial number from the `input_buffer` array, which has to be big enough for serial numbers of any conceivable length, into the `serial_number` array, which is just big enough to hold the number actually observed:

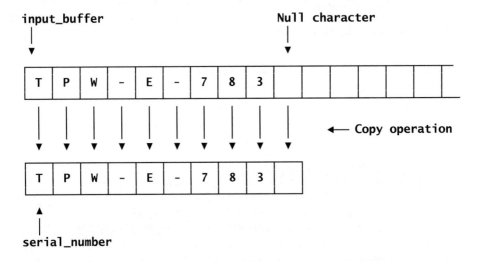

621 Note, incidentally, that both `input_buffer` and `serial_number` are pointers. However, because `input_buffer` is defined as an array name, it is a constant pointer, and `input_buffer` therefore cannot be reassigned. On the other hand, `serial_number` is a pointer variable, and can be reassigned.

622 At this point, you have the following definition for the one-argument `engine` constructor:

```
class engine {
  public: engine ( ) { }
          // New constructor:
          engine (char *input_buffer) {
            // Create new array just long enough:
            serial_number = new char[strlen(input_buffer) + 1];
            strcpy (serial_number, input_buffer);
          }
          virtual char* short_name ( ) {return "eng";}
};
```

623 After defining analogous constructors for the other car classes, you could arrange to deposit
     the serial number in each object by amending the new-car expressions. For example, in
     the current version of the `analyze_train` program, the new-car expression for `engine`
     objects is as follows:

```
new engine
```

Amended to take an argument, the expression would be as follows:

```
new engine (input_buffer)
```

624 Although you could define constructors for each car class that take `input_buffer` argu-
     ments, that solution is inelegant, because the `serial_number` member variable is a mem-
     ber variable in the `railroad_car` class, and, accordingly, the `serial_number` member
     variable should be assigned by a constructor in that `railroad_car` class.

625 Fortunately, you know you can have derived constructors call base-class constructors ex-
     plicitly. The following is a suitable base-class constructor, embedded in the `railroad_car`
     class definition:

```
class railroad_car {
  public: char *serial_number;
          railroad_car ( ) { }
          // New constructor:
          railroad_car (char *input_buffer) {
            // Create new array just long enough:
            serial_number = new char[strlen(input_buffer) + 1];
            // Copy string into new array:
            strcpy (serial_number, input_buffer);
          }
          virtual char* short_name ( ) {return "rrc";}
          virtual double capacity ( ) {return 0.0;}
};
```

The following defines an `engine` class constructor so as to make use of the one-parameter
`railroad_car` constructor:

```
class engine : public railroad_car {
  public: engine ( ) { }
          // New constructor:
          engine (char *input_buffer) : railroad_car (input_buffer)
            { }
          virtual char* short_name ( ) {return "eng";}
};
```

626   Note that the definition of a one-parameter box_car constructor makes use of both the one-parameter railroad_car constructor and, separated by a comma, the three-parameter box constructor. The box_car constructor establishes dimensions, and the railroad_car constructor records the serial number:

```
class box_car : public railroad_car, public box {
  public: // Constructors:
          box_car ( ) : box (10.5, 9.5, 40.0) { }
          box_car (char *input_buffer) : railroad_car (input_buffer),
                                         box (10.5, 9.5, 40.0)
            { }
          // Displayers:
          virtual char* short_name ( ) {return "box";}
          virtual double capacity ( ) {return volume ( );}
};
```

Also note that, as a matter of good programming practice, the definition contains not only the one-parameter constructor, but also a default, zero-parameter constructor.

627   Similar additions to the other car classes enable you to modify the class-object–creating for loop, as shown in the following version of the analyze_train program:

```
#include <iostream.h>
#include <string.h>
const double pi = 3.14159;
// ... Box and cylinder class definitions go here ...
class railroad_car {
  public: char *serial_number;
          railroad_car ( ) { }
          // New constructor:
          railroad_car (char *input_buffer) {
            // Create new array just long enough:
            serial_number = new char[strlen(input_buffer) + 1];
            // Copy string into new array:
            strcpy (serial_number, input_buffer);
          }
          virtual char* short_name ( ) {return "rrc";}
          virtual double capacity ( ) {return 0.0;}
};
```

```
class box_car : public railroad_car, public box {
  public: // Constructors:
          box_car ( ) : box (10.5, 9.5, 40.0) { }
          box_car (char *input_buffer) : railroad_car (input_buffer),
                                         box (10.5, 9.5, 40.0)
            { }
          // Displayers:
          virtual char* short_name ( ) {return "box";}
          virtual double capacity ( ) {return volume ( );}
};
// ... Other modified railroad car class definitions go here ...
railroad_car *train[100];
char input_buffer[100];
enum {eng_code = 'E', box_code = 'B', tnk_code = 'T', cab_code = 'C'};
char extract_car_code (char *input_buffer) {return input_buffer[4];}
main ( ) {
  int n, car_count;
  // Read serial number and create car class objects:
  for (car_count = 0; cin >> input_buffer; ++car_count) {
    // Construct new class object:
    switch (extract_car_code (input_buffer)) {
      case eng_code:
        train[car_count] = new engine (input_buffer);    break;
      case box_code:
        train[car_count] = new box_car (input_buffer);   break;
      case tnk_code:
        train[car_count] = new tank_car (input_buffer); break;
      case cab_code:
        train[car_count] = new caboose (input_buffer);   break;
    }
  }
  // Display report:
  for (n = 0; n < car_count; ++n) {
    // Display short name and capacity and terminate the line:
    cout << train[n] -> short_name ( )
         << "       "
         << train[n] -> capacity ( )
         << endl;
  }
}
```

628 Modify the program shown in Segment 627 such that it displays the railroad-car owner,
PRACTICE in addition to railroad car type and capacity, as in the following example:

```
TPW      eng      0
PPU      box      3990
NYC      box      3990
NYC      tnk      1539.38
TPW      cab      0
```

221

Avoid using the new operator in your solution.

- If you wish to create an array at run time to store a character string, **then** instantiate the following pattern:

  `character-pointer variable` = new char[`character count + 1`]

- If you want to use C++'s string-handling functions, **then** include the following line in your program:

  `#include <string.h>`

- If you want to determine the number of characters in a character array, **and** you have included #include <string.h> in your program, **then** instantiate the following pattern:

  `strlen( name of character array )`

- If you want to copy a string from one array into another, **and** you have included #include <string.h> in your program, **then** instantiate the following pattern:

  `strcpy ( name of target array , name of source array );`

43 HOW TO RECLAIM MEMORY WITH DELETE AND DESTRUCTORS

630 At this point, the latest version of the `analyze_train` program—the one shown in Segment 627—extracts serial numbers from a train-describing file, uses the numbers to identify car type, stores the numbers, and displays a report. Along the way, the program creates new class objects that are accessed through an array of pointers.

You soon learn about still another version of `analyze_train` that waits for you to type the name of a train file, whereupon it does its job, producing a new report. Then, the modified program repeats the wait–work cycle ad infinitum.

You soon see that the modified program creates class objects that become not only obsolete, but also inaccessible. That brings you to the heart of this section, where you learn how to reclaim the memory used for such class objects.

631 The `main` function in the version of `analyze_train` shown in Segment 627 reads serial numbers from the standard `cin` stream, which you know you can attach to a file using a command-line argument. Suppose that you want to make the following changes:

- You want your program to ask for a file name, which you type in after your program is called. Thus, there is to be no command-line argument.

- You want to move the bulk of the work from the `main` function into a new function, `do_analysis`, in preparation for doing the analysis repeatedly.

- You want your new `main` function to call on `do_analysis` whenever you type a file name.

632 First, assume that you have moved to the newly created `do_analysis` function the declarations and statements in the version of `main` in Segment 627. Some details need to be added to `do_analysis`, to be sure; for the moment, however, concentrate on what you need to do to obtain a file name in the new version of `main`.

Recall that the program, as it stands, defines `input_buffer` to be a character array. Accordingly, you can have the program insert a file name into that array:

```
cin >> input_buffer;
```

Then, once the program has a file name, you can have it attempt to open the corresponding file:

```
ifstream car_stream (input_buffer, ios::in);
```

633 When opening a file for reading, you should check to see whether the file was opened successfully. To check, you can take advantage of the fact that an unsuccessful attempt to open a file causes the value of the stream variable to be 0.

```
if (!car_stream) {
  cerror << "No such file." << endl;
  return 0;
}
```

634 Finally, as you know, it is good programming practice to close a file after you are finished reading from it:

```
car_stream.close ( );
```

635 To repeat a series of statements ad infinitum, you can insert them into a `while` loop in which the Boolean expression consists of just the number 1. Because 1 is not 0, the `while` loop will carry on until you type the `control-c` keychord—or the appropriate alternative recognized by your operating system.

```
while (1) {···}
```

636 Thus, you can have your `main` program ask for a file name, accept one, open it, check to be sure it is open, and pass the resulting input stream on to `do_analysis`, over and over, as follows:

```
main ( ) {
  // Read file name and call analysis function repeatedly:
  while (1) {
    cout << "Please type the name of a train file." << endl << ": ";
    cin >> input_buffer;
    // Open:
    ifstream car_stream (input_buffer, ios::in);
    // Check:
    if (!car_stream) {cout << "No such file." << endl; return 0;}
    // Analyze:
    do_analysis (car_stream);
    // Close
    car_stream.close ( );
  }
}
```

637 Now return your attention to `do_analysis`. The `do_analysis` function must have a return type, which happens to be `void`, and a parameter type, which must indicate that the argument belongs to the `ifstream` class. To prevent copying, the parameter is a call-by-reference parameter:

```
void do_analysis (ifstream &car_stream) {···}
```

638 You can write most of the rest of `do_analysis` by copying statements from the version of `main` in Segment 627 with just one small modification: Previously, serial numbers were read from the standard input stream:

```
for (car_count = 0; cin >> input_buffer; ++car_count) {···}
```

Now, they are read from the stream attached to the named input file:

```
for (car_count = 0; car_stream >> input_buffer; ++car_count) {···}
```

639 Assembling all file-handling elements into a new program, you have the following:

```cpp
#include <iostream.h>
#include<fstream.h>
#include<string.h>
const double pi = 3.14159;
// ... Class definitions go here ...
railroad_car *train[100];
char input_buffer[100];
enum {eng_code = 'E', box_code = 'B', tnk_code = 'T', cab_code = 'C'};
char extract_car_code (char *input_buffer) {return input_buffer[4];}
void do_analysis (ifstream &car_stream) {
  // Declare various integer variables:
  int n, car_count;
  // Read serial number and create car class objects:
  for (car_count = 0; car_stream >> input_buffer; ++car_count) {
    // Construct new class object:
    switch (extract_car_code (input_buffer)) {
      case eng_code:
        train[car_count] = new engine (input_buffer);
        break;
      case box_code:
        train[car_count] = new box_car (input_buffer);
        break;
      case tnk_code:
        train[car_count] = new tank_car (input_buffer);
        break;
      case cab_code:
        train[car_count] = new caboose (input_buffer);
        break;
    }
  }
  // ... Display report here ...
}
main ( ) {
  // Read file name and call analysis function repeatedly:
  while (1) {
    cout << "Please type the name of a train file." << endl << ": ";
    cin >> input_buffer;
    // Open the input file:
    ifstream car_stream (input_buffer, ios::in);
    // Give up if the input file does not exist:
    if (!car_stream) {cout << "No such file." << endl; return 0;}
    // Analyze:
    do_analysis (car_stream);
    // Close:
    car_stream.close ( );
  }
}
```

640   At this point, your new program is complete, and works fine, but if you run it long enough, it will fill up your computer's memory with useless class objects. To see why, note that, once one file—one that contains, say, three cars— has been analyzed, the memory involved in the analysis looks as follows:

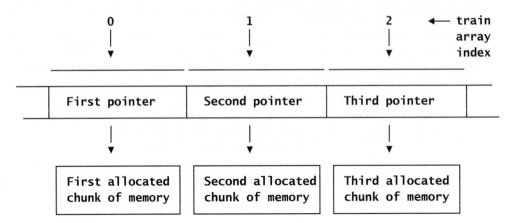

641   Now suppose that you provide a second file—one that also contains three cars. Your program allocates memory for three new class objects in addition to the memory previously allocated for three other class objects:

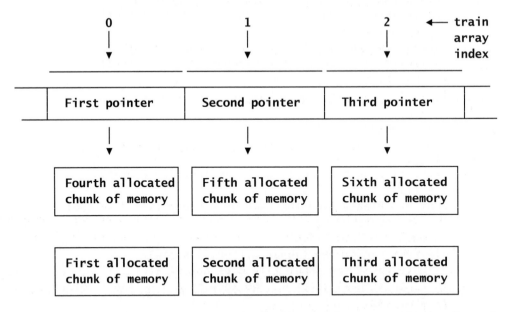

Now, however, there are no pointers to the first three of the memory chunks allocated at run time for class objects. Accordingly, those chunks are completely inaccessible.

642   Plainly, your program spins off inaccessible chunks of memory each time that it reads a file other than the first. If your program does nothing to reclaim those chunks, it eventually will run out of memory.

Whenever a chunk of memory becomes inaccessible, that chunk of memory is called **garbage**. Whenever a program creates garbage, the program has a **memory leak**.

643 Here are the conditions that lead to memory leaks:

- You define a pointer variable or a pointer array.

- You arrange for the pointer to point to a chunk of memory allocated by the new operator at run time.

- You subsequently arrange for the pointer to point to a different chunk of memory.

644 The following is one of the assignment statements in the current version of do_analysis:

```
train[car_count] = new engine (input_buffer);
```

To prevent the memory leak, you use the delete operator before you reassign a pointer and lose your access to the memory you want to reclaim. You can, for example, deploy the delete operator just before the allocation of new objects:

```
...
delete train[car_count];
switch (extract_car_code (input_buffer)) {
  case eng_code:
    train[car_count] = new engine (input_buffer);
    break;
  case box_code:
    train[car_count] = new box_car (input_buffer);
    break;
  case tnk_code:
    train[car_count] = new tank_car (input_buffer);
    break;
  case cab_code:
    train[car_count] = new caboose (input_buffer);
    break;
}
...
```

So situated, the delete operator reclaims memory previously used by previously created class objects. Once reclaimed, memory automatically becomes available for subsequent applications of the new operator.

The first time that do_analysis is called, the train array contains pointers to 0, because the elements of global arrays are initialized to 0 by the C++ compiler. Fortunately, delete does nothing when its argument is 0.

645 You might wonder why C++ does not reclaim memory automatically whenever a pointer is reassigned to a new object created by the new operator. The rationale is that chunks of memory accessed through a pointer are often accessible through more than one pointer. Accordingly, C++ cannot assume that reassignment of a single pointer makes a chunk of memory inaccessible.

646　Alas, although the revised do_analysis function uses the delete operator to reclaim the memory consumed by obsolete and inaccessible class objects, those objects themselves contain pointers to character arrays created at run time—the character arrays that store the serial numbers—and memory reserved for those character arrays is not yet reclaimed.

647　To reclaim the memory in a class-object character array, you take advantage of what are called **destructor functions**, which are member functions that run when the memory for a class object is reclaimed.

Like that of a constructor, the name of the destructor is based on the name of the class, but unlike the constructor name, the destructor name includes a tilde prefix. The following, for example, is the railroad_car class, augmented with a destructor that reclaims memory from the serial_number array:

```
class railroad_car {
  public: char *serial_number;
          // Constructors:
          railroad_car ( ) { }
          railroad_car (char *input_buffer) {
            // Create new array just long enough:
            serial_number = new char[strlen(input_buffer) + 1];
            // Copy string into new array:
            strcpy (serial_number, input_buffer);
          }
          // Destructor:
          ~railroad_car ( ) {
            cout << "Deleting a railroad serial number" << endl;
            delete [ ] serial_number;
          }
          // Other:
          virtual char* short_name ( ) {return "rrc";}
          virtual double capacity ( ) {return 0.0;}
};
```

Note that, when you use the delete operator to reclaim an array of objects, rather than an individual object, you place two brackets, [ ], between the delete operator and the array name. Because C++ keeps track of the lengths of all arrays created by the new operator, C++ can proceed to reclaim all the memory in such an array.

648　Now consider the following statement:

```
delete train[car_count];
```

On the face of it, the delete just reclaims the memory allocated for a class object. But reclaiming that memory activates the destructor for railroad_car objects, thus reclaiming the memory in which the car's name is stored.

649　You might think that the deletion of a railroad car in the train array would activate the appropriate engine, box car, tank car, or caboose destructor. As usual, however, C++ ordinarily does not note whether the objects in the train array, defined to be full of railroad_car objects, belong to a more specific railroad-car type. To force C++ to take into account more specific type information, you must, once again, invoke the virtual-function mechanism, this time on the destructor for the `railroad_car` class, by placing the symbol `virtual` before the destructor definition:

```
class railroad_car {
  public: char *serial_number;
          // Constructors:
          railroad_car ( ) { }
          railroad_car (char *input_buffer) {
            // Create new array just long enough:
            serial_number = new char[strlen(input_buffer) + 1];
            // Copy string into new array:
            strcpy (serial_number, input_buffer);
          }
          // Destructor:
          virtual ~railroad_car ( ) {
            cout << "Deleting a railroad serial number" << endl;
            delete [ ] serial_number;
          }
          // Other:
          virtual char* short_name ( ) {return "rrc";}
          virtual double capacity ( ) {return 0.0;}
};
```

By making the `railroad_car` destructor virtual, you tell C++ to treat all the lower-level destructors as virtual. Thus, a virtual destructor exposes destructors in derived classes.

650 Note that, in contrast to ordinary virtual functions, all the virtual destructors in a hierarchy have different names, rather than identical names, because their names are derived from the names of the classes in which they belong.

651 You may wish to use destructors that contain temporary output statements as an aid to debugging. Such destructors help you to ensure that they run when you think they do, thus helping you to prevent memory leaks. The following definition of the `box_car` class, for example, contains a destructor that only displays:

```
class box_car : public railroad_car, public box {
  public: // Constructors:
          box_car ( ) : box (10.5, 9.5, 40.0) { }
          box_car (char *input_buffer) : railroad_car (input_buffer),
                                 box (10.5, 9.5, 40.0)
            { }
          // Destructor:
          ~box_car ( ) {cout << "Destroying a box car" << endl;}
          // Members:
          virtual char* short_name ( ) {return "box";}
          virtual double capacity ( ) {return volume ( );}
};
```

652 Another way to prevent memory leaks is to keep track of the number of objects that you have created by having constructors and destructors increment and decrement an object counter. You could arrange for a global variable to be the object counter, but you will be a better programmer if you use what is called a **static member variable**.

Normal member variables are duplicated once for each class object. Static member variables are not—there is just one static member variable for the entire class in which the static member variable is defined. Accordingly, a static member variable is a convenient place to store information that pertains to a class as a whole.

653 The following revision of the `railroad_car` class definition shows you how to define a static member variable and how to initialize that member variable. Modified constructors and destructors maintain the static member-variable value, thus keeping track of the total number of railroad cars currently in existence:

```
class railroad_car {
  public: char *serial_number;
          // Constructors:
          railroad_car ( ) {++counter;}
          railroad_car (char *input_buffer) {
            // Keep track of the number:
            ++counter;
            // Create new array just long enough:
            serial_number = new char[strlen(input_buffer) + 1];
            // Copy string into new array:
            strcpy (serial_number, input_buffer);
          }
          // Destructor:
          virtual ~railroad_car ( ) {
            cout << "Destroying a railroad car; "
                 << --counter << " remain." << endl;
            delete [ ] serial_number;
          }
          // Other:
          virtual char* short_name ( ) {return "rrc";}
          virtual double capacity ( ) {return 0.0;}
  private: static int counter;
};
int railroad_car::counter = 0;
```

654 Note that the symbol `static` is used in connection with both member variables and, as
SIDE TRIP described in Segment 705, with global variables.

The meaning is different, however. Used in connection with a member variable, `static` means "there is just one of these member variables for the whole class," whereas used in connection with a global variable, `static` means "this variable is available in only those functions defined in this file."

655 In summary, you have the following version of `analyze_train`:

```cpp
#include <iostream.h>
#include<fstream.h>
#include<string.h>
const double pi = 3.14159;
// ... Box and cylinder class definitions go here ...
class railroad_car {
  public: char *serial_number;
          // Constructors:
          railroad_car ( ) {++counter;}
          railroad_car (char *input_buffer) {
            ++counter;
            serial_number = new char[strlen(input_buffer) + 1];
            strcpy (serial_number, input_buffer);
          }
          // Destructor:
          virtual ~railroad_car ( ) {
            cout << "Destroying a railroad car; "
                 << --counter << " remain." << endl;
            delete [ ] serial_number;
          }
          // Other:
          virtual char* short_name ( ) {return "rrc";}
          virtual double capacity ( ) {return 0.0;}
  private: static int counter;
};
int railroad_car::counter = 0;
// ... Other railroad-car class definitions go here ...
railroad_car *train[100];
char input_buffer[100];
enum {eng_code = 'E', box_code = 'B', tnk_code = 'T', cab_code = 'C'};
char extract_car_code (char *input_buffer) {return input_buffer[4];}
void do_analysis (ifstream &car_stream) {
  int n, car_count;
  for (car_count = 0; car_stream >> input_buffer; ++car_count) {
    delete train[car_count];
    switch (extract_car_code (input_buffer)) {
      case eng_code:
        train[car_count] = new engine (input_buffer); break;
      case box_code:
        train[car_count] = new box_car (input_buffer); break;
      // ... Entries for tank cars and cabooses ...
    }
  }
  car_stream.close ( );
  for (n = 0; n < car_count; ++n)
    cout << train[n] -> serial_number << "      "
         << train[n] -> short_name ( ) << "      "
         << train[n] -> capacity ( ) << endl;
}
```

```
main ( ) {
  // Read file name and call analysis function repeatedly:
  while (1) {
    cout << "Please type the name of a train file." << endl << ": ";
    cin >> input_buffer;
    // Open the input file:
    ifstream car_stream (input_buffer, ios::in);
    // Give up if the input file does not exist:
    if (!car_stream) {cout << "No such file." << endl; return 0;}
    // Analyze:
    do_analysis (car_stream);
    // Close:
    car_stream.close ( );
  }
}
```

656   Note that both the do_analysis function and the railroad_car class contain readily seen new–delete combinations.

Readily seen new–delete combinations is indicative of good programming practice, because you can determine at a glance that memory allocated by a new is eventually reclaimed by a delete. Thus, you can determine at a glance that the new does not cause a memory leak.

The lack of such pairing is considered extremely bad, because it makes memory management much more difficult.

657   Modify the program in Segment 655 such that each railroad car has as a short_name
PRACTICE   member variable. Then, redefine the constructors and short_name member function so as to make use of the new variable. Also, modify the appropriate destructor so that no garbage is left lying around.

658
HIGHLIGHTS

- Inaccessible memory is called garbage.

- Whenever a program creates garbage, the program is said to have a **memory leak**.

- If you wish to plug a memory leak caused by reassignment of a pointer, **then** instantiate one of the following patterns just before the pointer is reassigned:

  ```
  delete pointer name ;
  delete array name [ index ];
  delete [ ] array name ;
  ```

- A destructor is a member function that is run when the memory allocated for a class object is reclaimed.

- Destructors frequently reclaim memory in excess of that reserved for an object by applying the delete operator to member variables that hold array pointers.

- If a pointer is defined for a particular class, **and** the pointer is assigned at run time to an object belonging to a subclass of that defined class, **then** indicate that the destructor is virtual.

- As a rule, most destructors should be virtual destructors.

- In contrast to ordinary member variables, there is only one chunk of memory allocated for every member variable that you define to be static. You can use static member variables to store properties of a class as a whole.

- If you want to define a member variable to be static, **then** add the symbol `static` to that variables declaration.

44 HOW TO PREVENT OBJECT COPYING

659   In Section 43, you learned how to reclaim memory, preventing memory leaks, by using the `delete` operator and destructor functions. In this section, you learn more about memory management in general, and about copy constructors in particular.

660   Subtle problems arise when you define functions with call-by-value parameters that have class objects as values. You have already learned about one such problem: If the object handed to a function actually is a subclass of the parameter's class, only the superclass portion of the object is copied into the memory temporarily reserved for the parameter.

  Another, quite different, problem arises when you define your own destructor functions. In preparation for understanding the problem, you need to examine an example function that has a call-by-value `railroad_car` parameter.

661   Suppose that you decide to count the number of cars whose serial number begins with the three characters, NYC.

  One approach would be to determine whether each railroad car has such a number by way of a member function defined in the `railroad_car` class.

  Imagine, however, that you have no access to the `railroad_car` source code, so you are prevented from adding any member functions. You could try, nevertheless, to achieve your objective by defining an ordinary function, `check_owner`, that takes a railroad-car argument and character-string argument:

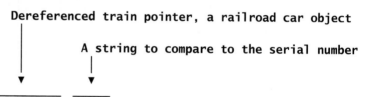

Dereferenced train pointer, a railroad car object

A string to compare to the serial number

```
check_owner (*(train[n]), "NYC")
```

  Once `check_owner` is defined, you can write statements that run `check_owner` over all the cars; increment a variable, `nyc_count`, whenever appropriate; and display a result:

```
int nyc_count = 0;
for (n = 0; n < car_count; ++n)
  if (check_owner (*(train[n]), "NYC"))
    ++nyc_count;
cout << "There are " << nyc_count << "NYC cars." << endl;
```

662   The `check_owner` function, defined next, exhibits a `railroad_car` parameter, a character-pointer parameter, and an integer return value, which is either 0 or 1 depending on whether the car belongs to the railroad specified by the character-pointer parameter. Note that the `check_owner` function uses `strncmp`, a function supplied by the string-handling library, which tests two strings to see whether a specified number of initial characters in the two strings are the same:

```
// DANGEROUS; contributes to difficult-to-find bug:
int check_owner (railroad_car r, char* s) {
  if (strncmp (s, r.serial_number, 3))
    return 0;
  else
    return 1;
}
```

663
SIDE TRIP Actually, the strncmp function checks two strings character by character until in encounters the null character in either string, or encounters mismatching characters, or reaches the specified limit on the number of characters. It returns 0 if the compared characters are all the same, -1 if the first mismatching character in the first string is represented by a integer smaller than that of the corresponding character in the second string, and 1 otherwise.

664 The reason for introducing check_owner is to have a believable function in hand with a class-object, call-by-value parameter. Now that you have it, note that a railroad_car object is copied whenever check_owner is called, because the parameter is a call-by-value parameter:

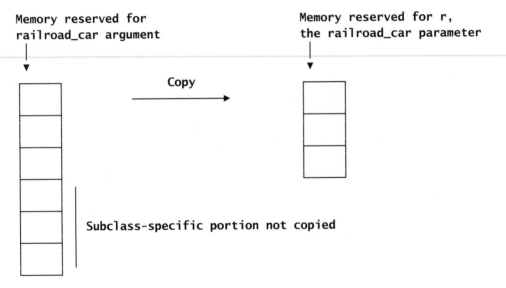

As you know, only the railroad-car portion of the object is copied, inasmuch as the parameter is declared to be a railroad-car parameter. In this particular situation, only the railroad-car portion is needed, however.

665 C++ programs copy objects using a **copy constructor**. The C++ compiler always creates a **default copy constructor** unless you supply one yourself, which you can learn about from C++ handbooks. For the moment, you need to know only that the default copy constructor works by copying the contents of the member variables.

Accordingly, if a member variable contains a pointer, the pointer is copied, but the target of the pointer is not copied. Each railroad-car class object contains a pointer to a serial number, for example. The default copy constructor copies the pointer, but does not copy the chunk of memory reserved for the serial number; that chunk of memory is shared:

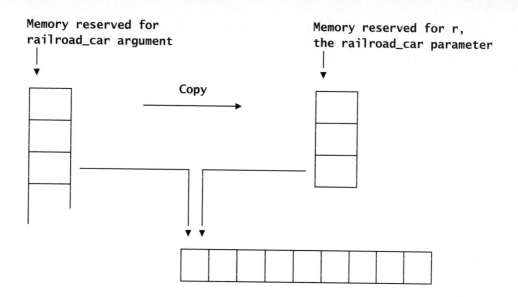

Memory reserved for
railroad_car argument

Memory reserved for r,
the railroad_car parameter

Copy

666   A problem emerges if you happen to define a destructor for the railroad_car class that reclaims the chunk of memory reserved for the serial number. In Section 43, you learned that you can define such a destructor in the railroad_car class definition as follows:

```
class railroad_car {
  public: char *serial_number;
          // Constructors:
          railroad_car ( ) { }
          railroad_car (char *input_buffer) {
            // Create new array just long enough:
            serial_number = new char[strlen(input_buffer) + 1];
            // Copy string into new array:
            strcpy (serial_number, input_buffer);
          }
          // Destructor:
          virtual ~railroad_car ( ) {
            delete [ ] serial_number;
          }
          // Other:
          virtual char* short_name ( ) {return "rrc";}
          virtual double capacity ( ) {return 0.0;}
};
```

667   The reason a problem emerges is that the destructor runs whenever the memory for a class object is reclaimed:

- As you know, memory is reclaimed when the delete operator is called explicitly.

- Memory is also reclaimed whenever you return from a function with a call-by-value class-object argument.

In the example, the destructor runs because the memory for a railroad-car copy is reclaimed, but, unfortunately, the destructor further reclaims the memory chunk allocated for the serial number, which is shared with the original object:

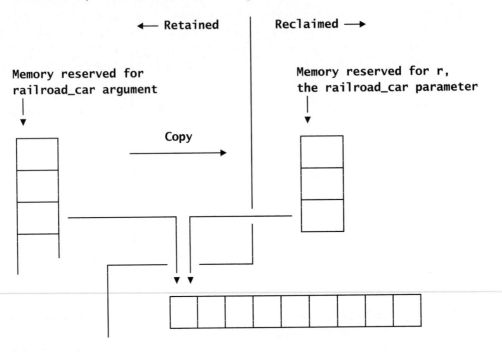

Thus, after the call to check_owner returns, the surviving railroad_car object has a pointer to memory that has been reclaimed:

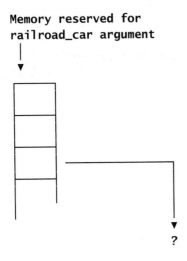

The pointer to reclaimed memory may still provide a serial number, when followed, for a while, until there is a need for the reclaimed memory. Eventually, however, the program is likely to stub its toe, for the reclaimed memory is likely to be overwritten by a subsequent call to the new operator.

The time separation between the flawed behavior and the resulting disaster makes the **excess-reclamation bug** extremely difficult to track down.

670 There are two ways to fix the excessive-reclamation problem introduced by the destructor. One way is to define your own copy constructor such that the entire serial number is copied, rather than only the pointer. Then, when the destructor reclaims the copy's car-number memory chunk, no harm is done to the original car-number memory chunk:

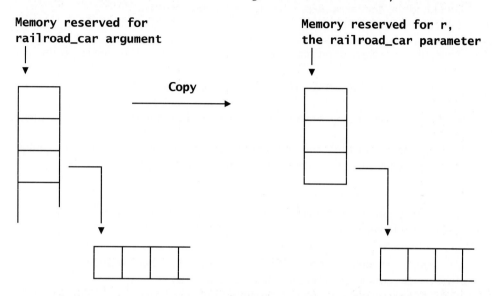

671 Another approach to the excessive-reclamation problem is to convert the parameter from a call-by-value parameter to a call-by-reference parameter. Then, no copy is made; no copy memory is reclaimed; and the destructor is never called:

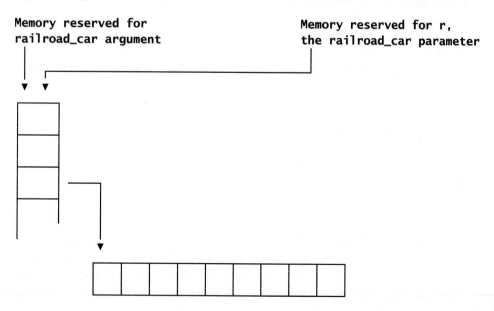

672 Of the two approaches, the conversion to use a call-by-reference parameter is generally the one preferred by virtue of the following philosophy-of-language point:

- Objects generally represent individuals in the real world. Any object creation, copying, or destruction should mimic corresponding actions in that real world.

It follows that objects should not be copied merely because a function is called, and objects should not be destroyed merely because a function returns.

673 Thus, there are three good reasons to avoid call-by-value class-object parameters:

- As you learned in Section 37, the subclass portion of a class argument is not copied.

- As you learned in this section, copying can lead to obscure excessive-reclamation bugs.

- Copying at call time and reclamation at return time go against the philosophy-of-language principle that identifies objects with real-world individuals.

674 The appropriate improvement to the `check_owner` function is to convert the parameter to call by reference:

```
// Improved; cannot contribute to excessive-reclamation bug:
int check_owner (railroad_car& r, char* s) {
  if (strncmp (s, r.serial_number, 3))
    return 0;
  else
    return 1;
}
```

675 Because your class-object parameters should be call-by-reference parameters, rather than call-by-value parameters, you may want to use a trick to prevent yourself from inadvertently introducing a call-by-value class-object parameter.

- Define your own copy constructor, thus displacing the default copy constructor that the C++ compiler would otherwise create.

- Ensure that your copy constructor cannot be called by placing it in the private part of its class definition.

Because your copy constructors are in the private parts of the class definitions in which they appear, any attempt at copying—introduced inadvertently by a call-by-value parameter—leads to a compiler error.

676 To define your own copy constructor for the `railroad_car` class, you proceed as follows:

```
class railroad_car {
  public: char *serial_number;
          // Constructors:
          railroad_car ( ) { }
          railroad_car (char *input_buffer) {
            // Create new array just long enough:
            serial_number = new char[strlen(input_buffer) + 1];
            // Copy string into new array:
            strcpy (serial_number, input_buffer);
          }
          // Destructor:
          virtual ~railroad_car ( ) {
            delete [ ] serial_number;
          }
          // Other:
          virtual char* short_name ( ) {return "rrc";}
          virtual double capacity ( ) {return 0.0;}
  private:
          // Never-to-be-called copy-constructor prototype:
          railroad_car (railroad_car&);
};
```

Note that it is enough to provide a function prototype; inasmuch as the function is never to be called, there is no need to provide a body.

It is also enough to provide a never-to-be-called copy-constructor function prototype in only the topmost class of every class hierarchy, because whenever any object in the class is copied, the topmost copy constructor has to be called.

677 Because of all the excessive-reclamation problems that come up when copy constructors are used in the presence of destructors, many experienced C++ programmers adhere to the following maxim:

- If you define a destructor in a class, define a copy constructor as well.

Usually, you will define the copy constructor to prevent copying.

678 You have learned that the use of railroad_car objects as call-by-value parameters can lead
PRACTICE to excessive reclamation bugs. The best way to avoid such bugs is to use call-by-reference parameters instead. Then, you ensure that you do not inadvertently use a call-by-value parameter by defining a private copy constructor.

Another way to avoid excessive reclamation is to rewrite the railroad_car destructor. Now it reads as follows:

```
virtual ~railroad_car ( ) {delete [ ] serial_number;}
```

You can change it to

```
virtual ~railroad_car ( ) { }
```

What is wrong with this alternative?

Suppose that you omit the copy constructor suggested for the `railroad_car` class, but you include the following copy constructors in the `box` and `cylinder` classes private portions:

```
box (box&);
cylinder (cylinder&);
```

Do these copy constructors prevent you from inadvertently copying `railroad_car` objects?

- Call-by-value class-object parameters can lead to excessive-reclamation bugs.

- You should avoid call-by-value class-object parameters.

- If you want to ensure that you have no call-by-value class-object parameters **then** insert the following copy-constructor function prototype into the private portion of the topmost class in each class hierarchy:

```
class name (class name &);
```

45 HOW TO ORGANIZE
A MULTIPLE-FILE PROGRAM

681 In Section 16, you learned about the organization of class hierarchies. In this section, you learn about the organization of files.

At this point, the `analyze_train` program has grown complex, so you might think about breaking in up into simple modules, one per file. In this section, you learn how to construct multiple-file programs.

682 Suppose, for the sake of illustration, that you decide to divide the `analyze_train` program into three files:

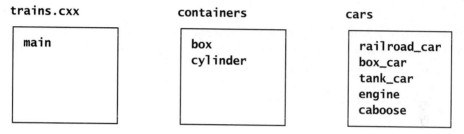

With the `analyze_train` program is so divided, you could use `#include` declarations to incorporate the text in the `containers` file and the `cars` file back into the `trains.cxx` file:

```
#include "containers"
#include "cars"
...
```

When the C++ compiler sees such `#include` declarations, it suspends its examination of the current file temporarily and pretends that the text of the included file is actually in the current file at that place:

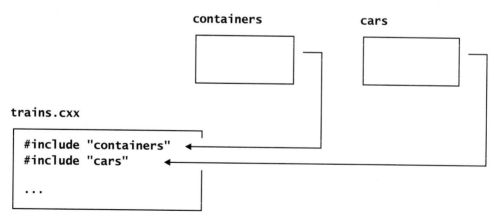

683 Note that, when a file specification is surrounded by double-quotation marks, "···", the C++ compiler attempts to find the file in the current directory—which is presumably the same one that contains the source-code file.

If that attempt fails, most compilers try harder, as you learn in Segment 694.

684   Although you may choose to put complete class definitions into included files, most seasoned C++ programmers divide class definitions into two files: a special **header file** and a **source file** that contains function definitions. As you learn later in this section, such division enables you to divide large programs into multiple, independently compilable files.

The general rule is that header files *should contain* only declarations; they *should not contain* any storage-allocating definitions.

Thus, header files should contain only member function prototypes, not member function definitions. The actual definitions of the member functions go in ordinary source-code files with cxx extensions.

By convention, you always give header files an h extension, for *header*, rather than a cxx extension.

685   Thus, you can divide the box and cylinder class definitions into two files: a header file and a source-code file:

```
// containers class definitions (h extension)


// box class definition:

class box {
  public: double height, width, length;
    // Prototypes:
    box ( )
    box (double, double, double)
    double volume ( )
};


// cylinder class definition

class cylinder {
  public: double radius, length;
    // Prototypes:
    cylinder ( )
    cylinder (double, double)
    double volume ( )
};
```

```
// Containers source-code file (cxx extension)

#include "containers.h"
const double pi = 3.14159;

box::box ( ) { }
box::box (double h, double w, double l) {
  height = h; width = w; length = l;
}
double box::volume ( ) {
  return height * width * length;
}

cylinder::cylinder ( ) { }
cylinder::cylinder (double r, double l) {
  radius = r; length = l;
}
double cylinder::volume ( ) {
  return pi * radius * radius * length;
}
```

You can, of course, divide the railroad-car class definitions into header and function files as well.

686   The class definitions and function prototypes in the containers.h and cars.h header files are all that the C++ compiler needs to compile the trains.cxx file. Similarly, the information in the containers.h header file is all that the C++ compiler needs to compile containers.cxx, and the cars.h header file is all that the C++ compiler needs to compile cars.cxx:

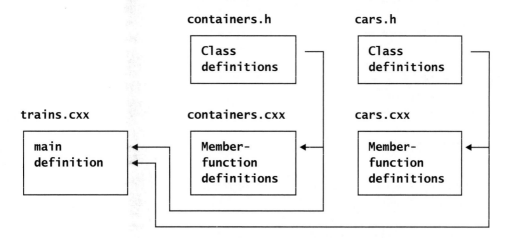

687   With the header files properly included, you can use the C++ compiler to compile each source-code file separately, producing object code. The object-code files, by convention, have o extensions:

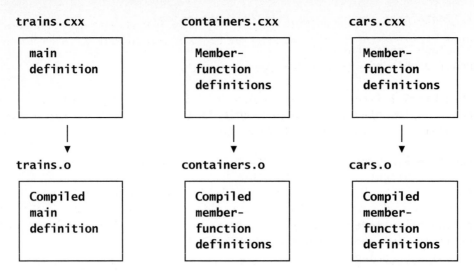

Most of the work required to translate source code into an executable program lies in producing object files. Fortunately, when you make changes in a big, multiple-file program, you need to recompile only the altered files; you leave unaltered files alone.

688 Later, you use the C++ compiler again to link the object files into an executable program:

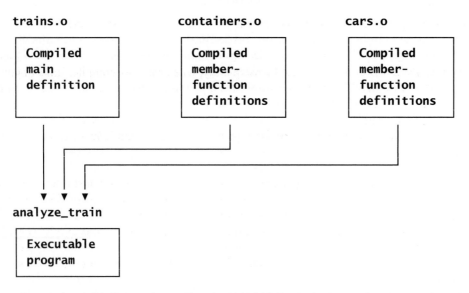

The process of linking object files requires relatively little work compared to the work required to produce object files from source-code files.

689 To produce an object file from a source-code file, you issue a command to the compiler with the -c option. In the following, for example, the compiler and linker, which happens to be named CC, produces a trains.o file:

```
CC -c trains.cxx
```

If you wish, you can produce several object files at once. In the following, for example, you produce three object files as though you had issued three commands to the C++ compiler.

```
CC -c trains.cxx containers.cxx cars.cxx
```

690 Once you have object files ready, you can link them into an executable program file with another command to the C++ compiler. In the following, the -o option instructs the C++ compiler to name the executable file `analyze_train`:

```
CC -o analyze_train trains.o containers.o cars.o
```

691 Note that, if you change just one source-code file, you need only to recompile it into an object file and link it with the object files previously produced from unchanged source-code files. You save time, because you do not have to wait for your C++ compiler to produce object code from most of your source-code files.

Suppose, for example, that you have a working `analyze_train` program, but you make a change in the `trains.cxx` source-code file. You therefore need to recompile `trains.cxx`:

```
CC -c trains.cxx
```

Then, you need to relink the object files:

```
CC -o analyze_train trains.o containers.o cars.o
```

You do not, however, need to recompile `containers.cxx` or `cars.cxx`.

692 Of course, you nearly always include header files, such as `iostream.h`, for functions supplied by C++ standard library. Consequently, when the C++ compiler links object files to create an executable program, it encounters functions for which it has seen function prototypes but no corresponding function definitions. Whenever that happens, the C++ compiler looks for the appropriate object code in a **standard library file**. The location of this standard library file generally is provided to the compiler when the compiler is installed.

693 Because there are many header files for the object code in the standard library file, each header file covers only a fraction of the functions in the standard library file. The reason is that many C++ compilers bring every function mentioned in a header file into your program, even those functions that you do not use. By creating multiple header files, a library's author makes it possible for you to use the library file selectively, reducing the degree to which your programs are bloated with functions that you do not use.

694 Note that, when a header file specification is surrounded by angle brackets < ··· >, the C++ compiler first looks for that header file in a directory known by your C++ compiler to contain header files for the standard library. Later on, when the C++ compiler needs the object code corresponding to the function prototypes in a header file, it looks for that object code in a directory known to contain the standard library file.

In contrast, when the file specification is surrounded by double-quotation marks, " ··· ", the C++ compiler first looks for the header file in the current directory—which is presumably the same one that contains the source-code file.

Whenever the first look produces no header file, most compilers look elsewhere. For file specifications with angle brackets, the second look is likely to be the current directory; for file specifications with double-quotation marks, the second look is likely to be the standard library's directory.

Many compilers also allow you to specify additional places to look by way of a command line argument.

695 Of course, if you change a header file, you must recompile all the source-code files in which that header file is included.

696 To gain a more complete understanding of multiple-file programs, you need to learn how to distribute not only class definitions, but also function prototypes and ordinary function definitions among header files and source-code files.

As an illustration, consider again the three-function version of the rabbit-calculating program introduced in Section 23. Recall that the purpose of the program is to calculate the number of rabbits after n months, given one newborn female rabbit at time 0.

The program contains three key functions:

```
int rabbits (int n) {
  if (n == 0 ¦¦ n == 1)
    return 1;
  else return previous_month (n) + penultimate_month (n);}
int previous_month (int n) {return rabbits ((n - 1));}
int penultimate_month (int n) {return rabbits ((n - 2));}
```

697 Suspending disbelief, suppose that you decide to "improve" the rabbits program by dividing it into three files, one for each of the three key functions. One file, rabbits.cxx, contains main and rabbits:

```
//  The rabbits.cxx file
#include <iostream.h>
// ... Space reserved to include files ...
int rabbits (int n) {
  if (n == 0 ¦¦ n == 1)
    return 1;
  else return previous_month (n) + penultimate_month (n);}
main ( ) {
  int months;
  cout << "Please supply the number of months.
       << endl;
  cin >> months;
  cout << "After "
       << months << " months, there are "
       << rabbits(months) << "rabbits."
       << endl;
}
```

The other files, `previous.cxx` and `penultimate.cxx` are simpler:

```
// The previous.cxx file
// ... Space reserved to include files ...
int previous_month (int n) {return rabbits ((n - 1));}

// The penultimate.cxx file
// ... Space reserved to include files ...
int penultimate_month (int n) {return rabbits ((n - 2));}
```

698   Having divided your program into three files, you now note that each file contains a function that uses at least one function defined in another file. Thus, you cannot compile any file without providing the C++ compiler with information about those externally defined functions by way of function prototypes. The usual approach is to place those function prototypes in header files, which you then include where needed in other files:

```
// The rabbits.h file
int rabbits (int);

// The previous.h file
int previous (int);

// The penultimate.h file
int penultimate (int);
```

699   A function prototype is a declaration, rather than a definition, because it provides the C++ compiler with information about a function that is defined elsewhere. Remember that the C++ compiler accepts repeated function prototypes, but complains whenever it encounters repeated function definitions.

700   Because the `rabbits.h` header file contains a function prototype for the `rabbits` function, `rabbits.h` provides the information the C++ compiler needs to compile the two other files, `previous.cxx` and `penultimate.cxx`. Accordingly, you should include `rabbits.h` in both `previous.cxx` and `penultimate.cxx`.

You should also include each header file in its corresponding source-code file. That way, should there be any discrepancy between the function prototype provided in the header file and the function definition provided in the source-code file, your C++ compiler should note the discrepancy and complain.

Thus, each of your source-code files should contain at least one included header file, and may contain several.

701   The following is the complete collection of `cxx` files that comprise the `rabbits` program:

```
// The rabbits.cxx file
#include <iostream.h>
#include "previous.h"
#include "penultimate.h"
int rabbits (int n) {
  if (n == 0 || n == 1)
     return 1;
   else return previous_month (n) + penultimate_month (n);}
main ( ) {
  int months;
  cout << "Please supply the number of months.
        << endl;
  cin >> months;
  cout << "After "
       << months << " months, there are "
       << rabbits(months) << "rabbits."
       << endl;
}

// The previous.cxx file
#include "previous.h"
#include "rabbits.h"
int previous_month (int n) {return rabbits ((n - 1));}

// The penultimate.cxx file
#include "penultimate.h"
#include "rabbits.h"
int penultimate_month (int n) {return rabbits ((n - 2));}
```

702   Next, you need to learn how to distribute global-variable declarations and global-variable definitions among header files and source-code files.

As explained in Segment 129, when you define a global variable, you tell the compiler to allocate a chunk of memory for the variable. Consider the following definition, for example:

```
int mode;
```

Such a definition, appearing outside of any function definition, tells the C++ compiler to allocate storage for the mode variable.

If you wish to make use of the mode global variable in another file, you must so inform the C++ compiler by inserting a declaration in that other file. When you *declare* a global variable, you tell the compiler that the global variable is *defined* in an object file available to the C++ linker when it is time to link together object files into an executable program.

703   To declare a global variable, you precede its type declaration with the symbol extern.

For example, suppose that the global variable named mode is used to decide which of various alternative computational paths are to be taken in functions defined in multiple files. Such a variable might, for example, control a speed-versus-accuracy tradeoff.

To be accessible in multiple files, `mode` must be defined in one file and declared in the others:

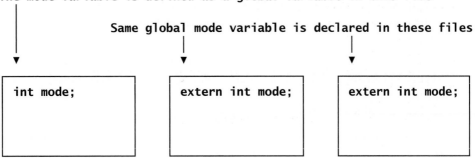

704   The most convenient place to declare global variables is, of course, in a header file that is included in every file where the global variable is evaluated or assigned.

Note that you *must not* include an initial value where `extern` is used. An initial value forces the C++ compiler to allocate memory for the variable, thus establishing the variable's definition, which can be done only once.

705   Of course, there are occasions when you want to keep the global variables in one file out
SIDE TRIP   of the way of the global variables in another file.

Suppose, for example, that you and a partner have divided the work of writing a program into two parts. Each of you works on a file full of functions. Both of you have employed a global variable named, accidentally, `mode`. Ordinarily, your separate use of that variable name will lead your C++ compiler to note a multiple-variable–definition error when those files are linked together.

Fortunately, if you add `static` to the definition of a global variable, then the value of that global variable is accessible to only those functions defined in the same file.

Accordingly, one or both of you can define the variable to be static:

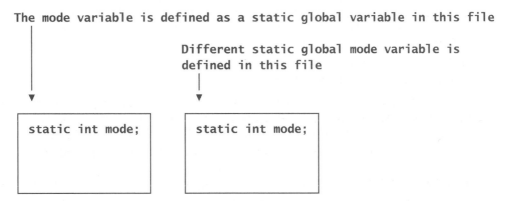

Because of the use of `static` in the variable definitions, the variables keep out of each other's way.

706 The following general rules will help you to keep global variable declarations and function declarations properly separated from their definitions:

- You must define global variables and functions only once. Accordingly, you must keep definitions out of header files, which are likely to be included into many source-code files.

- You may declare global variables (using **extern**) and functions (using function prototypes) repeatedly, so long as each declaration is the same. Accordingly, you can place such declarations in header files that you use to inform many source-code files about global variables and functions.

707 Given the rules for declarations and definitions, you now can reflect a bit on how class
SIDE TRIP definitions are distributed between header files and source-code files.

In particular, note that a class definition without internally defined member-function definitions is more properly called a declaration, because such a definition tells the C++ compiler what memory to allocate when an object belonging to the class is created, but it does not actually allocate any memory. Accordingly, the proper place for such a class definition is a header file.

708 C++ does not prevent you from defining member functions in class definitions provided in
SIDE TRIP header files. At first, such member-function definitions may seem to violate the principle that functions are to be defined only once, because header files are likely to be included in multiple source files.

Nevertheless, you can get away with such definitions, because the developers of C++ have gone to considerable trouble to make such definitions possible, albeit not preferred.

First, your C++ compiler tries to compile the member functions defined inside a class definition as **inline functions**.

Recall that, each time an ordinary function appears, the C++ compiler arranges for the calling function to suspend what it is doing. Then, the program assigns parameters to arguments, jumps to the body of the called function, returns a value from that called function, and resumes where it left off in the calling function.

In contrast, each time an inline function appears, the C++ compiler substitutes the body of the function at that place. There is no subsequent function call, with parameter assignment and value returning; instead, the body of the inline function becomes part of the body of the calling function.

Accordingly, when an inline function appears, the C++ compiler needs only to prepare to substitute its body into places where the function is called; no program memory is allocated for the function at the time the function definition appears. Thus, an inline function definition actually is more like a declaration than an ordinary definition.

709 Note, however, that the C++ compiler is committed only to *try* to compile internally de-
SIDE TRIP fined member functions as inline functions. If an internally defined member function is deemed too complex for the C++ compiler to compile, the C++ compiler actually, incredibly, produces a distinct version of the member function each time that the class definition reappears. If a header file contains such a class definition, and if that header file is included in 10 files, then 10 identical versions of the member function are compiled. Because a

distinct function is produced each time that the function definition is encountered in an included header file, there is—in a certain convoluted sense—no violation of the rule that each function definition must appear only once.

710 PRACTICE Suppose you have developed a system with the file dependencies indicated in the following diagram. Further suppose that you have developed appropriate header files, and that you have arranged for each of the ordinary files to include the appropriate header files.

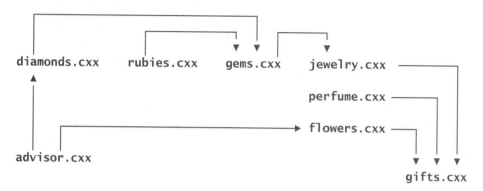

Now, suppose that gifts.h accidentally contains a definition for an ordinary function. Why would that function definition cause a problem when you try to compile the advisor program? How can you resolve the problem?

711 PRACTICE Suppose that the jewelry, perfume, and flowers files mentioned in Segment 710 all make use of a global variable named price_limit. Where should that variable be defined? Where should it be declared?

712 PRACTICE Suppose that the jewelry, perfume, and flowers files mentioned in Segment 710 accidentally happen to have global variables named urgency, all of which are to be considered separate. Where should these variables be defined? Where should they be declared?

713 HIGHLIGHTS

- Header files should contain class definitions, global variable declarations, and function prototypes for every class, global variable, and function that you expect to appear in more than one file.

- You may include member-function definitions in the bodies of class definitions that appear in header files. Externally defined member-function definitions must appear in source-code files; they cannot appear in header files that are included in more than one file.

- If you want to declare an ordinary function, **then** leave behind a function prototype:

  `return data type` `function name` `( data type of parameter 1 ,`
  `... ,`
  `data type of parameter n )`

- If you want to declare a global variable, **then** instantiate the following pattern:

  `extern` `data type` `variable name` `;`

- You can declare functions and variables as often as you like. You can define them only once.

- If you want to compile a set of files independently, **then** include appropriate header files **and** instantiate the following pattern:

  `CC -c` `first source specification` `···`

- If you want to link together a set of independently compiled files to form a working program, **then** instantiate the following pattern on one line:

  `CC -o` `executable file specification`
  `first object file specification`
  `···`

46 HOW TO COMPILE
A MULTIPLE-FILE PROGRAM

714 When you build big programs, with many header and source-code files, you eventually lose track of what depends on what. Accordingly, most operating systems that support C++ provide what is called the make utility. The basic idea is that you describe dependencies in a file that a compilation program uses to figure out what needs to be recompiled and relinked.

715 When you compile a multiple-file program using the make utility, the file describing dependencies is called a **makefile.**

Over the years, the make utility has come to offer more and more features, with a corresponding increase in syntactic complexity. Consequently, expert programmers often write makefiles that are extremely difficult for beginners to read. Nevertheless, simple makefiles are easy to write and read, even for C++ beginners, and you should learn to use them early on.

716 Recall that the executable file, analyze_train, described in Section 45, depends on three object files. This dependency is reflected in a makefile line in which analyze_train appears, followed by a colon, followed by a list of the depended-on files:

```
analyze_train: trains.o containers.o cars.o
```

A similar line asserts that the trains.o file depends on the trains.cxx file and two included header files:

```
trains.o: trains.cxx containers.h cars.h
```

Finally, the following lines assert that the object files containing member functions depend on both source code files and header files:

```
containers.o: containers.cxx containers.h
cars.o: cars.cxx cars.h containers.h
```

Note that dependency lines *must* begin in the first column—no spaces or tabs are permitted.

717 Makefiles also contain information about what to do when a depended-on file changes. This information is provided in command lines, each of which immediately follows a dependency line. The command line looks like a command that you would issue yourself if you were providing a command line by hand. For example, if you were to relink the object files to produce a new analyze_train program, you would issue the following command:

```
CC -o analyze_train trains.o containers.o cars.o
```

Note, however, that command lines in makefiles *must* begin with a tab character:

```
	CC -o analyze_train trains.o containers.o cars.o
```

718 Accordingly, a makefile for the analyze_train program would contain a dependency line describing analyze_train file dependencies and a corresponding command line:

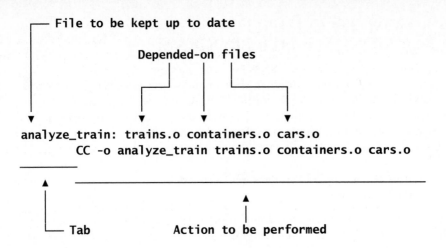

File to be kept up to date

Depended-on files

```
analyze_train: trains.o containers.o cars.o
        CC -o analyze_train trains.o containers.o cars.o
```

Tab   Action to be performed

719 The following is a complete makefile for the `analyze_train` program; note that the `make` utility interprets as comments lines beginning with # characters:

```
# makefile for analyze_train program

analyze_train: trains.o containers.o cars.o
        CC -o analyze_train trains.o containers.o cars.o

trains.o: trains.cxx containers.h cars.h
        CC -c trains.cxx

containers.o: containers.cxx containers.h
        CC -c containers.cxx

cars.o: cars.cxx cars.h containers.h
        CC -c cars.cxx
```

The `make` utility is smart enough to propagate changes properly through the dependencies. For example, noting a change to the `cars.cxx` file, `make` produces a new `cars.o` object-code file. Then, noting a change to the `cars.o` file, `make` produces a new `analyze_train` executable file.

720 With the makefile complete, and is named `makefile`, you need only to issue the following command to have every file in your program brought up to date:

```
make
```

If you wish, you can use another name for your makefile—say `Make_analyze_train`. Then, you supply that name to the make command:

```
make Make_analyze_train
```

721 Assume that the function-definition problem in the `gifts.h` file mentioned in Segment 710
PRACTICE has been resolved. Create a makefile for the `advisor` program.

- **If** you want to keep a multiple-file program up to date, **then** create a makefile named `makefile`, **and** issue the following command to your computer:

  `make`

- **If** you want to express how one program file depends on others, **then** instantiate the following pattern in your makefile, taking care to start in the first column:

  `file name : list of depended-on files`

- **If** you want to express what should be done when a change occurs in a depended-on file, **then** instantiate the following pattern, taking care to start with a tab:

  `compiler command`

  ▲
  └── Tab

47 HOW TO IMPLEMENT LISTS

723   In this section, you learn about storing objects in lists. There are several reasons why learning about lists is important, the most conspicuous of which is that the implementation of lists demonstrates that you can use C++ classes to implement programming-language features, as well as to represent domain-specific concepts.

Another reason to learn about lists is that list manipulation is a useful tool. When you use a list, instead of an ordinary array, you do not need to anticipate how many objects you will need to store, so you can conserve the space that would be wasted by safe worst-case estimates.

A third reason to learn about lists is that list manipulation provides a compelling context for the introduction of other C++ concepts such as *class friends* and *template functions*.

To work with lists in C++, you have to extend the language by defining new C++ classes and member functions. Understanding what you have to do is not easy, so once you have understood the material in this and the remaining sections, you can consider yourself well beyond the novice stage as a C++ programmer.

724   So far, you have seen `analyze_train` programs in which trains are represented as one-dimensional arrays of pointers to railroad-car objects. The principal defect of such a representation is that you always wonder whether you have allocated an array that is long enough to hold all possible trains, yet not so long as to waste a great deal of never-to-be-used space.

725   One alternative is to include a pointer to a railroad car in the definition of the `railroad_car` class itself. To create a train, you simply arrange for each `railroad_car` object in the train, except for the final one, to carry a pointer to the next railroad car. The last `railroad_car` object carries a pointer to 0, also known as the **null pointer**.

The following, for example, illustrates how you would arrange the pointers in a three-car train list:

Three railroad_car objects, with pointers inside:

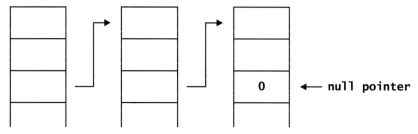

Such pointers are called **internal pointers,** because they are stored *inside* the class objects whose primary purpose is to describe domain-specific individuals.

726   When objects are linked together by pointers, the objects are said to be in a **list**. Each object in a list is called an **element** of the list.

727   For two reasons, most experienced programmers *rarely* use internal pointers to create lists:

- When you use internal pointers to create lists, you must add a new member variable to the class definition that defines the objects you want to tie together. You may not have access to that class definition; moreover, you always should be slow to muck around with existing, debugged class definitions.

- You may want to include particular railroad-car class objects in more than one list, such as a train list, a box-car list, a full-car list, or an old-car list. It would be incredibly awkward to add internal pointers for each such list.

728   Fortunately, you can create lists without using internal pointers. You can create a new class, the link class. Objects in this new class have two pointers; one points to the next link object, and the other points to a railroad_car object. The following illustrates the role of link objects in a three-car train list:

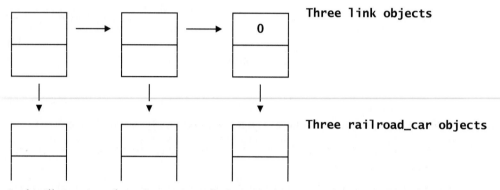

Three link objects

Three railroad_car objects

In this illustration, the pointers are called **external pointers**, because they are stored *outside* the class objects.

729   External pointers have the following advantages relative to internal pointers:

- You do not need to alter the class definition of the objects that you want to tie together.

- You can include particular railroad-car class objects in as many lists as you like, without further class redefinition.

- You can include objects that belong to railroad_car subclasses.

730   At this point, you are ready to learn about an implementation of lists using external pointers. This implementation involves not only a link class, but also a header class. Each header object, one per list, contains a pointer to the first link object. If the list is empty, the link pointer is the null pointer, as in the following illustration:

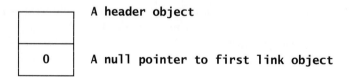

A header object

A null pointer to first link object

The following illustration shows a list that contains three cars:

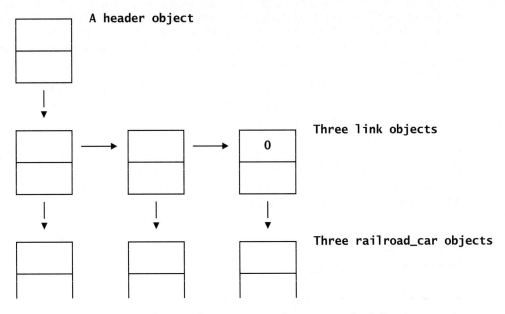

A header object

Three link objects

0

Three railroad_car objects

731   To design the **header** and **link** classes, you need to answer the following questions:

- What member variables do you need for the pointers involved?

- What member functions do you need to create lists, to add new list elements, and to access existing elements?

- Which member variables and member functions should be private, which should be protected, and which should be public?

For the moment, you can defer the private–protected–public question by making all member variables and member functions public. Later, with all the answers to the other questions behind you, you can make the adjustments that sensibly allocate the member variables and member functions to the appropriate portions of the class definitions.

732   In the **header** definition, you need to declare a pointer to the first **link** object; in the **link** definition, you need to declare a member variable for a pointer to the next **link** object and a member variable for a pointer to a **railroad_car** object. The definition of the **link** class must come first, because a **link** pointer appears in the definition of the **header** class:

```
class link {
  public:  link *next_link_pointer;
           railroad_car *element_pointer;
           ...
};
class header {
  public:  link *first_link_pointer;
           ...
};
```

733 Next, you need a way to create an empty list—one that has no link objects. More specifically, you need a header constructor that explicitly assigns first_link_pointer to the null pointer 0, such as in the following definition:

```
class header {
  public:  link *first_link_pointer;
           header ( ) {
             first_link_pointer = 0;
           }
           ...
};
```

734 Many programmers prefer to assign pointer variables to the null pointer by using the NULL macro:

```
class header {
  public:  link *first_link_pointer;
           header ( ) {
             first_link_pointer = NULL;
           }
           ...
};
```

As explained in Segment 136, the C++ compiler replaces the characters in macros before regular compilation begins. Instances of the NULL macro, which happens to be declared in the iostream.h header file, are replaced by 0. By using NULL instead of 0, you identify the places where 0 is used as a special pointer, rather than as an ordinary integer, thereby increasing program clarity.

735 You also need a function for adding an element to a list. In the simple implementation described here, all additions are made to the front of the list using the add member function. When you use add, you instantiate the following pattern:

```
A header variable
    │
    │    Name of the element-adding function
    │        │
    ▼        ▼
train.add ( pointer to a railroad_car object );
```

736 Because add works on header objects, add is a member function of the header class. Because add adds a pointer to a new railroad_car object, provided as an ordinary argument, add must have a parameter that is declared to be a pointer to a railroad_car object. Because there is to be no return value, add's return type is void:

```
class header {
  public:  link *first_link_pointer;
           header ( ) {
             first_link_pointer = NULL;
           }
           void add (railroad_car *new_element) {
             ...
           }
           ...
};
```

737 The work done by add involves several pointers. As an illustration of how add works, suppose that you want to add a third element onto a two-element list. First, add must create a new link object with pointers to the old first element and to the new object:

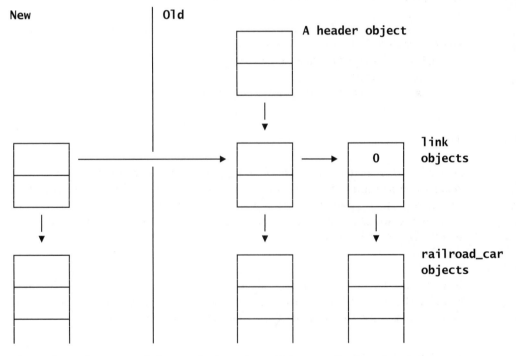

738 Note, then, that part of the work done by add is actually done by the two-argument constructor for the link class:

```
class link {
  public:
    link *next_link_pointer;
    railroad_car *element_pointer;
    link (railroad_car *e, link *l) {
      element_pointer = e;
      next_link_pointer = l;
    }
};
```

The link constructor is called when a new link object is created inside of the add member function:

```
class header {
  public:
    link *first_link_pointer;
    header ( ) {
      first_link_pointer = NULL;
    }
    void add (railroad_car *new_element) {
      first_link_pointer = new link (new_element, first_link_pointer);
      ...
    }
    ...
};
```

Note that the add member function arranges for the value of the first_link_pointer variable to be the address of the new link object. Thus, add reroutes the pointer in the header object to point to the new link:

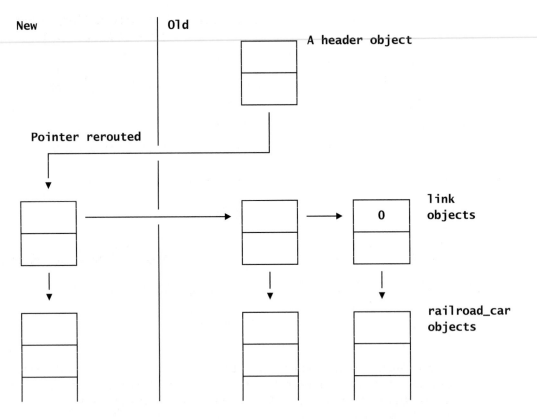

739 At this point, your definitions are such that you can construct an empty list and add elements to an existing list, but you cannot get at a list's elements. To get at the elements, you need the following:

- A pointer, `current_link_pointer`

- A function, `advance`, that advances `current_link_pointer` from one `link` to the next

- A function, `access`, that obtains a pointer to a `railroad_car` object from the `link` pointed at by `current_link_pointer`

- A function, endp, for *end* predicate, that determines whether `current_link_pointer`'s value is NULL

- A function, `reset`, that assigns the value of `current_link_pointer` to the value of `first_link_pointer`

740   Thus, to access the elements in a list, you have your program use `advance` to move `current_link_pointer`:

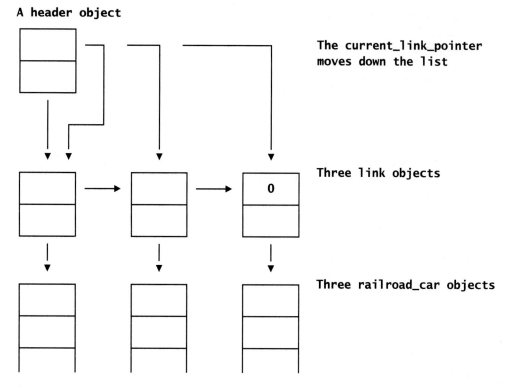

A header object

The current_link_pointer moves down the list

Three link objects

Three railroad_car objects

As your program moves `current_link_pointer` along, it can access elements using `access` until `endp` determines that there are no more elements. Then, your program can use `reset` to return `current_link_pointer` to its original position.

741   When lists are created or elements are added, `current_link_pointer` is assigned to the value of `first_link_pointer`:

```
class header {
  public:
    link *first_link_pointer;
    link *current_link_pointer;
    header ( ) {
      first_link_pointer = NULL;
      current_link_pointer = first_link_pointer;
    }
    void add (railroad_car *new_element) {
      first_link_pointer = new link (new_element, first_link_pointer);
      current_link_pointer = first_link_pointer;
    }
    ...
};
```

742 To advance the current_link_pointer down the list, you need advance, a member function that digs next_link_pointer out of the link identified by current_link_pointer:

```
class header {
  public:
    link *first_link_pointer;
    link *current_link_pointer;
    header ( ) {
      first_link_pointer = NULL;
      current_link_pointer = first_link_pointer;
    }
    ...
    void advance ( ) {
      current_link_pointer = current_link_pointer -> next_link_pointer;
    }
    ...
};
```

743 To get at element, you define access, which returns a pointer to a railroad_car object:

```
class header {
  public:
    link *first_link_pointer;
    link *current_link_pointer;
    header ( ) {
      first_link_pointer = NULL;
      current_link_pointer = first_link_pointer;
    }
    ...
    railroad_car* access ( ) {
      return current_link_pointer -> element_pointer;
    }
    ...
};
```

744   To determine whether a list has been traversed completely, you define endp. The endp predicate is easy to define, because, when you work on a pointer with the negation operation, the result is 0, of type int, if the pointer is the null pointer; otherwise, the result is 1, of type int:

```
class header {
  public:
    link *first_link_pointer;
    link *current_link_pointer;
    header ( ) {
      first_link_pointer = NULL;
      current_link_pointer = first_link_pointer;
    }
    ...
    int endp ( ) {
      return ! current_link_pointer;
    }
    ...
};
```

745   Finally, to reset the current_link_pointer so that it points to the first link, you define reset:

```
class header {
  public:
    link *first_link_pointer;
    link *current_link_pointer;
    header ( ) {
      first_link_pointer = NULL;
      current_link_pointer = first_link_pointer;
    }
    void add (railroad_car *new_element) {
      first_link_pointer = new link (new_element, first_link_pointer);
      current_link_pointer = first_link_pointer;
    }
    void advance ( ) {
      current_link_pointer = current_link_pointer -> next_link_pointer;
    }
    railroad_car* access ( ) {
      return current_link_pointer -> element_pointer;
    }
    int endp ( ) {
      return ! current_link_pointer;
    }
    void reset ( ) {
      current_link_pointer = first_link_pointer;
    }
};
```

At this point, you have the essential machinery required for manipulating lists. It is time to see that machinery at work in a revised version of the `analyze_train` program. It makes a list of railroad cars, and then displays the usual report:

```cpp
#include <iostream.h>
#include <string.h>
const double pi = 3.14159;
// ... Box, cylinder, and railroad-car class definitions go here ...
// Define list classes:
class link {
  public:
    link *next_link_pointer;
    railroad_car *element_pointer;
    link (railroad_car *e, link *l) {
      element_pointer = e;
      next_link_pointer = l;
    }
};
class header {
  public:
    link *first_link_pointer;
    link *current_link_pointer;
    header ( ) {
      first_link_pointer = NULL;
      current_link_pointer = first_link_pointer;
      }
    void add (railroad_car *new_element) {
      first_link_pointer = new link (new_element, first_link_pointer);
      current_link_pointer = first_link_pointer;
    }
    void advance ( ) {
      current_link_pointer = current_link_pointer -> next_link_pointer;
    }
    railroad_car* access ( ) {
      return current_link_pointer -> element_pointer;
    }
    int endp ( ) {
      return ! current_link_pointer;
    }
    void reset ( ) {
      current_link_pointer = first_link_pointer;
    }
};
// Define list header:
header train;
char input_buffer[100];
enum {eng_code = 'E', box_code = 'B', tnk_code = 'T', cab_code = 'C'};
char extract_car_code (char *input_buffer) {return input_buffer[4];}
```

```
main ( ) {
   // No initialization or increment expressions:
   for (; cin >> input_buffer;)
      switch (extract_car_code (input_buffer)) {
         case eng_code: train.add (new engine (input_buffer));    break;
         case box_code: train.add (new box_car (input_buffer));   break;
         case tnk_code: train.add (new tank_car (input_buffer));  break;
         case cab_code: train.add (new caboose (input_buffer));   break;
      }
   train.reset ( );
   // No initialization; increment expression advances list:
   for (; !train.endp ( ) ; train.advance ( ))
      // Display number, short name, and capacity and terminate the line:
      cout << train.access ( ) -> serial_number
           << "        "
           << train.access ( ) -> short_name ( )
           << "        "
           << train.access ( ) -> capacity ( )
           << endl;
}
```

—————————————————— Sample Data ——————————————————

```
TPW-E-783
PPU-B-422
NYC-B-988
NYC-T-988
TPW-C-271
```

—————————————————————— Result ——————————————————————

TPW-C-271	cab	0
NYC-T-988	tnk	1539.38
NYC-B-988	box	3990
PPU-B-422	box	3990
TPW-E-783	eng	0

Note that the preceding program in Segment 746 will work fine without the instance of the reset member function placed just before the list-traversing for loop. Nevertheless, it is always a good idea to reset current_link_pointer before traversing a list, just in case some distant part of your function leaves current_link_pointer assigned inappropriately.

747   Note that a counting variable is no longer needed in the for loop that constructs the list. Accordingly, initialization and increment expressions have disappeared:

```
for ( ; cin >> input_buffer; ) {···}
```

748   The for loop that displays the report also contains no counting variable:

```
for (; !train.endp ( ) ; train.advance ( )) {···}
```

The test expression merely checks `current_link_pointer`; if it is the null pointer, there is no next element, in which case the `for` loop terminates. The increment expression advances the list after the current element is processed.

749
SIDE TRIP There are many options when you want to extend C++ to work with lists. Accordingly, your extension is likely to differ from that of other programmers. Eventually, a standard library will emerge; for now, however, you are on your own.

750
SIDE TRIP A more complete implementation of lists would provide additional member functions, such as member functions for splicing a new element into the middle of a list, for adding a new element to the end of a list, for deleting an element from a list, and for copying a list.

751
SIDE TRIP In some languages—notably COMMONLISP—all sorts of list-creation and list-manipulation functions are built in. Working with lists in such languages is almost effortless.

752
PRACTICE Revise the `analyze_train` program such that only load-bearing cars are entered on the `trains` list.

753
PRACTICE Revise the `analyze_train` program such that all cars are entered on the `trains` list, but only load-bearing cars are reported on.

754
PRACTICE A popular alternative to storing `railroad_cars` in either ordinary arrays or lists is to store them in **self-expanding arrays**. A self-expanding array is an array that gets larger as more and more elements are added to it.

You can implement a self-expanding array as follows:

- Define a `self_expanding_array` class that contains a member variable assigned to an internal array of objects.

- Define class reader and writer member functions that read from and write into the internal array.

- Modify the writer such that, if a program attempts to write into a location that does not exist, a new, larger array is created, the old array is copied into the new array, and the old array is destroyed.

- Modify the reader such that, if a program attempts to read from a location that does not exist, an error message is displayed.

The following definition of the `Integer_array` class embodies the first two steps toward the creation of a self-expanding array of integers:

```
#include <iostream.h>
// Define global integer array:
class Integer_array {
  public: // Constructor:
          Integer_array ( ) {
            hidden_array = new int[100];
          }
          // Reader:
          int read_element (int n) {
            return hidden_array[n];
          }
          // Writer:
          void write_element (int n, int i) {
            hidden_array[n] = i;
          }
  private: int* hidden_array;
};
```

Modify the definition so as to complete the development.

- When objects are linked together by pointers, the objects form a list and each object is an element of the list. Unlike arrays, lists have no fixed size.

- You can create lists in many ways. One of the most popular is through a header class and a link class.

- A header objects for an empty list contains a null pointer, which is often written as NULL, rather than as 0.

- A header object for a nonempty list contains a pointer to a link object. All link objects contain a pointer to a list element and to the next link object in the list.

- List-manipulation functions generally include add, advance, access, endp, and reset.

- One way to visit all the elements in a list is to instantiate the following pattern:

  ```
  list name reset ( );
  for (; list name .access ( ) ; list name .advance ( )) {···}
  ```

756 In Section 47, you learned about the definition of two classes, header and link, that enable you to construct lists of railroad_car objects. So that you did not have to deal with too much complexity at once, all member variables and member functions in those two classes are in the public portion of the class definitions, where they are too freely accessible.

Of course, add, advance, access, endp, reset and the header constructor are used in the train program and therefore should be in the public portion of the header class. In this section, you learn how to make all other member variables and member functions inaccessible, except through those six functions, which constitute the public interface. Along the way, you learn about friends and why they are needed.

757 Note that the link class definition shown, for example, in Segment 746, includes two member variables, next_link_pointer and element_pointer, which you can reasonably suppose should be accessible to only the link constructor and to the member functions of the header class.

758 Accordingly, you might suppose that you should restrict access to those member variables by placing them in the private portion of the class definitions, thereby reducing the risk that you or some other programmer will abuse the values in those member variables accidentally. While you are at it, you might as well put the link constructor in the private portion of the link class, to protect it from abuse as well:

```
// An interim definition of link; as given, it does not work!
class link {
  private:
    link *next_link_pointer;
    railroad_car *element_pointer;
    link (railroad_car *e, link *l) {
      element_pointer = e;
      next_link_pointer = l;
    }
};
```

759 Similarly, the first_link_pointer and current_link_pointer member variables are included in the header class definition. You might reasonably suppose that they should be accessible only to the member functions of the header class:

```
// An interim definition of header; as given, it does not work!
class header {
  public:
    header ( ) {
      first_link_pointer = NULL;
      current_link_pointer = first_link_pointer;
    }
    void add (railroad_car *new_element) {
      first_link_pointer = new link (new_element, first_link_pointer);
      current_link_pointer = first_link_pointer;
    }
    void advance ( ) {
      current_link_pointer = current_link_pointer -> next_link_pointer;
    }
    railroad_car* access ( ) {
      return current_link_pointer -> element_pointer;
    }
    int endp ( ) {
      return ! current_link_pointer;
    }
    void reset ( ) {
      current_link_pointer = first_link_pointer;
    }
  private:
    link *first_link_pointer;
    link *current_link_pointer;
};
```

At this point, six member functions—add, advance, access, endp, reset, and header—remain generally accessible. Accordingly, as you may recall from Section 14, these six functions are said to constitute the public interface to the link and header classes.

Note, however, that moving the member variables and the constructor of the link class to the private portion of the class definition makes them inaccessible not only for general use, but also for the use of the member functions in the header class.

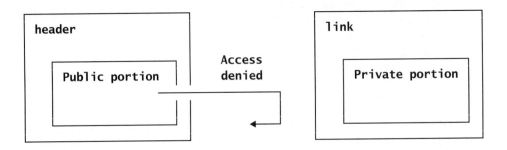

760   One possible, albeit *bad*, way to make the link member variables and constructor accessible is as follows:

- Put the member variables and the constructor in the protected portion of the class definition, instead of in the private portion.

- Make the `header` class a subclass of the `link` class.

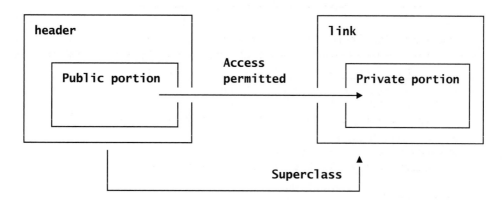

The reason this way to enable access is a bad one is that `header` objects are not specialized `link` objects. Accordingly, to construe one class as a derived class and the other as its base class would be bad conceptually. It would be bad practically as well, for then `header` objects would carry around `element_pointer` and `next_link_pointer` member variables as excess baggage.

761 Nevertheless, the member functions of the `header` class absolutely need access to the private member variables and to the private constructor of the `link` class. Accordingly, C++ provides a mechanism whereby the `link` class can grant complete access privileges to the member functions of the `header` class. To use this privilege-granting mechanism, you add a **friend declaration** to the definition of the `link` class:

```
class link {
  friend class header;
  private:
    link *next_link_pointer;
    railroad_car *element_pointer;
    link (railroad_car *e, link *l) {
      element_pointer = e;
      next_link_pointer = l;
    }
};
```

762 Once the friend declaration is included, the `header` class is said to be a friend of the `link` class. Then, all member variables and member functions in the `link` class acts as though they were public with respect to the member functions of the `header` class. Thus, the member functions of the `header` class can get at the constructor, `link`, and the member variables, `next_link_pointer` and `element_pointer`, in `link` objects.

275

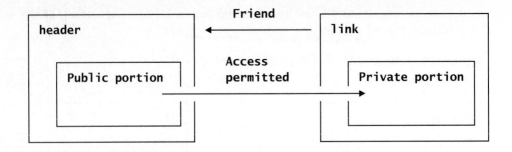

763   Here, then, are the revised, fully protected, class definitions:

```
class link {
  friend class header;
  private:
    link *next_link_pointer;
    railroad_car *element_pointer;
    link (railroad_car *e, link *l) {
      element_pointer = e;
      next_link_pointer = l;
    }
};
class header {
  public:
    header ( ) {
      first_link_pointer = NULL;
      current_link_pointer = first_link_pointer;
    }
    void add (railroad_car *new_element) {
      first_link_pointer = new link (new_element, first_link_pointer);
      current_link_pointer = first_link_pointer;
    }
    void advance ( ) {
      current_link_pointer = current_link_pointer -> next_link_pointer;
    }
    railroad_car* access ( ) {
      return current_link_pointer -> element_pointer;
    }
    int endp ( ) {
      return ! current_link_pointer;
    }
    void reset ( ) {
      current_link_pointer = first_link_pointer;
    }
  private:
    link *first_link_pointer;
    link *current_link_pointer;
};
```

764 Note that the friend declarations circumnavigate C++'s usual mechanisms for hiding data. Accordingly, you should use friend declarations sparingly and with great care.

765

- When you create lists, you should take care to restrict access to the `header` and `link` member variables by placing them in the private portion of the appropriate class definitions.

- Because the `header` class member functions require access to link member variables, and because the `header` class is not a natural subclass of the `link` class, you need to provide access by declaring the `header` class to be a friend of the `link` class.

- **If** you want one class to have access to the member variables and member functions in another, **then** declare that class to be a friend by instantiating the following pattern in the class with the member variables and member functions:

  ```
  friend class name of class to be granted access ;
  ```

49 HOW TO REUSE CLASS DEFINITIONS USING TEMPLATES

766　In Section 47 and Section 48, you learned how to use the header and link classes to make a list of railroad cars. The work was difficult, however, so you learn, in this section, how to package what you have done for reuse by exploiting C++'s template mechanism. Once you have defined template classes for lists, it is easy to create new lists, and you can forget about all the detail you have to struggle through to understand lists and templates.

Note, however, that the definition of template classes is merely illustrated with the use of lists. The template mechanism is a general feature of C++ with wide applicability.

767　Once you have a way to make lists of railroad cars, you could make lists of other objects—such as cylinders or integers—by editing the link and header class definitions by hand, replacing the railroad_car string of characters by another string of characters appropriate to the new type.

Of course, there are good reasons why creating list class definitions by manual editing of the existing header and link class definitions is a bad idea:

- Manual editing is error prone.

- Future improvements to the original class definitions would not propagate to the copied-and-edited class definitions without further, even more error-prone editing.

- You would have to have different names for header and link, corresponding to each type of object that you want to put into lists.

768　Fortunately, most C++ implementations provide a **template mechanism**, enabling you to define generic list and link template classes.

As a step toward understanding C++'s template mechanism, note that you can make the header and link classes shown in Segment 763 look like templates by substituting a heavy black bar, ■■■, for the railroad_car string:

```
class link {
  friend class header;
  private:
    link *next_link_pointer;
    ■■■ *element_pointer;
    link (■■■ *e, link *l) {
      element_pointer = e;
      next_link_pointer = l;
    }
};
```

```
class header {
  public:
    header ( ) {
      first_link_pointer = NULL;
      current_link_pointer = first_link_pointer;
    }
    void add (████ *new_element) {
      first_link_pointer = new link (new_element, first_link_pointer);
      current_link_pointer = first_link_pointer;
    }
    void advance ( ) {
      current_link_pointer = current_link_pointer -> next_link_pointer;
    }
    ████* access ( ) {
      return current_link_pointer -> element_pointer;
    }
    int endp ( ) {
      return ! current_link_pointer;
    }
    void reset ( ) {
      current_link_pointer = first_link_pointer;
    }
  private:
    link *first_link_pointer;
    link *current_link_pointer;
};
```

769 To convert the visual aids in Segment 768 into C++ templates, you must first add a prefix to each definition. That prefix announces that a template is coming and identifies one or more template parameters between brackets. In the following examples, the parameters have long names so that they are easy to understand:

```
template <class link_parameter>
class link {
  ...
};
template <class header_parameter>
class header {
  ...
};
```

770 Next, you must substitute the appropriate parameter names wherever black bars have appeared in Segment 768, and you must provide a specializing argument wherever another template class name is used. For example, whenever you refer to the header class inside the definition of the link class, you must provide an argument surrounded by brackets, thus specializing the header template to the same class as that to which the link is specialized.

```
template <class link_parameter> class link {
  friend class header<link_parameter> ;
  private:
    link *next_link_pointer;
    link_parameter *element_pointer;
    link (link_parameter *e, link *l) {
      element_pointer = e;
      next_link_pointer = l;
    }
};
```

Thus, the purpose of the template parameters is to set up slotlike locations into which the template mechanism eventually places instantiating symbols. In the railroad-car–list example, link_parameter is destined to be replaced by railroad_car when the template class is put to use.

771 Similarly, whenever a reference to the link class appears inside the definition of the header class, you must provide an argument inside brackets. Again, in the railroad-car–list example, header_parameter is destined to be replaced by railroad_car:

```
template <class header_parameter>
class header {
  public:
    header ( ) {
      first_link_pointer = NULL;
      current_link_pointer = first_link_pointer;
    }
    void add (header_parameter *new_element) {
      first_link_pointer =
        new link<header_parameter> (new_element, first_link_pointer);
      current_link_pointer = first_link_pointer;
    }
    void advance ( ) {
      current_link_pointer = current_link_pointer -> next_link_pointer;
    }
    header_parameter * access ( ) {
      return current_link_pointer -> element_pointer;
    }
    int endp ( ) {
      return ! current_link_pointer;
    }
    void reset ( ) {
      current_link_pointer = first_link_pointer;
    }
  private:
    link<header_parameter> *first_link_pointer;
    link<header_parameter> *current_link_pointer;
};
```

772 Now, you can have your program create a `railroad_car`-specific list using the generic header template class. In Section 47, the `analyze_train` program used a statement that defined the `train` variable to belong to the single-purpose `header` class:

header train;

Next, you can replace that statement with one that defines the `train` variable to belong to a parameterized version of the generic `header` class:

header<railroad_car> train;

This expression causes the `header` template class to be instantiated so as to deal with objects belonging to the `railroad_car` class.

Next, the `header` template class activates the `link` template class, because the `header` template class contains embedded `link<header_parameter>` expressions. Thus, the `link` class is also instantiated so as to deal with `railroad_cars`.

Note, that these instantiations do not prevent your program from building other lists of `railroad_car` objects, nor does it prevent your program from building lists of other kinds of objects. You can write programs that construct as many lists as you like for as many object types as you like.

773 Here, then, is the `analyze_train` program, newly revised to make use of the generic header template class:

```
#include <iostream.h>
#include <string.h>
const double pi = 3.14159;
// ... Box, cylinder, and railroad-car class definitions go here ...
// Define list classes:
template <class link_parameter>
class link {
  friend class header<link_parameter>;
  private:
    link *next_link_pointer;
    link_parameter *element_pointer;
    link (link_parameter *e, link *l) {
      element_pointer = e;
      next_link_pointer = l;
    }
};
```

282

```cpp
template <class header_parameter>
class header {
  public:
    header ( ) {
      first_link_pointer = NULL;
      current_link_pointer = first_link_pointer;
    }
    void add (header_parameter *new_element) {
      first_link_pointer =
        new link<header_parameter> (new_element, first_link_pointer);
      current_link_pointer = first_link_pointer;
    }
    void advance ( ) {
      current_link_pointer = current_link_pointer -> next_link_pointer;
    }
    header_parameter* access ( ) {
      return current_link_pointer -> element_pointer;
    }
    int endp ( ) {
      return ! current_link_pointer;
    }
    void reset ( ) {
      current_link_pointer = first_link_pointer;
    }
  private:
    link<header_parameter> *first_link_pointer;
    link<header_parameter> *current_link_pointer;
};
// Define list header:
header<railroad_car> train;
char input_buffer[100];
enum {eng_code = 'E', box_code = 'B', tnk_code = 'T', cab_code = 'C'};
char extract_car_code (char *input_buffer) {return input_buffer[4];}
main ( ) {
  // ... Train list is constructed here ...
  train.reset ( );
  // No initialization; increment expression advances list:
  for (; !train.endp ( ) ; train.advance ( ))
    // Display number, short name, and capacity and terminate the line:
    cout << train.access ( ) -> serial_number
         << "      "
         << train.access ( ) -> short_name ( )
         << "      "
         << train.access ( ) -> capacity ( )
         << endl;
}
```

774
PRACTICE
Use the template mechanism to define the box class such that the height, width, and length member variables may be any kind of number type.

775
PRACTICE
Use the template mechanism to define the self-expanding array class, which you developed in Segment 754, such that the array elements may be any kind of number type.

776
HIGHLIGHTS

- Using the template mechanism, you can define generic classes, and then specialize those generic class definitions to define specific classes.

- If you want to define a template class, **then** instantiate the following pattern:

    template < template parameters >
    class class name {···};

- If you want to declare a variable using a template class, **then** instantiate the following pattern:

    class name < template arguments > variable name ;

- You can extend C++ to handle lists using the template mechanism. To do so, you define a generic list header class and link class. Later, you specialize those generic class definitions to define specific classes.

50 HOW TO ITERATE OVER LISTS USING ITERATION CLASS OBJECTS

777 In Section 49, you learned how to reuse class definitions so that you can make lists out of any sort of object you like. As defined, however, traversing a list alters that list, because of the changes made to the `current_link_pointer` member variable. Such alteration is a problem if you ever need to have more than one traversal going simultaneously.

Accordingly, in this section, you learn about iteration classes, which allow you to separate list construction from list traversal, thereby enabling multiple simultaneous traversals.

778 Basically, `iterator` objects contain member variables that hold pointers to link objects. In the following diagram, for example, an `iterator` object has a pointer that happens, at the moment shown, to point to the second link in a railroad-car list:

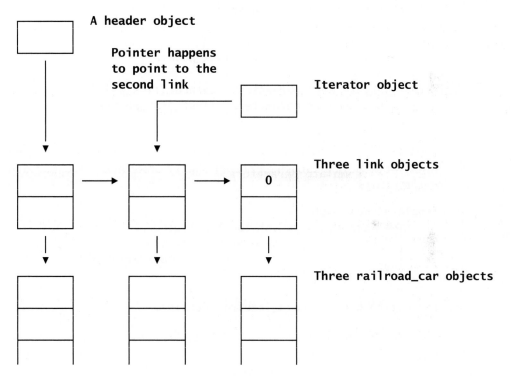

779 For full generality, you need to define the `iterator` class to be a template class. The first step is to establish that each `iterator` class object contains private pointers of the appropriate type:

```
template <class iterator_parameter>
class iterator {
    ...
    private: link<iterator_parameter>* current__link_pointer;
             link<iterator_parameter>* first_link_pointer;
};
```

780 Next, you need member functions to access the elements, advance `current_link_pointer` to the next `link` object, test if `current_link_pointer` is the null pointer, and reset the `current_link_pointer`. Conveniently, you can borrow all these member functions from the definition of the `header` template class:

```
template <class iterator_parameter>
class iterator {
  public:  ...
    iterator_parameter* access ( ) {
      return current_link_pointer -> element_pointer;
    }
    void advance ( ) {
      current_link_pointer = current_link_pointer -> next_link_pointer;
    }
    int endp ( ) {
      return ! current_link_pointer;
    }
    void reset ( ) {
      current_link_pointer = first_link_pointer;
    }
  private: link<iterator_parameter>* current_link_pointer;
           link<iterator_parameter>* first_link_pointer;
};
```

781 Defining the `iterator` constructor is not quite so simple. That constructor must get to the first link in a list by moving through the `header` object that is handed over as an argument in statements such as this:

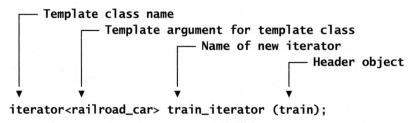

```
iterator<railroad_car> train_iterator (train);
```

782 First, as you begin to think about how to define the `iterator` constructor, note that the parameter declaration should indicate that the argument is to be handed over as is, rather than copied, for there is no point in copying the list header:

```
iterator (header<iterator_parameter>& header) {...}
```

Then, given a pointer to the `header` object, your constructor can obtain a pointer to the first `link` object as follows:

```
header.first_link_pointer
```

Next, you can assign the value of `header.first_link_pointer` to the `iterator` object's `first_link_pointer` member variable; then, you can assign the same value to the `iterator` object's `current_link_pointer` member variable:

```
    first_link_pointer = header.first_link_pointer;
    current_link_pointer = first_link_pointer;
```

783 Now, you can assemble a complete constructor function, here shown installed in the class
     definition:

```
template <class iterator_parameter>
class iterator {
  public:
    iterator (header<iterator_parameter>& header) {
      first_link_pointer = header.first_link_pointer;
      current_link_pointer = first_link_pointer;
    }
    iterator_parameter* access ( ) {
      return current_link_pointer -> element_pointer;
    }
    void advance ( ) {
      current_link_pointer = current_link_pointer -> next_link_pointer;
    }
    int endp ( ) {
      return ! current_link_pointer;
    }
    void reset ( ) {
      current_link_pointer = first_link_pointer;
    }
  private: link<iterator_parameter>* current_link_pointer;
           link<iterator_parameter>* first_link_pointer;
};
```

The constructor establishes the value of first_link_pointer, because the reset member
function needs that value to prepare the iterator for reuse. Note that both the header class
and the iterator class happen to have member variables named first_link_pointer.

784 Next, you must ensure that the iterator member functions have access to the header
     and link member variables by declaring the iterator class to be a friend of both the
     list class and the link class:

```
template <class link_parameter>
class link {
  friend class iterator<link_parameter>;
  friend class list<link_parameter>;
  ...
};
template <class parameter>
class list {
  friend class iterator<parameter>;
  ...
};
```

In the following program, the expression `railroad_car`, provided as a template argument in the expression `iterator<railroad_car> train_iterator (train)`, causes the iterator class to be instantiated so as to deal with railroad cars. The expression `train` provides the new iterator with access to a particular list of railroad cars.

```cpp
#include <iostream.h>
#include <string.h>
const double pi = 3.14159;
// ... Container, railroad-car, and list definitions go here ...
template <class iterator_parameter>
class iterator {
  public:
    iterator (header<iterator_parameter>& header) {
      first_link_pointer = header.first_link_pointer;
      current_link_pointer = first_link_pointer;
    }
    iterator_parameter* access ( ) {
      return current_link_pointer -> element_pointer;
    }
    void advance ( ) {
      current_link_pointer = current_link_pointer -> next_link_pointer;
    }
    int endp ( ) {
      return ! current_link_pointer;
    }
    void reset ( ) {
      current_link_pointer = first_link_pointer;
    }
  private: link<iterator_parameter>* current_link_pointer;
           link<iterator_parameter>* first_link_pointer;
};
// Define list header:
header<railroad_car> train;
char input_buffer[100];
enum {eng_code = 'E', box_code = 'B', tnk_code = 'T', cab_code = 'C'};
char extract_car_code (char *input_buffer) {return input_buffer[4];}
main ( ) {
  // ... Collect train elements as usual ...
  // Define and initialize iterator class object:
  iterator<railroad_car> train_iterator (train);
  // Iterate:
  train_iterator.reset ( );
  for (; !train_iterator.endp ( ) ; train_iterator.advance ( ))
    // Display number, short name, and capacity and terminate the line:
    cout << train_iterator.access ( ) -> serial_number << "      "
         << train_iterator.access ( ) -> short_name ( ) << "      "
         << train_iterator.access ( ) -> capacity ( ) << endl;
}
```

```
TPW-E-783
PPU-B-422
NYC-B-988
NYC-T-988
TPW-C-271
```

─────────────── Result ───────────────

TPW-C-271	cab	0
NYC-T-988	tnk	1539.38
NYC-B-988	box	3990
PPU-B-422	box	3990
TPW-E-783	eng	0

Note that you can remove the access, advance, endp, and reset member functions from the link_header class, forcing all list traversal to be done with a iterator object.

786
PRACTICE
The header, link, and iterator classes, as defined in Segment 785, work together such that car information is displayed in the opposite order from that in which car information is read from a file. Make all the revisions required to display the information in the same order. Do this revision by creating a second list whose elements are in the reversed order relative to the first.

787
PRACTICE
Augment the program in Segment 785 such that your augmented program compares the capacities of adjacent railroad cars and displays the results in a column:

TPW-E-783	eng	0	<
PPU-B-422	box	3990	=
NYC-B-988	box	3990	>
NYC-T-988	tnk	1539.38	>
TPW-C-271	cab	0	

788
HIGHLIGHTS

- If you have implemented lists, **and** you wish to perform an operation on all the elements in a list, **then** you should define the iterator class, **and** you should create an iterator object by instantiating the following pattern:

  iterator< object type > iterator name (list name);

- If you have implemented iterators, **and** you wish to work on the object pointed to by an iterator class object, **and** you have defined an access member function, **then** instantiate the following pattern:

  iterator name .access ( )

- If you have implemented iterators, **and** you wish to move an iterator class object's pointer to the next link in a list, **and** you have defined a advance member function, **then** instantiate the following pattern:

  iterator name .advance ( )

- **If** you have implemented iterators, **and** you wish to work on all the elements in a list, **and** you have created an iterator class object using a class with `access`, `advance`, `endp`, and `reset` member functions, **then** instantiate the following pattern:

```
iterator name .reset ( );
for (; iterator name .endp ( ) ; iterator name .advance ( )) {
    ··· iterator name .access ( ) ···
}
```

APPENDIX A:
OPERATOR PRECEDENCE

789   The following table lists C++'s precedence and associativity characteristics. Each box contains operators with equal precedence. The top box contains the highest-precedence operators.

Operator level	Associativity
::	left to right
( ) [ ] -> . sizeof(data type)	left to right
! ++ -- + (unary) - (unary) * (dereference) & (address of) new delete (data type)	right to left
* / %	left to right
+ -	left to right
<< >>	left to right
< <= > >=	left to right
== !=	left to right
&	left to right
^	left to right
¦	left to right
&&	left to right
¦¦	left to right
?:	right to left
= += -= *= /= %= &= ^= ¦= <<= >>=	right to left
,	left to right

Note that each data type, surrounded by parentheses, is considered an operator, namely a casting operator. Also, the parentheses following a function name are considered to be the function-call operator.

Three of the operators in the table are not described in the body of this text: &, ¦, and ^ are the **bitwise and, bitwise or,** and **bitwise exclusive or** operators.

APPENDIX B:
FORMATTED DISPLAY

790   The following table lists the specifications that are used in C++'s `printf` statements:

Specification	Argument type	What is displayed
%i	int	integer
%o	int	octal number
%x, %X	int	hexadecimal number
%c	int	character
%s	char pointer	string
%f	double	floating-point number
%e, %E	double	floating-point number with exponent
%%		the % character

791   The c, s, and % specifications are for characters, strings, and the insertion of percent signs.

Display character, percent sign, and string:

```
printf ("The character %c occupies 25%% of the string %s.\n",
                      'a',                              "abcd");
———————————————————— Result ————————————————————
The character a occupies 25% of the string abcd.
```

792   The o and x specifications are used for octal and hexadecimal numbers.

Display number in octal and hexadecimal:

```
printf ("In octal, 8 is %o, and in hexadecimal, 10 is %x or %X.\n",
                      8,                              10,   10);
———————————————————— Result ————————————————————
In octal, 8 is 10, and in hexadecimal, 10 is a or A.
```

793   The i specification is for integers. Note that xs are included in the `printf` statement to clarify the placement of padding characters.

Display short or integer or long:

```
printf ("x %i x\n", 816); printf ("x %i x\n", -816);
———————————————————— Result ————————————————————
x 816 x
x -816 x
```

Display with spaces, if necessary, to fill a six-character field:

```
printf ("x %6i x\n", 816); printf ("x %6i x\n", -816);
```
———————————————— Result ————————————————
```
x    816 x
x   -816 x
```

Display with spaces, if necessary, to fill a six-character field; if more than six characters are involved, display them all anyway:

```
printf ("x %6i x\n", 8160000); printf ("x %6i x\n", -8160000);
```
———————————————— Result ————————————————
```
x 8160000 x
x -8160000 x
```

Display with spaces, on the right, if necessary:

```
printf ("x %-6i x\n", 816); printf ("x %-6i x\n", -816);
```
———————————————— Result ————————————————
```
x 816    x
x -816   x
```

Always include sign:

```
printf ("x %+6i x\n", 816); printf ("x %+6i x\n", -816);
```
———————————————— Result ————————————————
```
x   +816 x
x   -816 x
```

Always include sign and pad on the right:

```
printf ("x %+-6i x\n", 816); printf ("x %+-6i x\n", -816);
```
———————————————— Result ————————————————
```
x +816   x
x -816   x
```

794 The f specification is for floating-point numbers. Note that xs are included in the printf statement to clarify the placement of padding characters.

Display float or double:

```
printf ("x %f x\n", 3.14159); printf ("x %f x\n", -3.14159);
```
———————————————— Result ————————————————
```
x 3.141590 x
x -3.141590 x
```

Display with two digits following the decimal point:

```
printf ("x %.2f x\n", 3.14159); printf ("x %.2f x\n", -3.14159);
```
————————————— Result —————————————
```
x 3.14 x
x -3.14 x
```

Display with spaces, if necessary, to fill a six-character field:

```
printf ("x %6.2f x\n", 3.14159); printf ("x %6.2f x\n", -3.14159);
```
————————————— Result —————————————
```
x   3.14 x
x  -3.14 x
```

Display with spaces, if necessary, to fill a six-character field; if more than six characters are involved, display them all anyway:

```
printf ("x %6f x\n", 3.14159); printf ("x %6f x\n", -3.14159);
```
————————————— Result —————————————
```
x 3.141590 x
x -3.141590 x
```

Display with spaces, on the right, if necessary:

```
printf ("x %-6.2f x\n", 3.14159); printf ("x %-6.2f x\n", -3.14159);
```
————————————— Result —————————————
```
x 3.14   x
x -3.14   x
```

Always include sign:

```
printf ("x %+6.2f x\n", 3.14159); printf ("x %+6.2f x\n", -3.14159);
```
————————————— Result —————————————
```
x  +3.14 x
x  -3.14 x
```

Always include sign and pad on the right:

```
printf ("x %+-6.2f x\n", 3.14159); printf ("x %+-6.2f x\n", -3.14159);
```
————————————— Result —————————————
```
x +3.14  x
x -3.14  x
```

795   The e specification is for printing floating-point numbers in scientific notation. Note that xs are included in the printf statement to clarify the placement of padding characters:

Display float or double:

```
printf ("x %e x\n", 27182.8); printf ("x %e x\n", -0.000271828);
printf ("Using E produces an upper-case E, as in x %E x.\n", 27182.8);
```
——————————————— Result ———————————————
```
x 2.718280e+04 x
x -2.718280e-04 x
Using E produces an upper-case E, as in x 2.718280E+04 x.
```

Display with two digits following the decimal point:

```
printf ("x %.2e x\n", 27182.8); printf ("x %.2e x\n", -0.000271828);
```
——————————————— Result ———————————————
```
x 2.72e+04 x
x -2.72e-04 x
```

Display with spaces, if necessary, to fill a 10-character field:

```
printf ("x %10.2e x\n", 27182.8);
printf ("x %10.2e x\n", -0.000271828);
```
——————————————— Result ———————————————
```
x    2.72e+04 x
x   -2.72e-04 x
```

Display with spaces, if necessary, to fill a 10-character field; if more than 10 characters are involved, display them all anyway:

```
printf ("x %10e x\n", 27182.8); printf ("x %10e x\n", -0.000271828);
```
——————————————— Result ———————————————
```
x 2.718280e+04 x
x -2.718280e-04 x
```

Display with spaces, on the right, if necessary:

```
printf ("x %-10.2e x\n", 27182.8);
printf ("x %-10.2e x\n", -0.000271828);
```
——————————————— Result ———————————————
```
x 2.72e+04   x
x -2.72e-04   x
```

Always include sign:

```
printf ("x %+10.2e x\n", 27182.8);
printf ("x %+10.2e x\n", -0.000271828);
```
───────────────────── Result ─────────────────────
```
x  +2.72e+04 x
x  -2.72e-04 x
```

Always include sign and pad on the right:

```
printf ("x %+-10.2e x\n", 27182.8);
printf ("x %+-10.2e x\n", -0.000271828);
```
───────────────────── Result ─────────────────────
```
x +2.72e+04  x
x -2.72e-04  x
```

COLOPHON

The author created camera-ready copy for this book using TEX, Donald E. Knuth's computer typesetting language.

He transformed the source text into PostScript files using the products of Y&Y, of Concord, Massachusetts. Pure Imaging, Inc., of Watertown, Massachusetts, produced film from the PostScript files.

The text was set primarily in 10-point Sabon Roman. The section headings were set in 14-point Sabon bold. The computer programs were set in 9-point Lucida Sans bold.

All programs shown with accompanying results were tested using the compiler produced by the Free Software Foundation, of Cambridge, Massachusetts. For information about the Free Software Foundation's C++ compiler, send a message to `gnu@prep.ai.mit.edu`.

Representative programs were also tested using compilers offered by Borland and by Microsoft.

INDEX